Learning a Foreign Language

A Handbook for Missionaries

by

Eugene A. Nida

Secretary for Translations
American Bible Society

Professor of Linguistics
Summer Institute of Linguistics
University of Oklahoma

Committee on Missionary Personnel
Division of Foreign Missions
National Council of the Churches of Christ in the U.S.A.
156 Fifth Avenue, New York 10, N. Y.

407
N549l
1950

Copyright 1950
Second Edition
Eugene A. Nida

PREFACE

This book on <u>Learning a Foreign Language</u> is designed especially for missionaries. Accordingly, the illustrations of linguistic problems are drawn principally from languages with which missionaries are primarily concerned and from the actual experience which missionaries have had with these languages.

The first three chapters treat the principles and procedures in language study and the following four chapters deal with some of the fundamental features of languages. In describing linguistic structure an attempt has been made to use nontechnical vocabulary wherever possible. In instances where this could not be done without considerable ambiguity or inaccuracy, every effort has been made to explain the technical words by simple illustrations.

In addition to its use as a guide for individual language study, this volume should prove helpful for elementary courses in linguistics offered in various seminaries, colleges, and Bible schools. However, teachers are advised to supplement the materials contained here by exercises and further illustrative data to be found in <u>Phonemics</u> (1947) by Kenneth L. Pike and <u>Morphology</u> (1949) by Eugene A. Nida. Both of these volumes are published by the University of Michigan Press, Ann Arbor, Michigan.

The following books and pamphlets have proved exceedingly valuable in the preparation of this volume:

- T. F. Cummings, <u>How to Learn a Language</u> (New York: privately published, Press of Frank H. Evory and Co., Albany, New York, 1916).
- L. Bloomfield, <u>Outline Guide for the Practical Study of Foreign Language</u> (Baltimore: Linguistic Society of America, 1942). Pp. 16.
- O. Jespersen, <u>How to Teach a Foreign Language</u> (London: Allen and Unwin, 1917). Pp. 194.
- H. E. Palmer, <u>The Scientific Study and Teaching of Languages</u> (London: George G. Harrap and Co., 1917). Pp. 328.

iv LEARNING A FOREIGN LANGUAGE

H. Sweet, The Practical Study of Languages (London: J. M. Dent and Sons, 1926). Pp. 278.

Ida C. Ward, Practical Suggestions for the Learning of an African Language in the Field (London: Oxford University Press, for the International African Institute, 1937). Pp. 39.

Full bibliographical footnotes accompany all published data cited in this volume, but there are many illustrations drawn from the writer's own field notes and from the contributions of missionary friends and former students, without whose help it would have been impossible to provide the necessary language data for such a volume. Acknowledgements are due the following individuals for contributions in their respective languages: Barrow Eskimo, Roy Ahmaogak and John McIntosh; Black Thai, Jean Funé; Futa-Fula, Harry Watkins; Huichol, John McIntosh; Ilamba, George Anderson; Jita, Sukuma, and Zinza, Donald Ebeling; Kekchi, William Sedat; Kipsigis, Earl Anderson; Kpelle, William Welmers; Loma, Wesley Sadler; Mende, H. Mitchell; Mongondow, J. M. Langeveld; Pame-Chichimeca, Anne Blackman and Lorna Gibson; Quechua (Chanca Dialect), Homer Emerson; Tepehua, Bethel Bower; Tojolabal, Julia Supple and Celia Mendenhall; Totonac, Herman and Bessie Aschmann; Yipounou, Leroy Pierson and Peter Stam III; Zapotec of the Isthmus, Velma Pickett and Marjory Nyman; and Zoque, William and Dorothy Wonderly.

New York   Eugene A. Nida
June, 1949

CONTENTS

Chapter	Page
1. LANGUAGES CAN AND MUST BE LEARNED	1
1.1 Popular Excuses	1
1.2 A False Evaluation of Ability	4
1.3 What Real Language Ability Can Mean	5
1.4 Reasons for Failure in Language Learning	8
2. PRINCIPLES OF LANGUAGE LEARNING	13
2.1 Start with a Clean Slate	13
2.2 Listening, Speaking, Reading, and Then Writing Constitute the Fundamental Order in Language Learning	21
2.3 Mimicry Is the Key to Language Learning	23
2.4 Language Learning Is Over-Learning	24
2.5 Language Learning Means Language Using	26
3. WAYS OF LEARNING A FOREIGN LANGUAGE	30
3.1 Popular Misconceptions	30
3.2 The Diversity of Language-Learning Methods	31
3.2.1 A Course with a Native Informant and a Linguistically Trained Guide	32
3.2.2 Instruction by a Private Tutor in a Nonaboriginal Language	35
3.2.2.1 Difficulties with Foreign Language Tutoring	36
3.2.2.2 What the Student Can Do to Help the Tutorial Program	38
3.2.2.2.1 A Better Textbook	38
3.2.2.2.2 A Phonemic Alphabet	39
3.2.2.2.3 Phrases for Memorizing and Drill	39
3.2.2.2.4 Reading Aloud and Listening to Reading	40
3.2.2.2.5 Speaking the Language	41
3.2.2.2.6 Criticism of Pronunciation	41
3.2.2.2.7 Supplementary Vocabulary	42
3.2.2.2.8 Associating with Native Speakers	43
3.2.2.2.9 Writing Down All New Words	44
3.2.2.2.10 Listening to the Radio	45
3.2.2.2.11 Going to Lectures and Public Entertainments	46

Chapter	Page
3.2.2.2.12 Attending Church.	47
3.2.2.2.13 Reading the Bible	47
3.2.2.2.14 Writing the Language.	48
3.2.2.2.15 Keeping Up in the Language.	49
3.2.3 Learning an Aboriginal Language from a Native Speaker.	51
3.2.3.1 The Typical Situation.	51
3.2.3.2 What the Student Can Do to Learn a Language from a Native Informant.	55
3.2.3.2.1 Reading Over the Grammar	55
3.2.3.2.2 Obtaining Some Practical Expressions	56
3.2.3.2.3 Writing the Native Expressions in the Best Way Possible.	58
3.2.3.2.4 Practicing All Expressions Until They Are Up to Speed	59
3.2.3.2.5 Obtaining at Least 200 Simple "Object" Words	60
3.2.3.2.6 Obtaining These "Object" Words in Possessive and Plural Formations	61
3.2.3.2.7 Obtaining Simple Verbs	64
3.2.3.2.8 Obtaining Verbs with Different Tenses, in the Negative, and in Questions	66
3.2.3.2.9 Obtaining Expressions Which Modify Nouns and Verbs.	69
3.2.3.2.10 Putting Words Together into Frames	72
3.2.3.2.11 Writing Down Texts.	75
3.2.3.2.12 Reading Texts and Listening to Them Read	77
3.2.3.2.13 Memorizing Stories.	77
3.2.3.2.14 Listening Constantly to the Language	78
3.2.3.2.15 Using the Language at Every Opportunity.	80
3.2.3.2.16 Making a Dictionary of the Language.	81
3.2.3.2.17 Seeking Constant Correction from Native Speakers.	82
4. MASTERING THE SOUNDS	85
4.1 Misconceptions about Phonetic Abilities.	87
4.2 What Makes the Sounds	88
4.3 The Principal Types of Speech Sounds	91
4.3.1 Consonants.	91

CONTENTS

Chapter	Page
4.3.1.1 Simple Stops	91
4.3.1.2 Double Stops	93
4.3.1.3 Clicks	94
4.3.1.4 Aspirated Stops	94
4.3.1.5 Affricated Stops	95
4.3.1.6 Glottalized Stops	96
4.3.1.7 Fricatives	97
4.3.1.8 Frictionless Consonants	99
4.3.1.8.1 Nasal Consonants	99
4.3.1.8.2 Laterals	100
4.3.1.8.3 Centrals	100
4.3.1.9 Vibrants	100
4.3.1.9.1 Flaps	100
4.3.1.9.2 Trills	101
4.3.1.10 A Chart of Consonants	101
4.3.2 Vowels	102
4.3.2.1 Nasalized Vowels	107
4.3.2.2 Glottalized Vowels	108
4.3.2.3 Long Vowels	108
4.3.2.4 Voiceless Vowels	110
4.3.2.5 Breathy Vowels	110
4.3.3 Prosodic Features	111
4.3.3.1 Tone	111
4.3.3.1.1 Contour Tone Languages	112
4.3.3.1.2 Register Tone Languages	114
4.3.3.2 Intonation	118
4.3.3.3 Stress	121
4.4 Types of Phonetic Problems	123
4.4.1 Similar Sounds	123
4.4.2 Similar Sounds but with Different Values in Other Languages	127
4.4.3 Strikingly Different Sounds	131
4.5 Mastering Foreign Sounds	133
4.6 A Usable Alphabet	139
4.6.1 The Usual Situation in a Written Language	139
4.6.2 A Phonemic Alphabet	141
4.6.3 Practical Solutions to the Alphabet Problem	144
4.7 Writing Down Sentences as the Native Informant Speaks	150

Chapter	Page
4.8 Appropriate Gestures	151
5. FIGURING OUT THE FORMS	153
5.1 The Minimal Meaningful Parts of Languages	153
5.2 Different Sizes of Words	154
5.3 Discovering the Morphemes	158
5.4 The Types of Phonemes that Make up Morphemes	161
5.5 Different Forms of Single Morphemes	163
5.6 Types of Morphemes	169
5.7 Determining the Extent of Words	173
5.8 The Parts of Speech	176
5.9 The Categories Expressed by Bound Forms	177
6. PUTTING WORDS TOGETHER	181
6.1 Different Syntactic Systems	182
6.2 The Arrangement of Words	187
6.2.1 Order	191
6.2.2 Juncture	192
6.2.3 Concord (Agreement)	194
6.2.4 Government	194
6.2.5 Cross Reference	197
6.3 Types of Syntactic Units	199
6.3.1 Sentence-Forming and Non-Sentence-Forming Constructions	200
6.3.2 Endocentric and Exocentric Constructions	201
6.3.3 Coordinate and Subordinate Constructions	203
6.3.4 Paratactic and Hypotactic Constructions	204
6.3.5 Immediate Constituents	204
6.4 Discovering the Syntactic Structure of a Language	207
6.5 Correcting Syntactic Errors	208
7. DISCOVERING THE MEANINGS	210
7.1 Popular Misconceptions	210
7.2 Basic Principles	213
7.2.1 There Are No Exact Synonyms within a Language	213
7.2.2 There Are No Exact Equivalents between Languages	213
7.2.3 Ambiguities Occur in All Languages	214
7.2.4 All Languages Exhibit Changes in the Meanings of Words	215

CONTENTS

Chapter	Page
7.2.5 Forms Have Areas of Meaning	216
7.2.6 Languages Subdivide Phenomena in Different Ways	218
7.2.7 Words Reflect Cultural Differences	221
7.3 The Process of Finding the Meanings of Forms	226
INDEX	229

Chapter 1

1. LANGUAGES CAN AND MUST BE LEARNED

Everything was in turmoil. Some of the boys at the mission school were huddled in groups talking in low, angry tones while others stared bitterly toward the home of the mission superintendent. The native school teachers tried to reason with the students but with little success. Finally, the native teachers came to the missionary and endeavored to explain again the basis of the difficulty and resultant misunderstanding, and as they pleaded, they said, "There can be no real peace between us unless you really speak our language." The trouble had arisen primarily because this devout, consecrated missionary was unable to understand and speak the native language effectively.

Such a tragedy is by no means unique. In one area of Africa the natives came to the British governor of the province and asked him through Arab interpreters, "Just what are the missionaries in our tribe trying to tell us? They seem like nice people, but we do not understand them." These missionaries, who had been suffering untold hardships in order to pioneer in a remote, disease-ridden region, had not in eight years succeeded in learning enough of the native language to communicate their vital message. Furthermore, none of them had ever taken the time to learn enough Arabic to use it adequately with the natives who did have an elementary knowledge of that trade language.

1.1 Popular Excuses

There is no valid reason for tragic failures in language learning, for languages can be learned. Children of six years of age in all cultures are able to speak their mother-tongue intelligibly and to discuss many things which missionaries seem never able to talk about. Naturally, we may then ask ourselves, "Why do we not learn a language as well as a child?" The reasons for our deficiencies are not difficult to discover. In the first place, as adult missionaries we have already acquired a set of language habits, and we have practiced them for fully twenty years, until they have become thoroughly a part of us. In the second place, we shelter our ego with all types of inhibitions and restraints. We are afraid of exposing our ignorance and of being laughed at, and as a result our speech becomes ridiculous. Of course, it is also true that we do not have native parents who fondly try to teach us, who never seem to tire of repeating words, and who praise us for our feeble efforts. Furthermore, we are not exposed to the taunting of other children who cruelly force conformity upon their playmates. In reality, we do not have many of the advantages afforded children, but, on the other hand, we have other advantages which come from analytical training and mature mental faculties. At times we tend to underestimate our childish woes and to forget the really strenuous efforts involved in learning to speak. Once the task is over, we forget any difficulties and assume that all was easy sledding.

Despite the many intricacies of strange languages, with their many peculiar sounds and utterly different grammars, missionaries have learned some of the most complicated languages in the world. For difficulties of vowels and tone no language appears to surpass Dinka in the Anglo-Egyptian Sudan, and yet Dr. Trudinger, translator of the Abwong dialect, has acquired an amazing facility in this extremely complex language. However, such ability has only come as the result of years of painstaking study and of constantly living and being with the people—sitting in the cattle kraals around dung fires, listening to stories of hunting exploits, fierce wars, and ancient lore, and then telling these ash-coated people the Good News as contained in the Book of books. Some missionaries have learned Eskimo with its long words and irregular forms, and others have mastered Navaho, with its highly involved verb paradigms consisting of stems and eleven sets of prefixes. No language is unlearnable, but languages do differ greatly in the degree and kind of complications.

There are many excuses given for missionaries' failures to learn foreign languages. One of the most common is the complaint of being too old before taking up the task. Of course, age is a type of liability, for habits become stronger as we get older, and our sensitive egos get more touchy; but the barrier of age has been greatly exaggerated. Old dogs can be taught

LANGUAGES CAN AND MUST BE LEARNED

new tricks, provided they really want to learn and will take the necessary steps to overcome their initial disadvantages. Mental alertness and a communicative personality will outweigh almost any disadvantage of age.

Some potential missionaries assume that because they are "tone deaf," they cannot learn another language, especially a tonal one. In the first place, this so-called tone deafness usually means that one is not able to "carry a tune," but that does not mean that the person is actually unable to recognize tone. If one is able to distinguish the declarative "Yes." from the interrogative "Yes?," he is not tone deaf. If, in speaking English, one uses the conventional intonational patterns, then he can also learn to make tonal distinctions in other languages. Undoubtedly he will have to work at the task more if his ear is less aware of tonal changes, but careful training can compensate for apparent woeful lack of natural ability. One well-known linguist, who has done considerable research in tonal languages, began his career with the serious handicap of poor musical aptitude, but by dint of persistent effort has succeeded in not only overcoming a liability but has developed remarkable acuteness in the analysis of tonal languages. People do not actually "sing" a tone language, in the sense of hitting precisely the same note whenever the same word recurs. The distinctions involve relative pitches, not absolute ones, and with persistent intelligent practice even the poorest student can make himself understood.

Some people assume that because they have never studied any foreign languages before going to the field, they are thereby handicapped for life. In some ways they may have some advantages over others, for some traditional courses in language teach many things which must be unlearned later. One missionary, who used to pride himself on being a "trained grammarian" (and he did have a number of years of traditional schooling in language), proved to be a terrible failure in learning a native language in Africa. Because the language did not conform to his idea of what a language should be like, he failed to appreciate its structure and to master its idiom.

One of the most common excuses for language inadequacy is lack of time. This is one very valid reason for language failure, and one which must be seriously considered. So-called technical missionaries, for example, doctors, nurses, agriculturalists, and industrialists, have often felt that the employment of their skills is so strategic that language facility is relatively unimportant. Evangelistic and educational missionaries are supposed to supplement the technicians' inadequacies. To an extent this reasoning is based upon the appreciation of efficiency in specialization, but fundamentally it introduces a serious error. The true missionary, whether technical or nontechnical, is not in the field to give of his skills, but rather to communicate the life of his Master. Technical tasks can be performed by government officials and employees of purely scientific and philanthropic organizations. The missionary has a greater calling, and the effective transmission of his message both by life and by word is of utmost importance. If the skill of a doctor has opened up some previously hostile area to the preaching of the gospel, he is the most effective one to present Christ. It is true that he cannot take the required time to do all the teaching and preaching. Much of this will necessarily fall to the responsibility of others, but natives will look to the doctor for spiritual guidance, for it is he who has been instrumental in breaking down prejudice.

Every missionary, regardless of his specialization, must be equipped to communicate to others the substance of his objective faith and the reality of his personal conviction. To tell men about the truth and to reveal the heart which has made that truth live requires skill in speaking the native language.

1.2 A False Evaluation of Ability

The missionary who is continually congratulated by the natives for his language ability frequently assumes that he is getting along famously. The truth is usually quite the opposite, for such statements result from the missionary's obviously faltering attempts to make his audience understand, and they are trying to encourage him to do better. When natives finally cease to make such statements, it is either because the missionary has so mastered the language that their attention is no longer called to the language problem or because they have simply given up hope that the missionary will ever improve. One missionary who had rather congratulated himself on his language ability was made humble again by the remark of a villager who, when asked whether he enjoyed the preaching service, said apologetically, "I'm sorry, your honor. You see I do not understand English." The missionary had actually been trying to speak the native's own language, and not English at all. A similar incident occurred to a German missionary in Japan who was unusually proud of his own rapid mastery of the Japanese language and so refused to use interpreters. One of the parishioners, however, revealed inadvertently how pitifully little was understood, when he commented to one of his friends, "The German language must not be too much different from Japanese." A most embarrassing rejoinder was made to a missionary who boldly asked his congregation whether he spoke their language intelligibly. "Well," replied one of the natives, "when you attempt to speak our language, we know at least that it is no other language which you are trying to talk."

Some missionaries have been deceived by the apparent understanding of the natives who live on the mission station and who become perfectly familiar with the missionary's own brand of the language. In actuality, they have learned the missionary's dialect, and in some cases they even imitate the missionary's speech to the point of developing a real mission-station jargon. Such localisms prove a real hindrance to effective evangelism, for the missionary often discovers that he cannot be understood beyond the limits of the immediate community. Often his reaction is to blame the extreme dialectal differences, though he may admit that the natives seem to get along all right in speaking with one another. In such circumstances one may be quite sure that the trouble lies with the missionary's mispronunciations and awkward grammatical forms.

1.3   What Real Language Ability Can Mean

The three keys to the Christian life are revelation, faith, and witness. The revelation is the Word of God; the faith is that God-given response which we make to the message; and the witness is the inevitable outflowing of our experience. To communicate this reality to others we must be able to speak. This does not mean just the ability to write out sermons and to deliver them in an intelligible form; it means the skill which enables one to engage in conversation with people, talking with them about their problems, beliefs, fears, desires, aspirations, and longings. Being able to frame appropriate sentences for a sermon is actually less important on the mission field than being able to respond intelligibly and spiritually to the intimate problems of the heart.

Some missionaries have taken the easy way out and have used interpreters for practically all of their ministry. It has been particularly common for missionaries among Indians in the United States to fall back on the use of interpreters, and nothing has been so unutterably tragic. In some instances the mission boards have even legislated against the use of the Indian language, and as a result missionary work has been in many cases unalterably crippled.

If interpreters are not good, they are doubly bad, for they interrupt the flow of the message and fail to reveal its contents adequately. If interpreters are good, then they can more profitably be trained to do the speaking themselves, following the instructions and suggestions of the missionary. Only those who have been forced to use interpreters can understand the fatal effects of such a procedure upon the message, for it is not so much the words uttered by the preacher as the fire burning within his soul which actually kindles conviction in others. For the most part, interpreters cannot communicate this characteristic of the personality.

The constant use of interpreters sometimes means that the missionary lapses into completely irrelevant types of illustrations. The missionary administrator who addressed a Japanese audience through an interpreter on the theme of "The Ships of God's Navy" and proceeded to talk about "Friendship, Fellowship, and Stewardship," was blind to the problems of language differences. One unfortunate missionary discovered after a number of years that his favorite interpreter had been consistently translating "only begotten Son" as "only forgotten Son," for the word "begotten" was unknown, and "forgotten" had the closest phonetic resemblance. Naturally the natives found it hard to understand how God could love the world so much and at the same time forget about His Son.

Being able to speak a language well means that one has gone through the process of learning not only the words of a language but the appropriate themes which are significant to the life of a people. Instead of drawing illustrations from urban American life, one may talk about the dangers that lurk along jungle paths, the essential processes in the planting of corn, and the strenuous requirements for success in hunting. Instead of trying to illustrate the wrong choice in a predicament by saying that "the man jumped from the frying pan into the fire," the missionary should know an equivalent proverb such as comes from West Africa, "The man was so afraid of the sword that he hid in the scabbard." If the missionary wants to talk about the epitome of human wisdom, there is no use speaking about Socrates or Einstein; but he can, if he is in some parts of the Gold Coast, speak about "an old man with but a single hair," for this is the metaphorical symbol of wisdom in those regions. Knowing a language should also mean knowing the people, and one must know people before it is possible to lead them into the truth.

Real language facility not only enables one to avoid the pitfalls occasioned by interpreters and to make one's message relevant to the life of the people, but it also helps to prevent those serious maladjustments and breakdowns which threaten the missionary's ministry. The deep frustration which many missionaries experience may be traced in numerous instances to poor language orientation. Being cut off from the sustaining social experiences of home and family are serious blows to one's personality integration, but if one fails to establish other vital links through free and intimate communication, sooner or later the personality tends to disintegrate or to find outlets which are meaningless or destructive as far as the Christian ministry is concerned. Maladjustments are particularly severe where a wife or a husband falls too far behind the other in language learning and through one discouragement after another finally gives up.

The learning of a language takes time, and some missionaries look upon such a period as almost an entire waste. On the contrary, they ought to be thankful, for those months and years before being thrown into the whirl of missionary activity and responsibilities make it easier to adjust to the difficult climate, the different foods, and the new and curious ways. Without such a delay in which one learns the foreign language and the customs, it is possible to ruin one's future work completely. Even in seemingly little things we can offend so easily. For example, in some parts of Africa and Latin America it is considered very dangerous to compliment a mother on the beauty of her child. To do so is to incur the responsibility for the possible death of the child. Any such words of praise are regarded by the natives as calling the attention of the evil spirits to the attractiveness of the child; and the child's death, even months later, may be attributed to the malignant influence of the well-intentioned missionary. Equally misunderstood among some tribes of Central Africa is our practice of affectionately patting children on the head, for the natives in those areas regard such an action as a direct threat to the soul of the child and a clear indication of evil intent. In certain places of the Congo one cannot point at a person with a finger without being regarded as very lewd and immoral. In such places the approved way to point is by sticking out the lower lip and jaw.

Language learning is more than simple mechanical ability to produce acoustic signals; it is a process by which we make vital contacts with a new community, a new manner of life, and a new system of thinking. To do this well is the basic requirement of effective missionary endeavor.

1.4 Reasons for Failure in Language Learning

Lack of time is the most common reason for failure in language learning. Of course, there are those rare individuals who seem to soak up languages like a sponge, but most of us are not in that category. Even when languages are seemingly simple, they exhibit all kinds of complications when we really attempt to master them. Some missionaries and mission boards seem to assume that languages of so-called primitive peoples are so essentially simple that they can be "picked up" as one carries on other responsibilities. It is true that languages differ considerably in difficulty, but primitive languages are by no means simpler as a class than traditionally written ones. Those who have been content with a superficial study of such a language usually end up with a very superficial knowledge. In general they use only a small percentage of the grammatical forms, being content to stumble along with two or three tenses, when the language may have seven or eight, and missing completely the tones of words and characteristic intonation of the sentences. Failure to take the required time to learn a language is costly, for the efficiency and character of one's life work is so largely determined by ability to communicate effectively.

Some of the failure to learn a language results from the wrong approach. Because of the traditional Latin-grammar approach to most European languages, it has been assumed that the same way of talking about and describing languages can be applied to any and all varieties of speech. Nothing could be further from the truth, for languages may be utterly different.[1] For example, in Muskogee, an Indian language of the south central United States, the numerals are conjugated just like verbs; in Maya, a language of Yucatan, Mexico, most of the words which appear to be conjunctions turn out to be possessed nouns; in Hupa, an Indian language of California, nouns may indicate tenses even as verbs do; and in Mongbandi, a Sudanic language of northern Congo, the tones on the subject pronouns show the difference between past, present, and future time. We simply must not force languages into the Latin mould and expect to understand their functioning.

Being taught the native language by some older missionary and without the constant presence of a native speaker can prove disastrous. The young missionary simply copies the probable mispronunciations and the idiosyncracies of the other missionary, rather than being guided constantly by what and how the native speaks. This does not mean, of course, that the experienced missionary cannot help tremendously in teaching the new missionary recruit. In fact, if the proper methods are used, exceptionally rapid progress may be made; but the important thing is to learn from the native, while the older missionary guides and directs the learning process.[2] There are unfortunately those missionaries who are so completely convinced of their infallibility in language matters that they insist on correcting the native speakers, even to the extent of contending that none of the natives actually pronounce their language correctly.

Another mistake in language learning is the habit of placing reading ahead of speaking. Undoubtedly there is much to

---

[1] For a nontechnical treatment of these problems see Eugene A. Nida, Linguistic Interludes (Glendale, California: Summer Institute of Linguistics, 1947).

[2] See Chapter 3 for a discussion of ways to learn a language.

be gained by reading, but printed symbols are only graphic symbols standing for acoustic (sound) symbols, and to learn a language we must make primary use of the primary system of symbolization, i.e., the spoken form of the language.

Frequently the circumstances for language learning are not the best. The missionary may lack the opportunities to hear the language spoken. For example, living in the comparative isolation of a hill-top mission station, he is not surrounded constantly by the language as he would be if he were living in a native village. The ideal situation is, of course, to live with the people in the villages; and though this is not regarded as possible in some areas of the world (for example, in Negro Africa), yet some missionaries have lived in native villages and their linguistic proficiency attests to the great advantages. One of the principal reasons for the remarkable language ability of many of the old missionary pioneers is the fact that they lived so much with the people, since they did not possess the means of isolating themselves in more comfortable surroundings. We do not mean that the conventional patterns of missionary life in many places are completely wrong, but we do mean that special efforts must be made to break down the social and linguistic barriers that arise from this form of segregation.

Failure to appreciate the nature of real language proficiency may also militate against one's accomplishments. It is relatively easy "to get by," for the natives are so polite and so intelligent that they understand what we ask for in spite of our awkward grammatical constructions. We can probably best describe the progressive stages in language learning in terms of the following five degrees:

1. Recognizing a few words and phrases and being able to make known one's very elemental needs. This involves a vocabulary of probably two or three hundred words.
2. A practical use of the language in very restricted circumstances, such as giving instructions to servants in the home and buying at the market place. At the same time, one is able to follow the gist of speeches, provided the subject matter is very familiar, e.g., sermons on well-known texts.
3. Understanding speeches with fair comprehension, following conversation (if the topic is not too removed

from one's experience), and ability to make speeches, if one prepares carefully in advance, or if one keeps well within a limited range of experience.
4. Understanding rapid conversation on practically all subjects and being able to participate in such conversation on familiar themes. One does not have to grope for correct grammatical forms, and for all practical purposes one is fluent in the language, though not necessarily expert.
5. Exhibiting complete facility as evidenced by ability to joke and pun, and to employ specialized idioms and proverbial statements in their proper contexts.

Of course, there are many degrees of proficiency within these five steps, but it should be noted that conversational ability, not speech-making, is the sign of proficiency. It is surprising the number of missionaries who never advance beyond the third stage. This is even true of some who have undertaken to translate parts of the Bible into the language they have been studying. Some valuable missionary work has been done by those who have not advanced beyond the third stage, but how much more effective it would have been if they had acquired further skill is evidenced by the truly excellent work done by those who have paid the price to know the words which unlock the door to the native's heart.

Because natives do not frequently voice their strong resentment about a missionary's linguistic failures, some have assumed that awkward forms and mispronunciations do not actually matter too much. That is far from being the case. One native approached a visiting missionary executive in Latin America and rather timidly and apologetically said, "Why is it that after ten years our missionary has not learned our language well? He hurts our ears." A people's language is their most distinctive possession; it is the shrine of their soul. In order to enter and appreciate this shrine, we must be familiar with its intricate and meaningful forms.

The business man can often succeed by using merely the trade language or the restricted vocabulary of barter, for his purpose is to get from the people something which the rest of the world wants and to give something which the natives can be induced to buy, regardless of the value of the article to the natives' own lives. The missionary, however, has a greater task, for he must convince men to accept the grace of God in Christ Jesus, which conflicts with much that native tradition holds dear and which demands complete allegiance. It is no trinket which the missionary comes to sell, but a way of life; and in order to explain the meaning of it, he must be able to converse about the most important and intimate features of native belief. The missionary finds that natives do not even mention many important aspects of their lives when using a trade language, even when they know such a language well. Some Mongbandi people in northern Congo explained their failure to mention their native beliefs to the missionaries by saying, "But how could we speak about that in Lingala?" Lingala was the trade language of all the area, but it was just that, a _trade_ language, and not the language of their heart and spirit. Only one who has heard natives "Oh" and "Ah" when they finally understand the message in their own language can appreciate the strategic importance of giving the Word in a man's own tongue.

Expert language ability helps to identify the missionary most effectively with the native society, and such identification is essential to a truly successful ministry. As missionaries we must work _in_ the field and not _on_ the field. It is not the geographical scope but the degree of cultural penetration which marks truly effective missionary enterprise, and there is no substitute for proper use of the native idiom. The native language is not only a means of entrance into the life, but it may be a defence against outside opposition. One missionary working in an Indian tribe in Latin America was threatened by the local priest, and the natives were instructed to drive him out, but they defended their missionary friend by saying, "We can't drive him away; he is one of us now. He speaks our language." This missionary had gone out and lived with a native family, and in this way he had acquired an amazing facility in one of the most complicated Indian languages of this hemisphere. His efforts were certainly not unrewarded in the response of the people to him and to his message.

Chapter 2

2. PRINCIPLES OF LANGUAGE LEARNING

Success in language learning requires close adherence to and thorough understanding of certain fundamental principles. These are not complicated, but they may seem strange, since they contradict so many traditional practices.

2.1 Start with a Clean Slate

Few people realize how very essential it is to drop all preconceptions about languages before beginning the study of a new one. It is a deceptive practice to teach the so-called "logic" of languages. Grammarians are forever giving "rules" for forms and trying to explain these rules by some complicated system of logical deductions. For example, we are told that the use of shall and will conforms to certain basic requirements of logic, but the rules are so complicated and arbitrary that no one follows them throughout. Furthermore, even the grammarians do not agree as to what should be done,[1] and they proceed to find so-called "glaring errors" in the writings of such men as Jowett, Wilde, Stevenson, Conan Doyle, Gladstone, Steele, Addison, Swift, and many others. It was actually not until 1765 that William Ward's Grammar of the English Language attempted to expound the rules on the basis of the "fundamental meanings" of the two words. The rules did not follow any described usage at the time, but were made almost entirely out of whole cloth. Far worse, however, than the multiplication of inane rules has been the tendency to vindicate all such statements by philosophical dictums about the logical structure of languages.

The relationships between words and the objects for which they stand as symbols do reflect some logical features, but we have made so much of this matter of logic and have attempted

---

[1] See a complete statement of this problem in Charles C. Fries, American English Grammar (New York: Appleton-Century, 1940).

so to universalize the concept, that students find it exceedingly strange and disconcerting when they undertake the study of a language that does not coincide with what has been taught as being the "natural and logical" expression of the human intelligence. For example, in Tarahumara, an Indian language of northern Mexico, there are no plural forms of nouns. The word <u>towíki</u> means "boy" or "boys." There is simply no difference in form. Of course, certain adjective-like words can be added to mean "many" or "few," but Tarahumara simply does not distinguish singular from plural by anything added to the noun.

If, however, we examine English carefully we will discover that there are many illogical aspects. For example, the verb <u>to be</u> has three entirely different forms in the present: <u>am</u>, <u>is</u>, and <u>are</u>. There is no other verb like this, and certainly this could be considered as "illogical." Certain so-called auxiliaries: <u>may</u>, <u>can</u>, <u>shall</u>, <u>will</u>, <u>must</u>, and <u>ought</u>, never occur as complete verbs, and all but one of them, namely <u>ought</u>, are followed immediately by a verb form without the introductory particle <u>to</u>, e.g., <u>can</u> <u>go</u>, <u>may</u> <u>sail</u>, <u>shall</u> <u>remain</u>, <u>will</u> <u>try</u>, and <u>must</u> <u>enter</u>. Ought, however, must always be introduced by this particle, e.g., <u>ought</u> <u>to</u> <u>remain</u> and <u>ought</u> <u>to</u> <u>go</u>. It is quite illogical that all but one of the auxiliaries should occur with one kind of construction and <u>ought</u> with another. Furthermore, <u>can</u>, <u>may</u>, <u>shall</u>, and <u>will</u> have past tense forms: <u>could</u>, <u>might</u>, <u>should</u>, and <u>would</u>; but <u>must</u> and <u>ought</u> have no such corresponding past formations. We could go on and on pointing out the illogical and contradictory nature of English and all languages, but perhaps the following anonymous poem, entitled "Why English Is So Hard," will help to point out the difficulties more adequately, though less scientifically:

Why English Is So Hard

We'll begin with a <u>box</u>, and the plural is <u>boxes</u>;
  But the plural of <u>ox</u> should be <u>oxen</u>, not <u>oxes</u>.
Then one fowl is <u>goose</u>, but two are called <u>geese</u>;
  Yet the plural of <u>moose</u> should never be <u>meese</u>.

You may find a lone <u>mouse</u> or a whole lot of <u>mice</u>,
  But the plural of <u>house</u> is <u>houses</u>, not <u>hice</u>.
If the plural of <u>man</u> is always called <u>men</u>,
  Why shouldn't the plural of <u>pan</u> be called <u>pen</u>?

PRINCIPLES OF LANGUAGE LEARNING

The cow in the plural may be cows or kine,
   But the plural of vow is vows, not vine.
And I speak of a foot, and you show me your feet,
   But I give you a boot—would a pair be called beet?

If one is a tooth and a whole set are teeth,
   Why shouldn't the plural of booth be called beeth?
If the singular is this, and the plural is these,
   Should the plural of kiss be nicknamed kese?

Then one may be that, and three may be those,
   Yet the plural of hat would never be hose;
We speak of a brother, and also of brethren,
   But though we say mother, we never say methren.

The masculine pronouns are he, his and him,
   But imagine the feminine she, shis, and shim!
So our English, I think you will all agree,
   Is the trickiest language you ever did see.

Even with all these irregularities, English is much more regular than many languages. Some people are, however, worried about such matters and insist on being told just why languages have such illogical formations. To find answers some people consult historical dictionaries of English, but that is no real help, for the irregularities do not vanish into thin air by projecting them backwards for several hundred years. Irregularities existed in Old English, in Proto-Germanic, in our reconstructed forms of Indo-European, and in what we know of Indo-Hittite. We cannot eliminate the illogical aspects of language by referring to their histories, nor blame them entirely on slovenly speakers or untutored children. In fact, if children had their way, they would regularize many features by such forms as foots, oxes, runned, fighted, and I is.

It is quite impossible for us to explain the "why's" of language. There is no reason, but a historical one, for any irregularities, and historical reasons are really not reasons. They are just statements that the irregularity has been in the language for a long time. It does not tell us just how the complexity arose. We do know something about these irregularities, namely, that they occur in all languages, that they are very persistent, especially if they occur in some frequently used form of the language, and that some irregularities are constantly disappearing and others being introduced. For example, in Old English the verbs step, laugh, and glide, were so-called irregular verbs, having different stem forms for the present, past, and past participle, but now these verbs are quite regular. On the other hand, ring, hide, and fling used to be regular in their formation but are now irregular. Changes in language are almost as unpredictable as styles of dresses, hats, and neckties. Of course, the changes are slower and less perceptible, but they are dependent upon the same social factors, for the acceptance or rejection of linguistic innovation is a social matter and as unpredictable as people.

One of the most persistent misconceptions about language is the belief that primitive languages are inadequate as means of communication. People have just assumed that since supposedly primitive peoples have a more or less simple material culture, they will of necessity have a restricted vocabulary, and that their language will reflect a general deficiency. A recent dictionary of Zulu[2] has approximately 30,000 entries and does not include thousands of regular derivative formations (e.g., verbs from nouns and nouns from verbs) which we would include in a comparable dictionary of English. Over 20,000 words have been listed in Maya and 27,000 in Aztec, but these figures are by no means exhaustive. Furthermore, extent of vocabulary is not necessarily a criterion of value. Shakespeare is said to have used approximately 24,000 different words, Milton some 17,000 and the English Bible only 7,200.[3]

Though some people will grant the fact that aboriginal[4] peoples have surprisingly large vocabularies, the conviction persists that such peoples could not have well-defined or complicated grammars. Note, however, the following forms in Congo Swahili:

ninapika "I hit"
nilipika "I have hit"

---

[2] C. M. Doke and B. W. Vilakazi, Zulu-English Dictionary (Johannesburg, South Africa: Witwatersrand University Press, 1948).

[3] A. L. Kroeber, Anthropology (New York: Harcourt, Brace, and Co., 1948), pp. 230-31.

[4] "Aboriginal" means that a society has not had a traditional form of written language.

nilimupika "I have hit him"
wunapikiwa "you (sg.) are hit"
nilinupikaka "I hit you (pl.) a long time ago"
wutakanipikizwa "you (sg.) will cause me to be hit"

The parts that go together to make up these various words are: ni- "I," na- "present tense," li- "perfect tense," mu- "him," -pika[5] "to hit," wu- "you (sg.)," -iw or -w "passive," nu- "you (pl.)," -ka "remote past tense," -iz "causative," taka- "future tense." These are just a very few of the thousands of combinations of prefixes and suffixes which can go with any verb. In fact, the structure of Congo Swahili is in many respects much more elaborate than Greek or Latin. It is ridiculous to talk about any primitive language as being inadequate. Not all aboriginal languages put parts together to make long involved words, but the grammar is there, whether the parts are coalesced into words or remain as separate units.[6]

The impression that natives throw their words together in an indiscriminate manner is quite wrong. There may be alternative ways of saying things, and the word order may be so different from English that it seems totally illogical, but there is always a basic pattern. Note, however, the following two sentences in Ilamba, a Bantu language of Tanganyika:

1. ke·nto kiakoe keko·lu kemoe kiameke·la eno·mba.[7]
 "Thing his big one is greater than a house."

2. lokani loakoe loko·lu lomoe loaoke·la oo·ta.
 "Word his big one is greater than a bow."

These two sentences mean (1) "His one big thing is greater than a house" and (2) "His one big (i.e., important) word surpasses (i.e., is greater in strength than) a bow." Note that the noun is the first word of the subject expression, while in English it would be the last, and that each word follows in a definite order, though different from English (cf. thing his big one with his one big thing). Furthermore, the adjectives show their agreement with the noun by the prefixes ki- or ke- in the

---

[5] See section 5.3 for further discussion of this stem.
[6] These problems are considered in Chapter 5.
[7] The tones are not written on the words.

first sentence and lo- in the second sentence. Even the verbs show reference to the subject by the subject prefixes ki- and lo-. In the verb kiameke·la the prefix me- shows that a noun like eno·mba "house" is the object, and in the verb loaoke·la the prefix o-, just before the stem -ke·la, shows that the object is a noun such as oo·ta. A language such as this cannot be said to have a "deficient grammar."

Some people have the impression that aboriginal languages are subject to all types of rapid changes because they are not reduced to writing. Strange as it may seem, the written languages seem to change much more rapidly than unwritten ones. For example, in Yucatan we can determine that during the last three hundred years Maya has changed much less in its structure and pronunciation than Spanish has. Of course, Maya has adopted many Spanish words, but so has the Spanish of Yucatan. However, we are not speaking here of vocabulary but of the grammatical structure, and in this respect the reducing of a language to writing is no guarantee in the least against change. In fact, languages seem to change directly in proportion to the density of communication, and the more a language is used by a greater concentration of people the more rapid will be its change. The new missionary need not worry about a native language changing so rapidly that he cannot keep up with it, simply because it has not been traditionally written. On the contrary, he will probably be irked by the comparative rigidity of the linguistic structure.

There are people who consider that learning some aboriginal language is not worth while, for, as they contend, it is bound to die out in ten or fifteen years. Such estimates are almost always too optimistic, for languages do not die out so abruptly. Of course, under the pressure of our agressive American way of life, numerous Indian languages of the United States have died out, but that is far from the situation in Europe, where some minority languages have persisted for generations, e.g., Welsh, Irish (which is now being revived), Scotch Gaelic, Breton, Romansch (spoken in Switzerland)—not to mention scores of local dialects which have a thriving literature. It is true that trade languages are spreading rapidly in many areas, e.g., Hausa in Nigeria and contiguous parts of West Africa, Swahili in East Africa, Lingala in the Congo, Spanish in Spanish America, Malay in the East Indies, and English in the

Pacific Islands. But native languages will persist for many years as a second language and may even be revived with the turn of political events. For example, in Indo-China it was the policy of the French government to push Annamese at the expense of the Thai languages, but in the political upheaval following World War II, Annamese was thrust aside and native education was undertaken in the Thai languages, with French as a trade language. The natives of Palau in the South Pacific have had a succession of Spanish, German, Japanese, and now English as trade languages, but they have retained their own language as a vital part of their lives and an entire New Testament has been translated into their language to meet the spiritual needs of a growing church.

Aboriginal languages are held in contempt by some because they are thought to have no literature. The mistake has been in assuming that literature is to be found only in books. Actually, many primitive peoples have vast quantities of literature, but the way in which it is passed from one generation to another is by word of mouth and not by written manuscript or printed page. A number of native and European scholars have spent years in accumulating the Zulu oral literary products, and they are amazed at their wealth and volume. The San Blas Indians of Panama possess a prodigious quantity of stories, legends, and poetry. In fact, before being able to candidate for the chieftainship, a man must memorize enough of such materials (most of them in a type of poetic form) that several days would be required to recite them all. Even the Homeric poems, which are still considered to be the greatest epic poetry of all times, were passed on for generations through a purely oral tradition. Their being committed to writing was only a relatively unimportant part of their cultural significance.

One final misconception about languages must be considered before we can clear the slate for constructive thinking about language. This concerns the popular idea that there is some basic form to all languages or that at least all the primitive languages have some fundamental characteristics in common. Such ideas are exceedingly old and very prevalent. Many scholars of past centuries related all strange languages to Hebrew, especially if no one knew much about such languages. For example, James Adair wrote in his <u>History of the American</u>

Indian (London, 1725), "The Indian language and dialects [i.e., those of America] appear to have the very idiom and genius of Hebrew...both in letters and signification, synonymous with the Hebrew language. It is a common and old remark that there is no language in which some Hebrew words are not to be found. Probably Hebrew was the first and only language."

Such ideas have persisted to the very present. For example, some missionaries have related one of the Bantu names for God Lesa to the Hebrew stem El occurring in Elohim (Genesis 1:1). The -sa portion has been dismissed as not important, and they have attempted to explain the discrepancy between El and Le- by the fact that Hebrew is written backwards. An even more absurd deduction as to the Hebrew origin of African languages (as well as an identification of the Lost Ten Tribes) was made by a missionary who concluded that because some of her students were mirror readers and writers (a well-recognized difficulty even with many American children) Hebrew must necessarily have been the ancestral language of the people. There are other people who have vainly attempted to relate all the languages of Africa to Egyptian. Our minds seem to be plagued by the desire to organize things and get them together, but the linguist soon dismisses such flights of fancy and returns to the basic task of describing languages as he finds them. When he does so, he discovers that there is absolutely no single structural characteristic running through all languages, and that so-called primitive languages are just as diverse as any other. There are indeed some characteristics in common to all languages. For example, we speak with our mouths and not with our ears; we have vowels and consonants; and we change the pitch of the voice; but these are not means of classifying linguistic types. One pseudo-linguist, however, attempted to classify languages as (1) vowel languages, (2) consonant languages, and (3) tonal languages.[8] Of course this is absurd. It would be just as

---

[8] What the man actually meant was that some languages have a predominance of syllables which end in a vowel and others are characterized by having many syllables ending in consonants, while certain languages are characterized by tonal distinctions. A classification on the basis of syllables is meaningless. Distinctive tones occur on all types of syllabic structures.

sensible to classify pies as consisting of three types: (1) crust, (2) filling, and (3) cheese. Naturally, all pies have crust and filling, and some are served with cheese. In the same fashion, all languages have vowels and consonants, and some make distinctions between individual words by means of tone.

It would be fine to be able to reduce all linguistic problems and language diversity to some simple structure or to find certain fundamental roots occurring in all the languages of the world, but the truth is that no such features exist, and so we are obliged to consider each language on its own merits. If we do, we shall discover amazingly usable devices for conveying important and subtle distinctions in meaning. If we fail to be understood, it will not be the deficiency of the language but our own ineptness in using its complex and highly refined system of symbols.

2.2 Listening, Speaking, Reading, and Then Writing Constitute the Fundamental Order in Language Learning

The scientifically valid procedure in language learning involves listening first, to be followed by speaking. Then comes reading, and finally the writing of the language. This is almost the reverse of the traditional methods. One of the reasons for this is that many teachers of foreign languages cannot themselves speak the language, and hence there is no chance to listen. Certainly the infrequent, clumsy, oral reading of the prescribed sentences in the textbook can scarcely be called speaking. What actually happens in so many instances is that the student begins by writing out sentences on the basis of the grammar rules. This is done almost from the first day, certainly before one has half a chance to become acquainted with the vocabulary or the flow of the language. We soon get involved in hundreds of intricate rules, some of them purely orthographic, e.g., in French and Hebrew, and we usually end up by "hating" grammar and detesting the language. But worst of all, we rarely learn to use the language, for though we may pass tests so as to graduate, our ability to carry on a conversation in the foreign language with a native speaker is almost nil. We even spend so much time with the Masoretic pointing of Hebrew vowels that we do not get a chance to read the language extensively, and in the end our only contact with Hebrew may be an infrequent use of an analytical Hebrew-Chaldee lexicon.

Our primary trouble is that we have tackled the study of language from the wrong end. We are like the man who thinks he can learn to swim by reading books about swimming. In actuality, we learn by doing. The grammatical rules are valuable as we plunge into the language and need some assistance. In the same way, advanced instructions about swimming are helpful as we learn something from actual experience in the water. But reading books never makes a swimmer and learning rules never makes a practical linguist.

By setting up listening, speaking, reading, and writing in this order, we do not imply that one must be able to understand everything before beginning to speak. It does mean, however, that we learn to speak by hearing someone else speak, and not by reading orally on the basis of certain "rules of pronunciation." When we hear words and expressions from a native speaker, we should of course imitate just as closely as possible, so that speaking follows immediately upon listening. Reading may begin rather soon if one is studying a language such as Spanish or German where the orthography represents the meaningful distinctions in sound; but if the language is French or English, then reading traditionally spelled words is a great disadvantage at first. It is better to use some so-called "phonetic alphabet" first until one has mastered several hundred phrases. Only then should one read the traditional orthography. In the case of Chinese, it is probably better to put off the reading process for several months and until such time as one has a rather good conversational ability for simple situations. Many linguists advise mastering a vocabulary of two or three thousand words before embarking on the difficult and quite different task of learning the Chinese symbols.

Some people object to placing reading in third place in the language-learning procedure, for they insist that they are visual-minded and that they can learn vocabulary much more easily from seeing it than from hearing it. To an extent this may be true, for our entire educational process has been such as to place great importance on the eye-gate. On the other hand, there is a much closer relationship between the auditory impression of a phrase and the motor action of reproducing this sound by the vocal organs than there is between the graphic symbolism on a page and the oral reproduction. The graphic symbolism must usually be transferred first into some type of corresponding acoustic impression before it can be uttered. Furthermore, auditory impressions are more frequently obtained in real situations, so that the expression and the environment are interrelated, and accordingly the recall is easier. Purely visual impressions are too often gained in artificial situations such as sitting at home reading a book, and hence the forms are not so easily associated with the action, as when we hear expressions used in connection with actual happenings.

Our special emphasis upon the auditory perception does not mean that we should set aside all the other factors in the memory process. We should listen to expressions (an auditory process), write them down (a motor process), read them (a visual process), and then pronounce them over and over (repeated motor processes). People differ in the importance which these various processes have in their memorization of materials. Some people find it very helpful to write a phrase several times. Others consider that seeing the phrase repeatedly is just as valuable for them. Still others apparently learn most rapidly by means of auditory impressions. Whatever one's special aptitudes are, these should be cultivated and improved. Nevertheless, one should constantly try to improve one's auditory memory. Our own civilization does very little for us in this way, for our training is predominantly a matter of sight. We are frequently astonished to find natives who cannot read and yet who can recite from memory entire books of the Bible. This is true of a number of people in Africa and the Orient. The auditory memory can be developed as well as any other, and anyone learning a language will do well to concentrate in so far as possible on improving this vital factor.

2.3   Mimicry Is the Key to Language Learning

People who mimic easily have a great advantage in learning a foreign language, providing, of course, they will mimic native speakers. However, some people who are good at mimicry become very self-conscious when they try to reproduce foreign sounds, and their natural ability may become relatively useless.

Language learning usually necessitates conscious mimicry. It means noticing carefully such matters as the position of the lips, the quality of the sounds, the speed of utterance, the intonation of the voice, the so-called "swing" of the sentences, and even the characteristic gestures. To mimic all such features may seem silly at first, but it is much sillier not to do so, even though one may make numerous mistakes. In general one must murder a language before mastering it, and part of the murdering process must begin at once. One of the great mistakes is thinking that the refining of the pronunciation may come later in the study, and that first one must get acquainted with the grammar and the vocabulary and acquire some conversational facility. Those who consciously delay their mimicry of foreign speakers will discover that they have acquired habits which remain with them for many months, and sometimes they are never overcome.

Mimicry consists of three phases: (1) acute and constant observation, (2) "throwing oneself into it," and (3) continual practice. The matter of observation will be treated in Chapter 4. What we must emphasize here is the necessity of throwing oneself into the mood. At first this conscious adopting of entirely different habits of speech may seem terribly awkward, in fact, even painfully displeasing. It goes against our grain, and we have a feeling that we may be offending people by the conscious way in which we imitate their every word and gesture. What seems odd to us is not, however, odd to them. Rather, our American manner of speech transferred into another language seems unutterably queer. Of course, there is the possibility that by our conscious and obvious mimicry we may offend some fastidious native speaker, but it is certain that failure to mimic would offend many more.

An important part of the mimicry process is continual practice. After a short time the mimicry does not seem so strange to us. In fact, it seems very natural, and we unconsciously find ourselves adopting entirely new speech "manners" when we begin to speak a foreign language.

2.4   Language Learning Is Over-Learning

Language must be automatic, or it is practically useless. The person who must stop to figure out the right forms or who

PRINCIPLES OF LANGUAGE LEARNING

must grope constantly for words has not learned a foreign language. Expressions must be on the tip of the tongue.

To acquire an automatic language facility requires three processes: (1) memorizing, (2) drill and repetition, (3) thinking in the foreign language. Some people have the weird idea that language consists primarily of grammatical forms and that the vocabulary is more or less inconsequential. Both forms and vocabulary are essential parts, and neither can be neglected. However, there is no point in just memorizing long series of paradigmatic forms, e.g., Spanish compro "I buy," compras "you (sg. familiar) buy," compra "he, she, it, you (sg. formal) buy," compramos "we buy," compráis "you (pl. familiar) buy," and compran "they, you (pl. formal) buy," unless one understands how such forms are used and how they can be combined into sentences. Similarly, it is quite useless to begin learning a language by memorizing a dictionary, even one with only the more common words listed. Languages are learned by words in meaningful combinations (see Chapter 3), but nevertheless, the words and forms must be learned. Perhaps it would be better if we did not use the word "memorize," for it conjures up all types of unpleasant associations—mastering long lists of vocabulary in a Greek grammar or of relatively impracticable grammatical rules about certain prepositions taking the genitive, others the dative, and still others the accusative case. By memorizing we do not mean learning forms out of context as is so often the case in poorly constructed grammars, but we do mean having the facts of a language down pat.

One of the most effective ways to memorize is to drill. This means constant repetition either to oneself, or preferably to a native speaker. Drilling can mean taking a number of short sentences in a language and going over and over them, first slowly and then more and more rapidly until they are up to normal speed. In fact, our practicing should at times be a bit faster than normal speed, so that when we actually use the forms, they will sound right. If one is able to drill with a native speaker, then this person can say the sentence first and the student can repeat, sometimes three or four times, and then go on to another similar expression. It may take hundreds of repetitions, but that is not too many if by them one gains automatic facility. Further instructions on drilling are contained in Chapter 3.

Thinking in a foreign language is absolutely essential. One cannot expect to speak with facility while going through the process of translating ideas from English into another language. Not only will the time required make the speech slow and jerky, but it is inevitable that the idiom and word order will be predominantly English, with the result that the sentences will sound extremely queer and foreign. One can practice thinking in a foreign language by making up imaginary conversations, constructing speeches, or recalling what one has heard or read in the foreign language. Even though one's vocabulary may be limited (for example, not more than a few hundred words), it is very important to experiment in formulating one's thinking by using the words and expressions of the language being acquired. At first, it may seem almost hopeless, but every time an English word or phrase pops into one's mind, it should be tossed out, and thinking should progress only as foreign words and phrases come to mind. One can begin by recalling the conversation when buying at the market. Or one may wish to construct some more effective arguments as to why the merchant should have come down further on the price. It is valuable to try to think through the sermon preached by the native evangelist or to construct another following some theme for which one has an adequate vocabulary.

In listening to someone else speak, we should attempt to think along in the foreign language, without attempting to translate the words into English. Despite our efforts to the contrary, we tend to translate automatically into English, so that a conscious effort to avoid this practice is absolutely necessary. One must let the foreign words have their own meanings and let them begin to "ring the bell" in one's thoughts.

We cannot overemphasize the necessity of complete automatic facility in a language. Speech must flow naturally and easily without any apparent mental contortions. Speech should be so automatic that one can say, "He let his mind slip into neutral while his tongue idled on."

2.5   Language Learning Means Language Using

A person never learns to play the piano simply by studying the mechanism of the instrument, observing the manual skill of others, and learning how to read music. Piano playing is an art and a skill, and it requires practice. No amount of technical knowledge about music can compensate for the necessary hours sitting at the piano and practicing progressively more complex musical selections. Furthermore, the beginning piano student does not learn to play pieces just by practicing scales and chords. He must attempt to play real pieces if he is ever going to learn to play them.

The same thing applies to a person learning a foreign language. A great deal of technical information about language structure and even the mastering of the paradigms (comparable to scales in music) will not make a skilled speaker. To learn to speak, one must speak. Of course, this does not mean starting out with a sermon, any more than the aspiring pianist begins with a Bach fugue. It does mean, however, that the ivory-tower attitude toward language learning dooms a person to failure. We must become surrounded by the constant hubbub of language use if we are to learn.

One of the most common errors in language learning is the failure to practice hearing. We have become so accustomed to the book technique of learning anything that we consider our time most profitably spent studying in the isolation of our libraries. This is folly for the student of foreign languages. He must get out where the language is spoken and where he can speak. To do this, he needs to look for real situations where the language can be used. Once when a new group of missionaries were entering a country in Latin America, one of the members of the group gallantly volunteered to do the marketing while the others seemed to think that such time was lost from more important "study." It turned out, of course, that the one doing the marketing progressed very rapidly in the use of the language, for he had excellent opportunities to use his limited knowledge of Spanish since marketing involved constant haggling over prices.

Missionaries in Africa have found it very valuable to go out and sit with the old men or school boys around the smoking fires of the native compounds. At first, the missionary may not be able to understand a thing of what is being said, but gradually recurring expressions seem to jump out of the stream of speech and conversation. After a time, the missionary may be able to ask questions of the people in the group or even contribute some tale from his own experience. <u>Only after one has learned to sit and listen can one profitably stand and speak.</u>

Another practical situation is visiting. This means simply chatting—about anything and everything. The missionary should not attempt to be preaching or arguing all the time. He must learn just to talk. His later evangelistic efforts will be much more valuable if he will only take the time to learn how to chat with people. Of course, this procedure does contradict many of our ideas about how a missionary should spend his time. Chatting with people may not seem very impressive to put down on a report to be sent to one's home constituency, but it is the indispensable introduction to the language and to the people.

We must not overlook the part that the missionary's personality plays in the learning of a language. Two young ladies working in an Indian tribe in Latin America showed conspicuous differences in practical language ability resulting from their personality contrasts. One of them was very vivacious, extrovertish, and talkative, but was considerably inferior in the structural analysis of the language and in the mastery of grammatical rules. The other was quieter, slower in speech, and much less inclined to express herself on every occasion and about everything that was happening. However, she was much the better technical linguist of the two. Nevertheless, as one may well guess, the first young lady learned to speak much better and more rapidly than the second. Being naturally talkative, interested in people and things, and feeling certain irrepressible desires to be communicative are great aids to language learning.

Some people are emotionally and psychologically incapable of not learning a language. One missionary wife complained when her husband insisted on transferring to South America during World War II. She had already learned French and Flemish, and she objected strenuously to the prospect of being required to learn Spanish. Her husband knowingly and humorously challenged her, "I dare you to keep quiet in any language." Sure enough, she also learned Spanish!

Language learning means plunging headlong into a series of completely different experiences. It means exposing oneself to situations where the use of the language is required. Making a trip alone where one must obtain food and lodging is a marvelous way to acquire vocabulary. It is amazing how words learned under such circumstances stick with one. The missionary will do well to take on word-using responsibilities or make of his circumstances a classroom for language learning. Building a house with native helpers can be an excellent means of learning the language—listening to their constant chattering, chiming in where possible, repeating over and over the names for various implements, always making suggestions with the aid of newly acquired words. Such an experience can prove even more valuable than hours of poring over poorly constructed grammatical rules, for we only learn to speak by speaking.

Chapter 3

WAYS OF LEARNING A FOREIGN LANGUAGE

When most of us think about learning a foreign language, our minds run to two extremes. One of these is of the poor missionary surrounded by cannibals gleefully sizing up their victim. We can imagine his desperate attempts to placate his captors and explain that he is really a very innocent person with perfectly friendly intentions. The other mental image of language learning is of a high school or college classroom where we struggled to answer questions about subjunctives, gerunds, ablatives, and supines—things that we never fully understood and never hoped to meet up with again. Numbers of potential missionaries have given up all thoughts of going to the foreign field simply because of their desperately distasteful experience with college French or seminary Greek; and many others feel certain that they could never go to certain areas of the world, for they are confident that they could never learn the language. Most of these ideas are based on complete misconceptions about language and the process of learning.

3.1 Popular Misconceptions

Most people have an exaggerated idea of the authority and value of a grammar and a dictionary. Some even think that they can learn a language by only these two books. Certain well-meaning souls have written to the Bible societies offering their services as Bible translators for work in their spare time. They admit that they do not know any foreign languages, but if the Bible Society will only send them a grammar and a dictionary of some language, they feel quite confident that they can translate the Bible, or at least portions of it, into that language. Such zeal is commendable, but the ignorance which such an offer reflects is unfortunate. Of course, the reason for this is the dominance of Latin study in our schooling. The only way in which we can learn Latin, Ancient Greek, and Hebrew is through books, but that is not true of living languages.

WAYS OF LEARNING A FOREIGN LANGUAGE

Even the best grammar of French cannot teach us to speak French, nor will it enable us to write good idiomatic French.

What frightens most missionary candidates about foreign languages is the thought of years of tedious, uninteresting study of some grammar and the slow painful reading of some insipid nursery stories, only to find that after all this he cannot understand a sentence of the language over the radio and cannot order a meal in a foreign restaurant. If after all that hard work there are no evident results, he wonders whether he could ever learn to speak a foreign language. Sometimes he builds up such a case against foreign language learning that he acquires a complex on the subject, and his protestations of inability are almost pathetic. He is like a person who has been forced to eat too much of some food and as a result acquires such an aversion for it that the very thought of having to swallow a small bit of it really makes him ill.

There are also those people who have been told that language learning consists primarily of reading the best literature. This, of course, can be a great help, but it is not the way to learn to speak. Furthermore, many of the literary productions of a language are in a very artificial dialect. One foreigner who came to the United States had concentrated on Shakespeare and the Bible as an introduction to the English language, but such phrases as "Unhand me!" and "When shall we depart from hence?" marked his speech as being odd, to say the least. Missionaries run the same risk of patterning their speech after Bible translations, for too often these translations are exceedingly awkward and stiff.

Some missionaries have felt obliged to learn only from the highly educated natives. It is admirable to want the "best," but it does not necessarily follow that a well-educated person is always a good teacher. In fact, some types of education, particularly the classical, conservative kinds, may make a person excessively pedantic. Furthermore, one who is desirous of being able to speak to all people must not restrict himself to imitating the speech of only the intelligentsia.

3.2 The Diversity of Language Learning Methods

There are numerous ways to learn a language. The missionary who finds himself among a tribe of people who do not speak a word of a language which he knows, must start by pointing out objects and mimicking certain actions. By listening carefully to natives around him, he learns the words which designate such objects and actions, and gradually he begins to piece the language fragments together.[1] This is no small job, but it is not impossible. In fact, the pressures of having to be communicative in order to live among monolingual people make the language learning process much more rapid than one might suspect.

At the opposite extreme of language learning there is the linguistically trained native speaker who can guide one's study of the language and who can provide the necessary drills, the concise explanations of grammatical problems, the scientifically constructed vocabulary lists, and the general cultural orientation, which is so important in really understanding a language and a people. Such trained teachers are very rare, so that one's actual experience usually falls some place between the two extremes of learning from monolingual natives and from linguistically trained native speakers.

It would be impossible for us to describe all the ways of learning a foreign language, but there are three principal methods: (1) a course with a native speaker as informant and a linguistically trained person to guide the study, (2) instruction by a private tutor in a language having grammars and an extensive literature, and (3) learning an aboriginal language with the aid of a native speaker who can use some intermediate language.

3.2.1 A Course with a Native Informant and a Linguistically Trained Guide

During the Second World War it was necessary to teach hundreds of men to speak languages for which there were few, if any, linguistically trained native speakers. It would have been folly to have the students imitate the pronunciation and usage of a non-native instructor, for the students assigned from the various branches of the armed services had to

---

[1] For a study of these monolingual procedures see Eugene A. Nida, Morphology (Ann Arbor, Michigan: University of Michigan Press, 1949).

WAYS OF LEARNING A FOREIGN LANGUAGE

acquire a practical use of the language. They needed to be able to communicate with native speakers of the language, and ability to do so effectively would mean life or death to themselves and to many others for whom they might act as interpreters. To meet these very practical needs a language program was worked out, and its results were highly successful. The following points are some of the most important features:

1. All forms and expressions are pronounced by the native speaker (i.e., the informant), and the students imitate his speech.
2. The linguistically trained instructor (actually just a "guide" for the course) points out the phonetic characteristics of the informant's speech and helps students overcome their difficulties in pronunciation by providing appropriate phonetic drills.
3. The course begins with simple words and phrases which may be used in actual situations, e.g., greetings, requests for directions, and means of identifying oneself to strangers.
4. The students write down words in a phonemic alphabet.[2]
5. The textbook materials are written in a phonemic alphabet (though in later sections of the book the traditional orthography may also be employed).
6. Grammatical explanations are introduced as required.[3] One studies the phrases and sentences first, and the grammatical explanations help one to understand what has been studied. This is opposite to the average grammar, which introduces grammatical rules first and

---

[2] Such an alphabet is often called a "phonetic alphabet." Strictly speaking, however, a phonetic alphabet indicates all types of very minute differences in sound, while a phonemic alphabet only indicates those distinctions in sound which make differences of meaning in a particular language. These problems will be discussed more fully in Chapter 4.

[3] The introduction of grammatical explanations makes this system quite different from and decidedly superior to the Berlitz method, which rejects any and all types of grammatical discussion. For adults, who have been trained by educational maturity to analyze and synthesize, it is a great advantage to have grammatical explanations.

then illustrates the rules by sentences which are often rather inane or silly.
7. The successive lessons are built around relatively familiar topics and actual situations, e.g., meeting people, occupations, one's home country, the weather, renting a room in a hotel, dressing, eating at the restaurant, sight-seeing, shopping, traveling by train, visiting the beach, going to the post office, and cashing a check at the bank.[4]

A number of textbooks prepared by linguists for the Intensive Language Training Program, sponsored by the Armed Forces, have been published by D. C. Heath and Co. and by Henry Holt and Co. These texts differ somewhat in value, but in many respects they are superior to other types of texts which on the whole give much less attention to learning to speak.

8. The sentence material in the text is generally in the form of dialogue. The student is expected to be able to carry on a similar dialogue with the informant and other members of the class.
9. The new vocabulary is introduced in meaningfully related groupings. For example, in a section on eating at the restaurant the necessary vocabulary is introduced so as to make conversation on the subject possible. This is quite different from many traditional grammars where words are introduced because they happen to belong to the first declension, the second declension, the first conjugation, the second conjugation, etc., rather than because there is some meaningful connection between the words.
10. The function of the linguistically trained instructor is simply to guide the study. He is there to suggest topics of conversation, supply necessary explanations of grammatically difficult points, indicate errors in pronunciation, and assist students to understand; but the students learn the pronunciation and the forms from the informant. The informant is the one who

---

[4] One of the finest modern grammars is *Spoken and Written French* by Francois Denoeu and Robert A. Hall, Jr. (Boston: D. C. Heath and Co., 1946).

provides the drill and the practice in listening and in the practical use of the language.
11. Supplementary reading is encouraged, but not at the expense of daily drill and practical use.
12. The informant and the instructor provide information about the customs, attitudes, and cultural backgrounds so that the language may be learned as an integral part of the total life of a people.

This method of language study is in many ways very different from the traditional approach. The primary distinctions are (1) greater emphasis upon hearing the language as spoken by a native, (2) the requirement of learning by speaking, (3) the acquisition of meaningfully related words and phrases, and (4) the subordination of the formal grammar to the practical requirements of language usage. It is not necessary to employ precisely this type of approach, but the fundamental features of such a learning-by-doing technique are essential if one is to learn to speak a language in a classroom.

Programs of this general type are being carried on at a number of universities, e.g., Yale, Cornell, the University of California at Berkeley, and the University of Michigan.[5] For the most part the results have been extremely gratifying, not only in the superior performance of the students, but in their more receptive and more intelligent attitude toward language study.

3.2.2   Instruction by a Private Tutor in a Nonaboriginal Language

Missionaries desiring to learn such languages as French, Spanish, Portuguese, Chinese, Burmese, and Malay frequently engage a native teacher to tutor them. In some places there are schools operated by mission boards or designed especially for English-speaking people, but even in these circumstances each student is usually given some tutorial instruction. Where there is a school in operation, the student will probably find his time fully occupied, but a number of the following suggestions might be carried out. Where, as is so commonly the case, instruction is given to a single missionary or a missionary

---

[5]Not all the foreign language courses at these institutions are necessarily conducted along these lines.

couple by a private tutor, it is imperative to make the best use of the time and attain the most rapid progress.

3.2.2.1 Difficulties with Foreign Language Tutoring

Some tutors are excellent; by their methods and their personalities they put across the subject with amazing ability. With the proper language orientation the missionary is able to make the best of such an opportunity. When, however, as is so frequently the case, the tutor is not good, the missionary must be able to compensate for certain deficiencies. To understand the problems we need to realize some of the reasons for difficulty.

Tutors make a common mistake by not speaking their own language enough. It is so easy for them to slip into the use of English whenever the slightest excuse is presented. The result is that sometimes the tutor learns more English than the missionary learns of the foreign language. In certain instances missionaries have discovered that the so-called "tutor" was really desirous of learning English, or at least of improving his knowledge of it, and had undertaken to teach as the easiest way to accomplish his purpose.

Much of European and Oriental learning is pedagogically traditional and filled with the memorizing of rules and lists of forms. Of course, memorizing rules about one's own language (one already spoken) is not so meaningless as memorizing rules about a foreign language. But often the result is that the missionary learns the grammar but does not learn the language. Rules can be very helpful, but unless they are presented in some meaningful, practical way, they are quite useless. One cannot take time to recite a rule mentally before uttering the next word in a sentence.

Frequently foreign language tutors use very old, traditionally constructed grammars. In many cases they use the very grammars which they themselves studied in school, but such grammars were probably constructed for native speakers and not for foreigners, and there is a vast difference. Such grammars may be very valuable in advanced studies, but they are almost worthless to the beginner.

Since the language teaching given to native speakers is oriented very largely in the direction of proper writing and spelling of the language, tutors often carry over the same tendency in teaching foreign pupils. This seems particularly true of tutors in French, where the spelling is complicated and many educated people take considerable cultural pride in orthographic correctness. Tutors may also find that it is relatively easy to assign written exercises, for the correction of them is more or less mechanical. Also the student frequently seems to prefer such an approach since it agrees with the usual foreign language instruction in college, and he acquires a false sense of language accomplishment by improving his ability to work out written sentences.

The average tutor is very weak on phonetics. He has probably had no training along this line, and he cannot be expected to provide adequate explanations. What would happen, however, if an English-speaking missionary were asked to explain the difference between the p in peak and the p in speak? He would probably say that they are the same, but that is far from the case. The p in peak is followed by a relatively strong puff of air, called "aspiration," but the p in speak is not followed by a puff of air. The same contrasts exist in the t's of take and steak and the k's of Kate and skate.[6] These are kinds of phonetic facts about a language that are rarely noticed by native speakers, and it is very unusual to find a tutor who can explain such facts about the sounds of his mother tongue. Of course, he can tell us whether the sounds have a natural "ring" to them, but we must be prepared to supplement his lack of phonetic training.

Foreign language tutors are often more valuable for advanced students than for beginners. In some instances they lack the necessary patience to do the required drilling; and we can scarcely blame them, for drilling may be very monotonous unless the teacher has certain definite goals and takes interest in the quality of his students' pronunciation. It is commonly thought that more skill is required to teach advanced courses of a language than beginning ones. This is actually not the case. It does require greater knowledge, perhaps, to

---

[6] To test these contrasts place the back of the hand within a quarter of an inch of the mouth and pronounce the words. The difference in the amount of air which follows the various p's, t's, and k's may be readily noticed.

lecture on literature and the historical development of a language, but teaching beginning language courses requires very specialized training, and this is often lacking in tutors. Another reason why tutors may be less valuable for beginners is their own primary interest in the more advanced stages. They are naturally more interested in pleasant conversation, literary features, and refining one's language facility; and hence, they prove much more helpful to the more advanced student.

If one is planning to spend a year in language study and cultural orientation in some country of Europe before going on to a colonial area, it is very profitable to have already taken an intensive course in some university which provides the <u>right</u> type of language courses. Having acquired some conversational ability in the language and a basic understanding of the structure, one is able to profit much more from the year's time in Europe. Rather than having to struggle along with tutors poorly equipped to teach beginners, one can be improving his language ability and making use of the precious months to get acquainted with the people and make those most important contacts with Europeans.

3.2.2.2 <u>What the Student Can Do to Help the Tutorial Program</u>

After all that has been said about the inadequacies of some tutors, one may well wonder if there is anything that can be done to improve on their methods, or lack of methods. Actually, there is much that can be done, but one must be tactful and considerate In most circumstances tutors will probably be delighted with any constructive suggestions, for more often than not, they find themselves floundering about trying desperately to do a good job, and realizing that in many instances they are not succeeding as they should.

3.2.2.2.1 <u>A Better Textbook</u>

In some cases it is possible to suggest the use of a better textbook. One should be sure, however, that it really is better, but since some antiquated language texts could scarcely be worse, one has a good chance of discovering a text which will be more adequate.[7]

---

[7] See section 3.2.1.

3.2.2.2.2 A Phonemic Alphabet

In studying a language like German or Spanish, where one can always predict from the traditional spelling how the word will be pronounced, it is not necessary to have a supplementary phonemic alphabet.[8] However, for a language such as French it is necessary to have some way of writing down words so that one can reproduce them with the appropriate sounds. The traditional spelling is only an approximate guide. In studying a language like Chinese it is absolutely necessary to have some romanized phonemic alphabet, for it is impossible to advance properly in language study if one tries to master the characters and the spoken language at the same time. For languages such as Annamese, where the native system of writing comes closer to representing the distinctions in sound, it is still necessary to develop some system of writing. These problems will be discussed more fully in Chapter 4.

3.2.2.2.3 Phrases for Memorizing and Drill

When the tutor does not provide drill materials, the student can prepare his own. He should begin with common, everyday, practical phrases such as, "Good morning."[9] "How are you?" "Where is the market?" "How much is the bread?" "Where is the railroad station?" "Can I help you?" "Thank you!" "I am very happy to meet you." "Please speak more slowly!" "I do not speak French." See Chapters 5, 6 and 7 for further suggestions.

One should make a collection of useful phrases which are encountered in studying the language. One may begin with anywhere from ten to twenty new phrases each day. However, one should not try to assimilate more new phrases each day than can be "linguistically digested," but should continue to add a number of phrases each day for a week's time. All the phrases should be reviewed ten or twenty times each day.

---

[8]See Chapter 3, footnote 2.
[9]Of course, these phrases must not be translated literally into another language. It is the cultural equivalent which we must obtain, and by "cultural equivalent" we mean that expression which would be used by the foreign speaker in a corresponding situation.

That means that if one begins with ten phrases the first day, ten phrases more the second day, ten phrases the third day, and so on through the week, a total of sixty phrases will be studied by the end of the week. If one goes over each phrase at least ten times, the phrases adopted the first day will have been studied sixty times by the end of the week. When the next week begins, ten new phrases should be added, and the first ten phrases begun the first day may be dropped. Some students, however, should continue to accumulate and review expressions for two or three weeks before beginning to drop the ones first acquired. The basic procedure is to add a certain number of phrases each day and to drop a similar number that have been reviewed for the longest period of time. At the end of each week, however, one should review all the phrases. If any of the original phrases have been forgotten, these should be reincorporated into the active list again. By the time one has followed this procedure for six months, it will be amazing how many phrases have been learned.

In speaking about these items for drill, we have purposely not spoken about "words" but rather "phrases." One should not memorize words as isolated items, but in meaningful combinations. Furthermore, it is valuable to make all phrases complete sentences as far as possible.

3.2.2.2.4   Reading Aloud and Listening to Reading

One of the most helpful ways to get acquainted with a language is to read aloud while the tutor listens and corrects one's pronunciation. The tutor may then read the same paragraph or another while the student listens intently to understand the meaning and to note carefully the pronunciation. Newspapers generally provide the best materials for language learning. The vocabulary is alive (not dead scholastic "stuff") and the happenings (or the interpretations of the happenings) are culturally significant.

As one improves in language ability, it will be found that more and more time may be profitably given to reading the newspapers which represent all the various political views. Listening to reading can be valuable in learning to pick up phrases through the ears. Furthermore, the subjects mentioned in the newspaper can provide topics for simple conversation. The student can ask in the foreign language for an explanation of some word or idiom, insisting that the tutor explain it, if at all possible, in the foreign language and not in English.

While it is very important to read outstanding books written in any foreign language that one is studying, newspapers, current magazines, and political propaganda may actually be more valuable to the missionary, for he must learn to understand and appreciate the contemporary problems of a foreign power. There is no substitute for newspapers and similar current materials to introduce one to the vital issues of the day.

3.2.2.2.5 Speaking the Language

The student should insist on speaking the foreign language with one's tutor on every possible occasion. One may even need to study in advance in order to ask appropriate questions about the lesson. One may also plan conversation with the tutor. For example, one may construct a series of sentences which will inquire as to the tutor's educational training, his home, his family, and his travels. One should insist that the tutor attempt to answer these questions in his own language; and even though many of the words are not understood, further questions should be used to keep the process going.

Another way of developing conversation is to plan certain comments and questions on subjects concerning which one has read in the papers. If the tutor's political affiliation can be discovered, then pertinent questions may sometimes stimulate a volume of interesting comments. Using the language in this way is worth much more than the mechanical recitation of rules or the correcting of one's copy-book sentences.

3.2.2.2.6 Criticism of Pronunciation

Inducing a tutor to be constantly critical of one's pronunciation is a big task. The tendency is to overlook the student's pathetic efforts to make some of the difficult sounds, and after a few weeks the tutor either becomes tired of trying to correct the errors or becomes so accustomed to the student's errors that they no longer seem to be quite so intolerable. Whatever the reason may be, one must not permit laxity about matters of pronunciation. Wrong forms of words and awkward sentence structure can be forgiven if only a speaker uses a half-way decent pronunciation. Furthermore, the incorrect forms can be readily supplied by the listener, but bungling of sounds may make entire sentences unintelligible. We could very well understand a foreigner who said with good English pronunciation "My foots went sleepy," but this same sentence in correct grammatical form but with utterly foreign pronunciations of the consonants and vowels would be scarcely intelligible. No doubt all of us have had the experience of speaking with foreigners who have had a very good knowledge of English grammar and vocabulary but who could scarcely make themselves understood, simply because they missed the English sounds so badly. The very same thing is true of us as speakers of foreign languages. Chapter 4 deals further with many of these problems of sounds.

3.2.2.2.7   Supplementary Vocabulary

The vocabularies listed in many textbooks are very poorly designed since they are more frequently chosen because of their grammatical forms than because of their meaningful relationships. Accordingly, the student must often supplement these deficiencies. Two principles should guide him: (1) the choice of meaningfully related words and (2) the memorization of vocabulary in phrases.

Vocabulary should be chosen because of association. One can set up ten or fifteen different sets of initial vocabularies. These may include words about the kitchen, the bedroom, traveling on a train, going to an office, buying vegetables, going through customs, or asking one's way around town. Either by using a dictionary or asking one's tutor or those with whom one is living, one can get such words for the kitchen as "stove, pan, pot, knife, fork, spoon, bread, flour, rag, salt, coal, wood." The choice of words is dependent upon the articles which people actually have in their kitchens. Articles in the bedroom may include "bed, chair, washstand, water, glass, cup, closet, sheet, blanket, window." Here, again, the thing to do is to look around and get the words for the very things which are in one's room. Similar vocabulary may be developed for all the common experiences.

But these words should not be learned as separate items. They should be incorporated into phrases, so that they can be used. For example, for some of the kitchen items one may have the following phrases: "the stove is hot," "the pan is cold," "the pot is big," and "the knife is sharp." Instead of just learning the words for things, one ends up by learning much more of the vocabulary than one dreamed of at first. But there is no value in knowing words for things if one can say nothing about such things or is unable to understand simple, typical statements made about them. Furthermore parts of these sentences can be reshuffled, so that one can also say "the pan is hot," "the stove is cold," and "the knife is big." Putting words into new combinations is the essence of language use, but one cannot discover the framework of sentences without learning some of them.

3.2.2.2.8   Associating with Native Speakers

To room and board with a local family is a tremendous asset in language learning. Furthermore, living in the home of a national provides one with experiences and insight that cannot be gained in any other way. A week's living in a home is worth a month's reading about the life of a people.

In many countries the main meal of the day is quite a long, drawn-out affair, but it provides wonderful opportunities for conversation. One may ask questions about current happenings, inquire about customs and practices (not with any sense of superiority but out of sympathetic interest), or provide interesting bits of anecdotal material from one's own experience. Two things are, however, to be strictly avoided: (1) any criticism of foreign, non-American ways and (2) bragging about America. The student should conform in the matter of eating habits, for example, in the manner of holding the knife and fork, in using a napkin to wipe the mouth with ceremonial frequency, in saying the right things at the beginning and end of the meal. All these little matters are important indicators of culture and refinement. Of course, one will at first make many mistakes, but being willing to be the object of a certain amount of friendly derision will only endear a person to his foreign hosts.

One should be particularly thoughtful about making any

and all types of complimentary statements about a foreign country. There are always many very fine things to compliment, e.g., museums, old churches, fine libraries, attractive gardens, flower markets, exquisite needle work, beautifully bound books, and courteous manners. One should seek opportunities to talk about such things. The very mention of such matters will often start pleasant conversations.

In almost all European and Oriental households there is some elderly person who is potentially a wonderful language informant. Often they have all sorts of time to chat and talk, and they are flattered by attention and appropriate compliments. They really make wonderful friends and can be a real help to the missionary in understanding the language and the people. Their lives are often rich, and their cultural heritage is priceless. Visiting by the hour with such persons constitutes some of the most valuable language training possible. Frequently one is able to give new hope and life to such elderly persons as one tells them about the Good News, which has prompted one to be a missionary. One is a missionary whether in Europe or Africa or the Amazon jungle, and the proper type of missionary will discover innumerable ways to witness of his joy and faith.

3.2.2.2.9 *Writing Down All New Words*

At first, this type of injunction is impossible of fulfillment, for there are just too many new words; but one should never get into the lazy habit of continually guessing at what one is reading or hearing. In many instances it is helpful to read a great deal without looking up the meaning of each word, for the context alone teaches us the meanings of many words. On the other hand, we can deceive ourselves into thinking that we understand when we really do not.

There is also a value in taking the time to look up new words and to write them down. This helps us to fix the words in our minds, and by reviewing these lists frequently we can increase our vocabulary very rapidly. When writing down a word, however, it is important to include an entire phrase so that the word may have a context, and thus it will be much more meaningful and useful to us.

It is quite a nuisance to have a dictionary and notebook

with us all the time while riding in streetcars, trains, and busses, or waiting in stations. Hence, we can just jot the word down on a slip of paper and then look up its meaning later, or all new words and phrases in the newspapers or magazines may be circled with a red pencil, and then in the evening such expressions can be readily found again, looked up in a dictionary, and written down in a notebook. The value of this procedure is proved by the almost inevitable experience which follows. After looking up such a word and fixing it firmly in mind, it will be amazing how many times that very word is encountered within the next few days and how often one can use it in conversation.

3.2.2.2.10   Listening to the Radio

Listening to the radio may at first seem to be a sheer waste of time, for the sentences appear to be just one solid blur of noise at a rapid rate of utterance. This is the impression left by any strange language. The radio seems much more difficult to understand than people with whom we speak personally. There are several reasons for this: (1) we cannot watch the speaker (we learn a great deal from facial expressions and gestures), (2) we cannot interpose any questions so as to understand the gist of the subject, and (3) we have no way of guessing the topic by sizing up the type of speaker.

As we continue to listen to the radio, we begin to pick out familiar words and phrases. We may find that the news commentator is easier to understand than anyone else because he is talking about things we have been reading about in the paper. A few key words may give us the clue to what is being said, and then we become all ears to pick out other phrases which we can almost anticipate from what we have read. After a time, we become so accustomed to the language that we begin to follow almost everything that is said, and we are rather amazed at how much "slower" the announcers seem to speak. What happens, of course, is that our ears become more perceptive.

The difficult thing about listening to a foreign language is our perception lag. We pick up two or three words, but by the time their meaning has begun to dawn on us, the speaker has gone on to something else, and we simply cannot fill in the remaining portion. While we have been concentrating on one part, we have lost the subsequent words; and even though they may be perfectly familiar to us in reading, we just do not "hear" them. Because our auditory perception is slow, we cannot pick up meaningful units as rapidly as they are being uttered. Speeding up this process requires practice. We must learn to hear a language just as we must learn to speak, and both hearing and speaking must become automatic.

Some people insist that certain languages are spoken more rapidly than others. Scientific observations contradict this impression. Individual speakers may differ greatly in average speed of utterance, but the average speed of speakers of all languages is approximately the same. The reason we are impressed by the apparent speed of foreign languages is our inability to keep up with the flow of meaningful units.

3.2.2.2.11 Going to Lectures and Public Entertainments

One of the finest ways of acquiring practice in hearing a language is to attend lectures given in a foreign university. Sometimes there is a slight charge, but often it is possible to get permission to attend as an auditor without fees. The subject which is being discussed is not of primary importance, though, of course, the broader the field, e.g., history, political science, art and literature, the more extensive will be the vocabulary employed. For those who have done graduate work in some specialized field in the United States, it is often possible to make profitable contacts with foreign scientists who are interested in the same area of study. Since so much of the technical vocabulary of specific sciences is common throughout all the Indo-European language area, it is sometimes possible to advance rapidly in language proficiency through concentration on vocabulary, the roots of which may be somewhat familiar.

Civic programs of all types provide good language opportunities. Political and dedicatory speeches are usually long, and their actual content may be somewhat boring; but as devices for getting practice in listening for words and phrases, they are hard to beat. For one who is learning a language there is no such thing as a really dull speech, for the speaker

WAYS OF LEARNING A FOREIGN LANGUAGE

who repeats himself is giving the missionary a grand opportunity to become fully familiar with new vocabulary.

Various types of dramatic performances have proved to be excellent aids for those learning a foreign language. The speech forms used are often quite different from the type used in formal addresses and in many ways much closer to that of ordinary conversation. The story of such dramas may also be very important in learning to understand the people, for the playwright in his plot is interpreting the aspirations, disappointments, and drives which account for much that one will find in the foreign culture.

3.2.2.2.12 Attending Church

It might seem unnecessary to encourage missionaries to attend church, but aside from the spiritual blessings received attendance has a very practical value. Religious vocabulary is often quite different from the vocabulary in colloquial use. Even the grammatical forms may differ. For example, in Spanish the pastor in speaking to his congregation may use the plural familiar forms, but that would not be done in most types of gatherings. Grammatical forms used in prayer may also be very different from the speech used in everyday situations. Hence, for the sake of vocabulary and grammatical forms, the missionary needs to be perfectly familiar with the religious language.

We must not think for a moment that specialized religious vocabulary and grammatical forms are found only in other languages. English possesses a very specialized religious vocabulary and characteristic grammatical forms used in prayer, e.g., thou, thee, sayest, and doeth. Such forms are so difficult for some foreigners in our own country that they frequently refrain from prayer in public because they are unable to use them. Certain English-speaking religious groups have almost made a fetish of such obsolescent grammatical forms, and hence we must not be too harsh in our criticism of the "religious language" of other cultures.

3.2.2.2.13 Reading the Bible

Many missionaries have found that reading the Bible is one of the best ways of picking up vocabulary quickly. In many instances they use diglot publications with English on one page or in one column and the foreign language opposite. This saves looking up words in a dictionary. Part of one's missionary task is to become familiar with the Bible in the language of those people with whom he works. Accordingly, Bible reading as a means of language learning has a double advantage.

One must be cautioned, however, against using the Bible indiscriminately as a guide for the grammatical forms of the language. In the first place, the Bible may be translated into a rather archaic form of the language. This is true, for example, of the Cipriano de Valera version in Spanish. If one used such forms and idioms in conversation, it would seem as much out of place as it would if one tried to converse in English by using the expressions of the King James Version of the Bible. In the second place, translations rarely succeed in breaking away completely from the linguistic form of the language which underlies the translation. As a result, the word order may be somewhat awkward and strange. Many missionary translations of the Bible are particularly bad in this regard and are in need of revision. A little inquiry as to the available translations in any language will enable one to exercise caution about how far one is to assume that the forms are usable in modern speech.

3.2.2.2.14   Writing the Language

It may seem like an oversight that writing the language is to be discussed so late in the list of language-learning techniques. However, there is purpose in this. Writing down the language is very important, but laboriously looking up of word after word in the dictionary and checking these in the grammar to be sure of the form can be a boring and unprofitable task. It is something like the procedure in the courses in Greek or Latin composition which some of us had to take in college.

We should learn to write the foreign language, but not until we have learned to express ourselves orally. This is in keeping with the second principle discussed in Chapter 2, where we noted that the proper order is hearing, speaking, reading, and then writing.

In writing one should endeavor to select topics which have personal interest, e.g., "My First Impressions of Paris," "Getting Seasick," "Difficulties in Learning French," or "What I Think of American Foreign Policy." One should not attempt to produce a flowery style, but rather, a simple, straightforward explanation of events, impressions, and reactions. One's tutor can then go over such materials and point out the unnatural word order, the incorrect idioms, the mistakes in grammatical forms, and the spelling errors. At first, these will be distressingly numerous, for what seems to pass as acceptable in conversation looks glaringly bad when written down. However, as one continues to write more and more, the old mistakes will be overcome and gradually one will learn to express oneself in writing. It is particularly important to familiarize oneself with proper forms for letter writing, for one is constantly called upon to correspond with officials and business firms. Being able to use the proper salutations (some of which may be extremely long and idiomatic) may mean success or failure in such negotiations.

3.2.2.2.15 <u>Keeping Up in the Language</u>

Unused skills are readily lost, and this is especially true of language ability. Many missionaries study French or Portuguese in Europe and then go to colonial areas where they are required to carry on their work almost entirely in some native language. They may have very infrequent contacts with government officials or business men, but such contacts as they do have may be tremendously important. However, one usually does not use the French or Portuguese[10] enough to keep fully fluent, and hence the missionary's hard-earned facility is rapidly lost.

---

[10]This same situation applies to Chinese, which one may have learned in Peiping before being transferred to Southwest China for work among aboriginal tribes. The same is also true of those who work among aboriginals of India and Latin America. Wherever there is a governmentally important trade language covering a native language community and the missionary's ministry is in the native language, this same problem will arise, and similar solutions must be found.

This problem of keeping up a language on the field may be solved in a number of ways, but it is very important to have had enough of the language before going to the colonial area. If one has only acquired a smattering of the language before discontinuing study in Europe and switching one's primary attention to a native language, there is too much of a tendency for the missionary to avoid possible contacts with French or Portuguese speakers, for he is painfully aware of his own limitations. Furthermore, Europeans readily sense this frustration and tend to avoid the missionary so as not to embarrass him. The result is disastrous, both from the standpoint of the missionary's language facility and from the standpoint of successful government relationships.

To keep up in the language the missionary should take the necessary time to read periodicals and newspapers printed in the European language, listen to radio broadcasts in the language, and cultivate the friendship of Europeans in the area. One missionary in Congo, whose ability in French and whose warm-hearted sympathy has led him to develop many friendships among Belgians, has a very important ministry among those people. Not only has he given great spiritual help to scores of officials and business men, but he has enriched his own life and benefited his missionary work in a remarkable manner. Another means of language practice is to speak the European language in the home or on the mission station among missionaries. This would not only benefit the missionaries and indirectly the natives who aspire to learn the language of the colonial power, but would do much to remove the suspicion which many government officials have concerning the activities of English-speaking missionaries.

Just as a matter of social etiquette missionaries should not speak English if there is any chance of a non-English-speaking person overhearing them. Constant use of the language of the country is essential in the cultivation of good relations. We Americans are often annoyed at foreigners who converse with each other in a foreign language. Some of us may suspect such people of making unkind remarks about us or of passing on secret information which may be harmful to us. In these days, when suspicions run rampant throughout the world, we must take every precaution; and in doing so, we shall be keeping up and improving our language ability.

WAYS OF LEARNING A FOREIGN LANGUAGE 51

3.2.3　　Learning an Aboriginal Language from a Native Speaker

Missionaries are frequently required to learn an aboriginal language directly from a native speaker. If absolutely no previous linguistic work has been done in the language, the missionary should by all means take a preliminary course in linguistics.[11] In most instances, however, some preliminary work has been done,[12] but the quality of the work and the extent of the linguistic analysis differ very greatly.

3.2.3.1　　The Typical Situation

Perhaps it is impossible to depict a typical situation, for it seems that the nature of the linguistic work in aboriginal languages differs with each language. Yet, there are some features which stand out as being quite typical, and in order to appreciate what the new missionary may do to improve the situation or at least make the best of it, we need to discuss the problem fully.

One will usually find a grammar which has been constructed by some older missionary. Sometimes it is far enough advanced to have been mimeographed, and in a few rare instances even printed. Some of these grammars are very good, but many of them are quite limited, that is, they

---

[11] Such courses are offered at a number of universities, e.g., University of California, University of Indiana, Yale, Cornell, University of Michigan, Kennedy School of Missions, and the Summer Institute of Linguistics. This latter institution specializes in preparing missionaries for pioneer linguistic work and has published a number of textbooks specifically designed to aid missionaries in this task.

[12] Publication of the Bible or parts of it is now being carried on in approximately 650 languages, though the total of all languages which have received something of the Bible as of January 1949 is 1108. There are still at least 1000 languages which have nothing of the Bible and with which very little if any linguistic work has been done. However, in the larger language areas, in which the great majority of missionaries work, some language analysis and Bible translating has been done. This book is especially written for this latter group of missionaries.

only discuss some of the more obvious features of the language. A number of these grammars take Latin as the typical mold and fit everything into its pattern. Sometimes there are a number of out-and-out mistakes, which may even constitute the basis of the language examinations. In one area in Central Africa the natives who help teach the missionaries their language take pains to explain that some forms are "missionary language" but that other forms are the way they themselves speak. These native teachers have found it necessary to teach the "missionary language" because certain of the older missionaries have insisted that the forms of the grammar are "correct" regardless of what the natives say. Hence, they have required the younger missionaries to pass the language exams based upon the "missionary language." This tendency to regularize and organize the native speech is completely unjustified. Correctness of form is what native speakers say, not what some foreigner thinks they should say.[13]

In certain instances the native language is taught by some older missionary, and this is often done without the constant presence of a native speaker. The result is that younger missionaries imitate the mistakes of older ones, and there grows up a "mission station" dialect. Sometimes older missionaries do have native speakers present; but in certain of these cases the missionary instructor has so brow-beaten the poor informant that he has been made a mere puppet, repeating automatically the forms that are suggested to him by the instructor and even imitating the instructor's pronunciation. Of course, the situation is not like this everywhere. Some older missionaries make expert teachers and the new missionary is able to profit a great deal by their years of experience. However, the new missionary must sometimes undertake compensating study in order to avoid some of the deficiencies in the instruction given by older missionaries.

Even before a grammar has been formulated, missionaries usually construct a kind of elementary dictionary. Dictionaries can be very useful, but they need to be recognized

---

[13] See a full discussion of these problems in Linguistic Interludes (Glendale, California: Summer Institute of Linguistics, 1947), pp. 40-61, and Bible Translating (New York: American Bible Society, 1947), pp. 11-30, 241-79.

for precisely what they are, namely, "elementary" dictionaries. The discussion under any one word should not be expected to cover all the meanings or even many of the more common idioms. Such dictionaries are not the final statement on the language; they should be the jumping-off point for further study and observation.

One of the great difficulties entailed in learning a foreign language from a native speaker is his relatively limited understanding and use of English or whatever intermediate language is used. The informant probably finds it very difficult to explain or to illustrate many of the subtler distinctions in his language; and furthermore, the intermediate language may not indicate precisely all the differences in form which he may make in his mother tongue, and vice versa. It is folly to ask any informant, "Why do you use the subjunctive form in this sentence?" It would be equally difficult for us to explain why we say I think he is crazy and I move he be elected, in which one verb requires is in the dependent clause and the other requires be. There is no way of explaining "why" such things occur either in English or in any other language. Rather, we should ask the informant, "When do you use such-and-such a form?" or "Do you use the form in the following sentence...?" We should inquire "how" and "when," but never "why" a form is used.

The missionary is often handicapped in learning an aboriginal language because he has no written materials in the language except translated stories or Bible texts. Naturally, the first thing which missionaries do is to translate what they think the young, growing church will require, and they rarely consider it valuable to write down native stories and legends to assist them in studying the grammatical structure of the language. As a result, the new missionary finds that the only things which he may read in the language are translations from English or some other European language, and often such translations are slavishly literal. To overcome this difficulty is not easy.

There is also the problem of dialects. This may be very acute, for the differences may be great in various parts of a tribe. However, missionaries tend to exaggerate such matters, largely because of their own inadequate knowledge of the language. They frequently complain about the grievous problems confronting them and cite their difficulty in being understood fifteen miles away from the station. In many cases one finds that the natives appear to have no difficulty whatsoever in speaking with natives of other dialects. What is frequently the trouble is the missionary's own imperfect use of the language, so that only those who live near the mission station and have had an opportunity to hear the missionary on numerous occasions can make out what he is saying.

However, there are many dialect differences in tribal languages, even as there are in all languages. In the United States we recognize differences in pronunciations of words, grammatical forms, and meanings. For example, certain dialects of the South and North differ markedly, and with only a limited knowledge of English we would find adjustment from one to the other rather complicated; but for those who know English well, there is no difficulty in understanding or making oneself understood. We realize that in some places a paper bag used in grocery stores is called a <u>poke</u>, in other places a <u>bag</u>, and in still other areas a <u>sack</u>. What some people call a <u>skillet</u>, others may call a <u>spider</u> or a <u>frying pan</u>; and what some insist is <u>corn bread</u>, others may call either <u>Johnny cake</u>, <u>corn pone</u>, <u>pone bread</u>, or <u>hoe cake</u>.

Rather than attempting to study several dialects at once, the missionary should concentrate on a single dialect and learn it well. By doing this he can make the transfer to other dialects with much less difficulty than if he attempts to compress dialect distinctions into his initial studies. Whether he selects one or another dialect to begin his study will depend upon a number of factors, which are primarily sociological and not linguistic. Some dialects have greater prestige and may be understood more extensively than others. If this is so, one will do well to concentrate on such a dialect of the language, but one should not be deceived by the protestations of natives who claim that their dialect and theirs only is the proper form of speech. The same thing is claimed by almost every group of people on earth. It is not so much the so-called intrinsic worth or correctness of a dialect that counts, but whether the dialect is used by those who carry on the affairs of the tribe. Similarly, English forms are not "correct" or "incorrect" simply because some grammarian claims them

WAYS OF LEARNING A FOREIGN LANGUAGE 55

to be so, but their acceptability is primarily determined by those who carry on the affairs of the English-speaking world.[14]

3.2.3.2 What the Student Can Do to Learn a Language from a Native Informant

The procedure for the new missionary varies depending upon the existence of some regular language classes or school. When there is a program already worked out, the student must compensate for the deficiencies by following some of the suggestions listed below.[15] In the great majority of cases, however, the missionary is told in effect, "Here is the grammar, and here is your native teacher; now you are to learn the language." Most people thrust into such a situation without any idea of how to proceed are in a hopeless dither. It should be understood that we cannot outline the program from start to finish, but some of the following steps in procedure may enable one to forge ahead and actually learn a language.

3.2.3.2.1 Reading Over the Grammar

This does not mean that one should attempt to memorize the grammar. It simply means that one should become familiar with what one is likely to find in the language. It is so much easier to appreciate and understand a foreign country if one has first read some travel guides. In the same way, a grammar can be a travel guide for one's learning of a new language. Such travel guides and grammars are not to be memorized, but they will provide important information along the route, and what may seem meaningless or arbitrary may be seen to fit into the larger framework of the language.

---

[14] For a fuller discussion of this problem see Eugene A. Nida, Bible Translating, pp. 31-49.

[15] The new missionary should be cautioned against trying to reform the language program from the start. His suggestions, unless they are made with consummate tact, may not be appreciated. However, if by employing some supplementary devices himself, he can exhibit exceptional skill in the language learning program, then there is a good probability that such procedures will be incorporated into the regular course.

3.2.3.2.2   Obtaining Some Practical Expressions

Elicit from the informant at least 200 practical expressions such as: "What is your name?"[16] "I am glad to know you." "My name is ..." "Where do you live?" "Where do you come from?" "What kind of work do you do?" "How many children do you have?" "Is your father still living?" "Is your mother still living?" "Have you gone to school?" "Where do you go to school?" "What do you study?" "Where is the waterhole?" "Where is the trading post?" "Will you sell me some bananas?" "How much are the bananas?" "I am hungry." "I am thirsty." "I am tired." "I must go home now." "I hope I will see you again." "What day is it?" "Will you help me, please?"[17] "Thank you!" "I enjoyed the food very much." "You are very kind." "I am sorry that I cannot speak your language." "I am trying to learn." "What is the name of that?" "Repeat it, please." "Will you speak more slowly?" "The sounds are very difficult for me." "Excuse my bad speaking." "I will try to learn." "Will you please bring me the food?" "You are a very good cook." "I enjoy the food very much." "Where is the mission?" "Where is the church?" "Where is the school?" "Where is the hospital?" "What are you doing?" "May I help you?" "You work very well." "Show me how to do that!"

Upon arrival at the mission station one should construct about 200 practical expressions which one feels certain will come in handy. These should be written down on separate slips of paper, and drill should begin immediately. These expressions should be gone over with the informant, and the

---

[16] One must use judgment in such anthropological matters as asking for names, for in certain areas it is not considered proper to inquire concerning a person's name, at least, not until one is very well acquainted. Similarly, all the forms suggested here must be adapted to the local situation.

[17] A number of languages do not have special expressions to indicate polite forms of requests, but one should be very careful to use them in languages where they do occur. Furthermore, missionaries will do well to address natives with polite forms, especially older natives, even though other Europeans, e.g., government officials and business men, do not use such forms.

pronunciation should be carefully checked so that it will be as close to the native speech as possible. One should note especially the intonation (i.e., the musical pattern) of the sentences. Particular care must be given to questions, for we as English speakers tend to raise our voices at the end of a question, and in many languages that is not done.

Some people may be concerned about this suggestion to learn some common expressions without first mastering the grammar that underlies them. Well, the grammar is to follow; first comes the practical use of phrases. We must get into the water before instruction in swimming does much good. So it is with language; we must begin to speak in order to learn how to speak.

In memorizing phrases we need to avoid associations which depend upon the order of items listed on a page. Some people have written out lists of words and phrases and then have always reviewed them starting at the top and going down the page. Sometimes the result is an ability to recall forms, once the list has been started, but these people have difficulty in picking out items apart from their association with other items on the list. To avoid this one finds that listing phrases on separate slips and then constantly reshuffling the slips will keep a person from being tied to one particular order.

Some students feel obliged to spend a long time concentrating on one particular form, believing that by prolonged concentration they can thoroughly rivet such an item in their minds. This may be true, but most people discover that it is more valuable to review an item briefly over a period of several days than to concentrate on a form for the equivalent amount of time on just one day. For example, to spend five seconds on ten successive days has much more value in training one's recall ability than to spend fifty seconds on just one day. Reviewing is the key to learning.

Memorizing sentences and drilling on them will not do any good unless one uses them. Furthermore, one must use them on every possible occasion. If the opportunities are not abundant enough, then one must go out around the mission station or village trying out these expressions. Of course, the natives may assume that one understands much more of the language than is actually the case, but "getting in over one's head" will not hurt anything but one's pride, and that needs annihilation anyway. One can always explain apologetically that as yet the language has not been sufficiently learned, but it will be amazing how much can be assimilated from practical situations in which one is forced to try to speak and explain, even if it is only to admit one's ignorance.

3.2.3.2.3 <u>Writing the Native Expressions in the Best Way Possible</u>

The next chapter will deal with problems of phonetics and alphabets which one may use in transcribing the sounds of a language. Usually one finds that the system of spelling (i.e., the orthography) is inadequate. For example, there may be seven different vowel sounds that make differences in the meanings of words, but the alphabet used may indicate only five. Very often the language makes differences of meaning by differences of tones, and these may be neglected entirely in the traditional orthography. This does not mean that the missionary has to throw out the spelling already used and take up the complicated International Phonetic System. Of course, if he has mastered some such system of phonetic notation, he can use it to great advantage in his own language study, but one can usually employ the alphabet already in use and just add some marks to the vowels and consonants to indicate the necessary distinctions. For example, if one <u>e</u> sound is more like the vowel of <u>bait</u> and another is like the vowel of <u>bet</u>, then one can mark all the vowels that sound like the vowel of <u>bait</u> with an acute accent, e.g., <u>é</u>. These problems will be discussed at length in the next chapter. What we want to say here is simply that the various sounds should be marked so as to help in recognizing and reproducing them. The system one employs does not make any difference provided it is consistent.

The marking of the tones of a sentence may be much more difficult, but one can always write phrases with a broad, generalized indication of their "melody." For example, in writing the following Spanish sentences one can draw a line right through the words to indicate the rise and fall of the voice, and the acute accents may indicate the emphasized syllables:

La semána pasáda me llevaron a la playa

"Last week they took me to the beach."

Dónde estarán nuestros asientos
"Where will our seats be?"[18]

There are other possible melodic patterns for these Spanish sentences, but such alternatives should not prevent one from noting carefully the musical form of each phrase and imitating it just as much as any other feature. In some languages one must preserve very strict relationships between various musical levels. For example, in Mongbandi, a Sudanic language of northern Congo, the following sentence would be completely unintelligible without the proper tonal differences:

ha he mbi ge pe da   "Speak to me here behind the house."

Drawing lines through the words to indicate the rising and falling musical features is very clumsy, and in the next chapter we will discuss some other devices; but before one has analyzed the major tonal features of the language, these wavy lines are very helpful and should be used. Some people think that the intonation of a sentence will just naturally come after one has learned enough of the words and grammar, but that is not so. The sentence melody must be learned in the same way as any other feature, and it should be learned right from the start.

3.2.3.2.4   Practicing All Expressions Until They Are Up to Speed

We must constantly bear in mind three phonetic facts: (1) the consonants and vowels, (2) the musical pitch of the phrase, and (3) the speed of utterance. This may seem like placing too much emphasis upon speed, but by doing so we are only pointing out the necessity of speaking at the native's normal rate, and not with the stumbling, halting enunciation which so often characterizes our utterances if we do not force ourselves to attain automatic control and facility. Proper speed of utterance should be practiced from the first, rather than being left to later stages of language study. The reason for

---

[18]See S. N. Trevino, Spoken Spanish (Boston: D. C. Heath and Co., 1945). There are certain alternate intonational patterns for such Spanish sentences.

this will become more evident when we consider in the next chapter how sounds spoken in rapid speech often differ from those in slow, interrupted speech.

3.2.3.2.5 Obtaining at Least 200 Simple "Object" Words

In learning a language from an informant where there is no adequate textbook to guide one's work, one should start by eliciting the names for concrete things, e.g., tree, grass, sun, cloud, dog, goat, house, man, and woman. These objects can be pointed to, and they are likely to be as short as any words in the language. One should, however, group the words by areas of meaning. Instead of asking for such words as "head, pants, cow, banana" in this jumbled order, it is well to subdivide the words into such classes as body parts, clothing, objects about the house, relationships between people, articles used in native occupations, fauna, and flora.

Naturally one must ask for culturally relevant items. It would be ridiculous to inquire of some Amazon River Indian his words for "sand-storm, camel, and dates," but these terms would be very pertinent for one learning Colloquial Arabic in the Anglo-Egyptian Sudan.

One must avoid minute distinctions. For example, in asking for body parts, one need not distinguish "arm, biceps, elbow, forearm, arm-pit, wrist, hand, finger, and thumb." For initial lists of words it is quite enough to ask for "arm, hand, finger." Even so one may find that the distinctions are too minute, or at least not pertinent, for some languages use the same word for "arm" and "hand."

There are many culturally pertinent features which one should note in taking down lists of words. For example, in the Kiowa language the word for "floor" and "ground" is the same. In terms of the Kiowa aboriginal culture on the Great Plains it is no wonder that the same native word was used. In some languages a word may have a very wide meaning. For example, in many of the languages of central Africa the word meaning "to cut" in the primary sense of "to cut wood" is also used in the phrases "to cut water" (i.e., "to carry water"), "to cut a palaver" (i.e., "to judge a case"), and "to cut a job" (i.e., "to finish the work"). (See Chapter 7 for further illustrations of problems connected with the meanings of words.)

We cannot suggest a list of words which is usable in all areas, but the following groups will give at least some idea of the types of words to elicit:

Body Parts: "head, hair of the head, nose, eye, ear, neck, arm, hand, finger, stomach, heart, leg, foot, toe, bone, blood, flesh."

Clothing: "hat, shirt, pants, blouse, skirt, sandals, beads, face paint, body paint."

Objects about the House: "knife, spoon, ladle, water container, animal skin, bed, hammock, fire, mush, bread, meal, grinding stone, banana, meat."

Relationships between People: "father, mother, daughter, son, sister, brother, uncle, aunt, brother-in-law, sister-in-law."[19]

Articles Used in Native Occupations: "machete (large knife), hoe, dibble stick, plow, seed, hammer, saw, forge, iron, axe, plank, vines for tying, canoe, paddle, bow, arrow, spear, gun."

Fauna: "horse, cow, ox, pig, dog, cat, sheep, goat, lion, tiger, jaguar, elephant, snake, monkey, eagle, buzzard, fly, flea, spider, ant, termite."

Flora: "tree, bush, grass, vine, flower, palm, fern, corn plant, wheat plant, banana tree, orange tree."

Geographical and Astronomical Objects: "river, stream, rapids, lake, hill, mountain, valley, forest, star, sun, moon, cloud."

3.2.3.2.6   Obtaining These "Object" Words in Possessive and Plural Formations

One of the ways in which we use "object" words is to possess them. We want to be able to say "my head, your (sg.)

---

[19] One is likely to have a great deal of difficulty with such words, for there may be distinct sets of terms depending upon (1) whether a man or a woman is speaking, (2) whether someone is younger or older than another person, and (3) whether the relative is on one's father's or mother's side of the house. One should not be too concerned if the native terms seem very irregular and strange. Further inquiry after one knows the language better will resolve most of the difficulties.

head, his head, our heads, your (pl.) heads, their heads." Similarly we combine such possessive pronominal elements with all types of words, e.g., "my hat, your skirt, his pants, her blouse, our sandals, their bed." Sometimes these possessive pronouns are separate words, and sometimes they are combined with the noun to form a single word. In Mongbandi the possessed forms for "heart" are as follows:

    bế mbī "my heart"[20]
    bế mò "your (sg.) heart"
    bế lò "his, her heart"
    bế ʔɛ́ "our heart(s)"
    bế ʔį́ "your (pl.) heart(s)"
    bế ʔálà "their heart(s)"

From hearing a native pronounce these forms we cannot tell whether the expressions consist of one word or two, and we really do not need to know at first. (See Chapters 5 and 6 for a discussion of such problems.) We should, however, note that there are distinct differences in the pitches of the words and that the noun bế "heart" has the same form whether it is one heart or more than one heart. The word bế is either singular or plural. This may seem very strange, for we are so accustomed to making important distinctions between singular and plural nouns, but in many languages such a difference in the forms of the words is not to be found.

In Tzeltal, a Mayan language of southern Mexico, we find quite different types of forms from what we noted in Mongbandi, e.g..

    kot'an "my heart"
    awot'an "your (sg.) heart"
    yot'an "his, her heart"
    kot'antik "our hearts"
    awot'anik "your (pl.) hearts"
    yot'anik "their hearts"

---

[20] The special signs in the Mongbandi words have the following values: [ɛ] is like the vowel in English <u>bet</u>; [ʔ] is a kind of catch in the throat (called a glottal stop); [̨] (a hook under the vowel) indicates that the vowel is pronounced partially through the nose; the acute accent [´] means that the syllable is relatively high; the grave accent [`] means that the syllable is relatively low, and the horizontal accent [¯] means that the pitch of the syllable is midway between the high and the low syllables.

This series may seem very jumbled, for the first parts of the words are the same in the singular and the plural, but the second part is different with plural possessors. The part that means "heart" is -ot'an, but it is very difficult to get an informant to give this form, for "hearts" are normally spoken of as being possessed by someone or something. One does not encounter a lot of unpossessed "hearts" in Tzeltal.

The set of forms in Tzeltal is really quite regular, and practically all the other nouns which begin with vowels[21] occur with these same combinations of forms placed in front of the noun (i.e., prefixes) and other forms placed after the noun (i.e., suffixes). Students who enjoy analyzing such combinations (i.e., pulling the grammatical pieces apart) can do so, but for those who find it difficult or uninteresting to follow an analytical approach, the forms can be learned just as they are found.

We must not expect that all words will be possessed in the same way. If, for example, in Tzeltal we should ask for the possessed forms of k'ab "hand" we would get quite different forms:

        hk'ab "my hand"
        ak'ab "your (sg.) hand"
        sk'ab "his, her hand"
        etc.

It may seem very arbitrary that words beginning with a vowel (with preposed glottal stop) should have one set of prefixes and those beginning with consonants (other than the glottal stop) should have other prefixes. Of course, this complicates the task of learning a language, but it is just as much a part of Tzeltal as the fact that the plural of English boy is boys and the plural of English child is children. Such irregularities are to be found in all languages.

In asking for possessed forms one must be quite certain that the informant understands what is being requested. When the missionary says, "How do you say 'your house'?" the informant may reply with a form meaning "my house." He has interpreted the question as referring to his own house, rather than to a translation of the form "your house." After a little

---

[21] There is a basic glottal stop before all such so-called initial vowels.

explanation, however, and careful attention to the forms that are given, it is usually quite easy to untangle such complications.

We must ask for sensible forms. To ask a native for the plural of "sun" or "moon" may prove ridiculous. He may not know that the sun of our solar system is only one of many and that some planets have several moons However, he may be able to make up such forms even though he has not heard them. On the other hand, the word "moons" may refer to "months," and "suns" may be a designation of "days."

Similarly, one must exercise caution about certain possessives. A missionary once asked an informant for "my world," to which the native replied, "But nobody can own the whole world." If informants object to certain forms as being impossible, one should go on to other forms. It would be ridiculous to insist on an English-speaking person giving the plural of wheat. He would claim it is just wheat. Of course, he could make up the form wheats, but it would sound very strange to him; and a form which sounds strange to a native speaker is no form for a missionary to start using.

3.2.3.2.7 Obtaining Simple Verbs

In eliciting verb forms from an informant one should observe the following principles:
  a. Select simple, demonstrable words. For example, the native equivalents for "walking, running, hunting, jumping, seeing, hearing, smelling, speaking, hitting" are much more easily obtained than "thinking, trying, becoming, seeming, being."
  b. Employ full sentences. Never ask for infinitives, e.g., "to jump, to run, to walk." Rather, use third person singular forms such as "he is running, he is walking, he is jumping." One can then obtain forms for the other persons, e.g., "I am running, you (sg.) are running, we are running," etc.
  c. Begin with verbs which usually do not require an object.[22] For example, one may elicit such forms as

---

[22] Verbs that do not occur with an object are called "intransitive," and those which occur with an object are "transitive."

"he is running, he is walking, he is swimming, he is falling, he is jumping, he is dancing, he is eating." After obtaining some of these verbs with various persons, one can elicit such expressions as "he is eating it, he is following him, he is seeing her, he is hearing him, he is hitting them, he is calling us." Such expressions can then be expanded to include all the different types of subjects and objects. Sometimes this is quite complicated, for the possibilities may be numerous and very irregular (see Chapter 5). Whenever a language combines both the subject and the object pronouns with the verb root, we can expect serious difficulties, even though the forms may not be too irregular. A glance at the following forms from Congo Swahili will show what some of the typical problems are:

ninakupika "I hit you (sg.)"[23]
ninamupika "I hit him"
ninanupika "I hit you (pl.)"
ninawapika "I hit them"
wunanipika "you (sg.) hit me"
wunamupika "you (sg.) hit him"
wunatupika "you (sg.) hit us"
wunawapika "you (sg.) hit them"
ananipika "he hits me"
anakupika "he hits you (sg.)"
anamupika "he hits him"
anatupika "he hits us"
ananupika "he hits you (pl.)"
anawapika "he hits them"
tunakupika "we hit you (sg.)"
tunamupika "we hit him"
tunanupika "we hit you (pl.)"
tunawapika "we hit them"
munanipika "you (pl.) hit me"
munamupika "you (pl.) hit him"
munatupika "you (pl.) hit us"
munawapika "you (pl.) hit them"
wananipika "they hit me"
wanakupika "they hit you (sg.)"

---

[23] This is the present tense.

wanamupika "they hit him"
wanatupika "they hit us"
wananupika "they hit you (pl.)"
wanawapika "they hit them"

At first, one will want to find all these forms with a few verbs; and then if everything seems to be perfectly regular, one can easily make up the forms of other words on the pattern of these. It would be ridiculous to learn the full paradigms of all the verbs in any Bantu language, for there are thousands upon thousands of possible combinations of subjects, objects, tenses (the time of action), modes (the psychological character of the action, e.g., declarative, doubtful, potential, unreal), aspects (the type of action, e.g., continuous, frequent, repeated), and voice (the relationship between the participants and the action, e.g., active [where the subject performs the action], passive [where the subject is acted upon], reflexive [where the subject acts upon himself], and reciprocal [where the various participants act reciprocally upon each other]).

3.2.3.2.8 Obtaining Verbs with Different Tenses, in the Negative, and in Questions

Verbs may have many different forms to express many different relationships.[24] In the beginning stages of language study, we do need to be able to distinguish past, present, and future tenses, indicate a negative form, and ask a question. This is not, however, quite so easy as it may sound, for many languages do not distinguish between certain tenses. For example, in Pame-Chichimeca, a language of Mexico, the form laháo? means "I am drinking" or "I was drinking." This verb form indicates a continuous action but makes no distinction between the present or the past time. Similarly, in Zoque, another language of Mexico, the word kenpa means "he looks, he will look." In this instance there is no distinction between present and future. We must be prepared for all kinds of strange differences between languages, but in general we will find some way of distinguishing past actions, present actions, and future actions. In some languages we may even find too

___
[24]For a full discussion of such problems see Eugene A. Nida, Morphology (Ann Arbor, Michigan: University of Michigan Press, 1949).

many distinctions—too many, that is, for our ease of learning, but excellent for distinguishing fine shades of meaning. For example, in Sukuma, a Bantu language of Tanganyika, there are four past tenses: (1) immediate past, (2) proximate past, (3) intermediate past, and (4) remote past:
1. tòà·lólà "we looked (less than two hours ago)"[25]
2. tòà·lólàgà "we looked (this morning some time)"
3. tòà·lórìrè "we looked (yesterday, or the day before)"
4. tòkàlòrà "we looked (any time prior to the day before yesterday)"

Sometimes the negative of a verb is very simply expressed by adding a negative particle. For example, in Spanish we may add _no_ before the verb or the pronouns that go with the verb, e.g.,

tengo "I have"
no tengo "I do not have"
lo puso "he placed it"
no lo puso "he did not place it"

In English we use _not_, but usually with a so-called auxiliary verb, in a negative-verb phrase, e.g.,

I _came_
I did _not_ come

In Congo Swahili there is a special set of forms for the negative, e.g.,

sitakupika "I do not hit you (sg.)"
hatakupika "he does not hit you (sg.)"
hatutakupika "we do not hit you (sg.)"
hawatakupika "they do not hit you (sg.)"

It seems quite irregular to have _si_- with the first person "I" and _ha_- used with all the other types of subjects, but that is just how irregular languages can be. One can and must expect anything and everything in languages.

Questions may be formed in a number of ways. In some instances just the intonation of the voice indicates a question, e.g., John _really came_? vs. John _really came_. Frequently there are little interrogative particles that tell us that the

---

[25] See the tables of phonetic symbols in Chapter 4 (sections 4.3.1.10 and 4.3.2) for an explanation of the values of the symbols used.

sentence is a question. This is the case in Chontal of Tabasco, a Mayan language. In still other languages there may be special forms of the verb to indicate that the sentence is a question and not a statement.

If the missionary has a fairly adequate grammar of his language, many of the problems which we have been discussing will have already been explained, and much of the difficulty will be overcome immediately. It is always well, however, to check the statements of the grammar with the forms which an informant supplies, for there may be mistakes in the grammar. Furthermore, in the average grammar prepared by missionaries one usually finds that many forms are omitted.

If there is no such elementary grammar and if the missionary has had to elicit all these forms from his informant, it may seem that the mass of material written down is almost undigestible. This depends, of course, on the way in which it is written down. It is convenient to make out a series of forms on 3" x 5" slips of paper. One can get eight or ten forms of a verb on such a slip, e.g., all the persons in one of the tenses. These slips may then be used for memorizing purposes, may be shuffled and filed so as to group similar verbs together (see Chapter 5), and may also be used as a kind of practical grammar-dictionary of the language.

This emphasis on digging out so many forms may seem to contradict the principles cited in the previous chapter. There we insisted upon learning words in combinations and not as isolated units. The principles, however, still apply; and though we may have to do some exploration work in the language in order to discover something about its forms, it does not mean that we should sit down and memorize all the singular and plural forms of the nouns as so much sheer memory work. We must learn the forms, but not by memorizing lists of isolated words. It is much more meaningful to put such words into combinations. If no other easy construction suggests itself, one can drill on singular and plural nouns by putting them in combination with the phrase "I see..." Accordingly, the sentences will be

"I see a horse"
"I see horses"
"I see a cow"
"I see cows"   etc.

These singulars and plurals can, however, be combined in a number of ways, e.g.,

"The horse ran"
"The horses ran"
"The fine horse"
"The fine horses"
"We drove the horse"
"We drove the horses"
etc.

Not all of the combinations of words need to be full sentences, but it is very convenient and helpful to have them constitute sentences, for then we are learning complete utterances. What so often handicaps our practical use of a language is our tendency to learn isolated parts of sentences. We need to learn the frameworks into which such parts fit.

3.2.3.2.9 Obtaining Expressions Which Modify Nouns and Verbs

We can do a great deal of talking with just nouns, pronouns, and verbs. However, we also need to get some qualifying expressions in order to extend our ability to express ourselves. The qualifying words for nouns may be grouped as follows:

a. Numerals: "one, two, three, four, five, six," etc.
b. Pointing and location expressions: "this, that, near, far, (those) in the house, (the woman) by the well."
c. Quantity: "few, many, some, much."
d. Quality expressions: "good, bad, tall, short, big, little, expensive, cheap, strong, weak, wealthy, poor, red, yellow, green, blue, white, black."

Some illustrative qualifying expressions for verbs may be grouped as follows:

a. Numerals: "once, twice, three times, four times," etc.
b. Pointing and location expressions: "here, there, near, far, in sight, out of sight, (went) to town, (fell) from the tree."
c. Quantity expressions: "much, little, some, often, rarely."
d. Quality expressions: "well, badly, quickly, slowly, powerfully, weakly, loudly, quietly."

We would be inclined to consider most, if not all, of the first groups of words as adjectives, since they would modify nouns in English, and we would judge most of the second types of expressions to be adverbs. However, if we insist on these categories in other languages, we shall be badly mistaken in many instances. For example, as noted in section 1.4, in Muskogee, an Indian language of the United States, the numerals are really verbs and have all the basic forms that verbs have. Likewise in many languages the words that we consider as adjectives, e.g., "good, bad, tall, short, thick, thin" turn out to be verbs. In the Abwong dialect of Dinka, a language of the Anglo-Egyptian Sudan, the words which correspond to English "recently, not yet, quickly, earnestly, always" are auxiliary verbs. However, the equivalent of "slowly" is a regular adverbial particle. In Navaho the equivalent of English "highway" is two verb expressions. The first is a dependent form, and the second the main verb. The Navaho expression translated literally would be "being-broad it-roads." The stems "broad" and "road" are basically verbs.

It is not absolutely necessary for a person learning a language to analyze all the parts of speech. Such an approach may make language learning easier, but it is never a substitute for being able to manipulate the forms. Furthermore, regardless of how strange and unusual the grammatical constructions are, they are not just haphazard combinations of words. They reveal a system, and the only way to learn how to use such a system is to use it.

Like all other words attributives are to be mastered by learning them in combinations with other words. For example, we not only learn to count, but to count things, e.g.,

"one horse, two horses, three horses, four horses," etc.
"one house, two houses, three houses, four houses," etc.

Often counting is not so easy as one might think. For example, in Burmese the expression "one person" consists of lú tayauʔ, of which lú means "person," ta- means "one," and -yauʔ is a classifier used when one is counting human beings. There are twenty-one principal classifiers of this type, and the following are typical examples listed under the classifier and with the numeral "one."[26]

---

[26] See William Cornyn, Outline of Burmese Grammar, Language Dissertation No. 24, (Baltimore: Linguistic Society of America, 1944), p. 27.

châun "long and slender things": khêdán tachâun "one pencil"
káun "animals": myau? takáun "one monkey"
khûn "words, utterances": zagâ takhûn "one word, sentence, utterance."
le? "tools, weapons": dâ tale? "one knife"
lôun "spherical or cubical things": tittá talôun "one box"
phe? "one of a pair": myessí taphe? "one eye"
pín "trees, hairs, threads": ?amwêi tapín "one hair of the body"
sháun "buildings": câun tasháun "one monastery"
thé "articles of clothing": bâumbí tathé "one pair of pants"

These same classifiers occur with all the numerals. In counting people one would use phrases as follows:

lú tayau? "one person"
lú hnayau? "two persons"
lú θôunyau? "three persons"
lú lêiyau? "four persons"
lú ŋâyau? "five persons"
etc.

Numerical classifiers are found in many Oriental languages. In fact, they have sometimes been considered as typical of Oriental languages, but their occurrence is not restricted to the Far East. In Maya, spoken in Yucatan, Mexico, there are similar types of numerical classifiers.[27] For example, in counting people or animals one says huntul "one," ka?atul "two," oštul "three," kantul "four," and ho?tul "five," This system does not go beyond five because the Spanish numerical system is used for higher numbers. If one is counting miscellaneous inanimate things, the numerals are hump'el "one," ka?ap'el "two," ošp'el "three," etc. The following classifiers, illustrated with the numeral "one," may be used:

-kul "trees": hunkul ša?an "one palm tree"
-to? "objects wrapped up in small quantities": hunto? ta?ab "a package of salt"
-lot "a handful": hunlot iši?im "a handful of corn"

---

[27] Of course, this does not mean that Maya is thus related to Oriental languages. It is just an interesting parallelism.

-kuč "loads carried on the back": hunkuč čuuk "a sack of charcoal"
-c'it "one or more from a class of objects": hunc'it haʔas "one banana"
-p'is "a measurement": hump'is nok' "a measure of cloth"
-ten "occurrences": hunten "once"
-buh "things divided into equal parts": humbuh luč "one half of a gourd"

There are equally complicated features about many other types of attributives to nouns and verbs, some of which will be considered in Chapter 6. These illustrations should be enough to warn us against taking anything for granted. Differences are precisely the features which provide each language with its individuality, and make of it an instrument for conveying important ideas in an impressive way. Each language has its own subtle distinctions and refinements of meaning and form. To appreciate these qualities and to use them effectively, rather than to complain about their strangeness, will mean much to one's language progress and mastery.

3.2.3.2.10   Putting Words Together into Frames

We have already been illustrating a number of frames, but most of them have been of the substitution type. Substitution frames are sentences or phrases which will allow the substitution of some part. The portion which remains unchanged may be said to constitute the "frame," and the portion which changes is the "substitution." The following is such a frame:

"The man saw the child."
"The man called the child."
"The man chased the child."
"The man caught the child."
"The man whipped the child."
etc.

With such a sentence we could substitute at least three different portions:
1. The subject, e.g.,
"The man saw the child."
"The woman saw the child."

"The boy saw the child."
etc.
2. The object, e.g.,
"The man saw the child."
"The man saw the house."
"The man saw the horse."
"The man saw the dog."
etc.
3. The verb, already illustrated above.

Of course, it is also possible to substitute different qualifiers of "man" and "child," e.g.,
"A man saw a child."
"This man saw that child."
"Some man saw this child."
etc.

This last type of substitution frame makes more than one substitution at once, and hence may be technically called a multiple-substitution frame, in contrast to a single-substitution frame, illustrated above.

Another important type of frame is the "expandible frame." This consists of substituting different and more extensive expressions or of simply adding attributives to already existing parts of phrases or sentences. A typical expandible frame would be the following:
"The man saw the child."
"The old man saw the little child."
"The poor old man rarely saw the ragged little child."
"The rather poor old man very rarely saw the extremely ragged little child."
etc.

By substituting different words as well as more extended phrases, one could construct the following:
"The man saw the child."
"The old fellow hit the poor boy."
"The stingy mean rascal almost destroyed the little house of blocks."
etc.

These last three sentences do not resemble each other very much, but they consist of precisely the same types of units, namely, a noun expression as subject, a verb expression, and a noun expression as object. Learning to build up sentences in this fashion is a basic feature of language learning.

If a person tries to elicit various sentences like these from his informant, complications may arise because they do not seem to have any importance or meaningful relationship. Hence, it is very valuable to try to follow some central theme in the construction of a series of sentences having a related structure. For example, one may obtain the following type of series:

"The boy saw a monkey."
"The boy chased the monkey."
"The monkey stopped."
"The monkey screeched at the boy."
"The boy was afraid of the monkey."
"The boy fled from the monkey."
"The monkey chased the boy."
"The boy ran out of the forest."
"The boy cried."
"The monkey laughed."

This series of sentences follows a kind of narrative and is constructed on a very simple framework, namely, a subject expression and a verb expression, with or without an object or some type of locative[28] attributive. The forms in a native language might not be as simple as this, and the informant might insist that some connectives, such as "then," "therefore," "because," and "since" should be added. Such syntactic refinements are all the better. The important thing is to be able to use one's vocabulary in certain straightforward sentences. After a while, such sentence frames become second-nature, and then one actually begins to speak a language. But first one must elicit such series and notice the particular ways in which the words go together. By restricting oneself at the beginning to certain fixed structures employing a limited vocabulary, it is much easier to learn how to speak. In fact, if one must choose between a limited vocabulary but a thorough knowledge of some of the basic grammatical frames and an extensive vocabulary but without a practical mastery of such syntactic structures, one should always choose the first. New words and phrases may be rapidly added to known

---

[28] That is, a form which indicates a location.

frames, but it is the ignorance of such frames which retards the language student so much. In Chapter 6 we will note some of the important differences between the frames used in various languages.

3.2.3.2.11 Writing Down Texts

In addition to providing oneself plenty of opportunities to hear natives speak, it is also very helpful to take down from dictation as many native stories, legends, proverbs, and conversations as possible. We need to be able to read over such texts and analyze their structure.

It is difficult to get such texts, for though an informant may be a superb story-teller as long as he is spinning his yearns to admiring listeners as they huddle around the campfire, he may ruin his tale by reducing it to a few prosaic sentences, once he is forced to dictate slowly while the student laboriously writes it down. With some practice, however, the informant will probably improve, especially, if his minor successes are praised, and fuller forms of expression are encouraged. One cannot begin the process of taking down text right at first. That is why we have outlined so many other preliminary steps. One must become accustomed to the sounds, many of the constantly recurring grammatical forms, and at least some of the basic vocabulary. Otherwise, a person becomes totally lost.

In writing down stories, it is best to let the informant proceed without any interruptions. To interrupt is often to spoil the continuity of the story and to dampen the informant's enthusiasm. When the story has been fully transcribed, one can go back over it phrase by phrase, correcting the transcription and finding out the meanings of the words and phrases. How these texts can be used to analyze the language structure will be indicated more fully in Chapters 5 and 6, but there are some observations which may be easily made, e.g.,

    1. Where does the subject usually come in the sentence?
    2. Where does the verb usually come in the sentence?
    3. Are the sentences conspicuously long, or are most of them short?[29]

---

[29] They are likely to be shorter in such dictation than in the average type of utterance.

4. Do the various kinds of words occur in a rigid sentence order, or do they seem to hop all around?
5. Are many of the words rather long (five or six syllables), or do most of the words consist of only a syllable or two.
6. Are there many connective words between sentences, e.g., "when, then, because, for, but, and, accordingly"?

Even these very elementary observations will begin to tell us a great deal about the language and the way the words go together. One of the big advantages of texts is that they reveal many additional frames which one may learn and then fill in with other words and phrases.

There are many different types of texts, and the variety should not be overlooked, for styles may differ considerably. The most common types of texts are greetings, conversation, personal narrative, traditional legends, poetry, and proverbs. Greetings are usually very highly formalized. Conversation often employs many clipped, shortened expressions. For example, in English we may say Howdy! in place of How do you do? and Smatter? for What is the matter? Similar developments occur in many languages. Personal narrative is usually the least specialized type of language form. Traditional legends may have many forms of expression which require an intimate knowledge of a people's history and ethnology. Native poetry may be very intricate with many archaic or pseudo-archaic expressions, so that one should not attempt to write down and analyze such forms until one has acquired considerable facility in the ordinary forms. Proverbs often tend to be very cryptic; in fact, they are sometimes intentionally so. It is very important to learn them for they are often an entering wedge to society and intellectual respectability. Certainly a knowledge of the proverbs of some African tribe will mean much more by way of prestige and gaining a hearing from the native peoples than any number of earned or honorary degrees strung after one's name. In fact, one's ability to employ the native proverbs at the appropriate time and place is the criterion of learning in some parts of the world. In central Africa it would be ridiculous to talk about "locking the barn door after the horse has been stolen" when one might much better use a native equivalent such as, "After the prince fell into the stream, they built a bridge."

3.2.3.2.12 Reading Texts and Listening to Them Read

One of the difficulties about learning to "hear" a language is that we do not have the opportunity to listen frequently to the same types of material. By reading over texts several times we become familiar with the words and the forms, and by encouraging the native informant to correct us constantly we are able to improve our pronunciation. However, we also need the experience of having such material read to us, and read several times. By hearing the same thing over and over we begin to identify more and more of the meaningful units. By this means we are "tuning" our ears to the language.

When a text becomes rather familiar, the content should be made the basis of conversation with the informant. One may ask questions about the why's and wherefore's of the action, the customs alluded to, and other versions of the story. If the story has any parallels known to the missionary, it is helpful to attempt to tell this other story to the informant. People are always fascinated by some tale similar to their own, and it begins to strengthen the bonds of mutual understanding.

3.2.3.2.13 Memorizing Stories

One of the best ways to acquire a number of grammatical frames and to endear oneself to natives is to memorize some favorite tales. It will show them that the missionary has great respect for native patterns of life[30] and will provide an almost endless source of entertainment. Some missionaries have become locally famous almost overnight by reciting some ancient legend with all the traditional rhetorical trappings. Of course, the missionary is not concerned about being renowned, but knowing the cultural heritage of a people is basic to understanding them. Being able to recite native stories not only demonstrates such knowledge and accordingly engenders confidence, but it also provides the missionary with a wealth of sentence frames to be used in talking about other things much more important to himself and to the people as well.

---

[30] With proper caution this need not in any way compromise the missionary's work or message.

3.2.3.2.14 Listening Constantly to the Language

One cannot learn without listening, but to provide oneself with opportunities for listening to a native language is not always easy. In Latin America and the Orient those who wish to learn a native language have usually had to go right out and live in the villages or in native quarters of large cities where they are constantly surrounded by it. This is really the only satisfactory procedure. In Negro Africa missionaries generally have felt that they could not live in native villages, though some missionaries have done so and certain of them have gained much in linguistic accomplishments as a result. Regardless, however, of the local obstructions and difficulties, a person must organize his program so that he can constantly hear the language. If he is in Africa, he can certainly do as many missionaries have, namely, sit around the campfires at night. It may mean squatting inside some dusty, smoky kraal near a fire of dried dung, but that may be the only way to hear the language for two or three hours each day. During working hours the people are usually scattered. The missionary on a station always has the opportunity to attend native services, and in many places there are various services during the day for workmen, schoolboys, house help, etc. In Africa one of the best places to listen to the language is at the native law courts. If one has been properly introduced to the chief, it is usually possible to get permission to attend. Hour after hour and sometimes day after day, the people plead their causes with all the subtlety of professional lawyers and all the accumulated knowledge of a hoary tradition. Anyone who wants to imbibe the wisdom of Africa can nowhere find it better presented than in the native courts.

Where it is possible, one should attempt to live with a native family. This is not only important for learning the language, but also for learning about the people. One of the principal difficulties, however, is the food, but as one missionary has said, "The one who claims that 'Where He leads me I will follow,' must also learn the meaning of 'What He feeds me I will swallow.'" Nevertheless, one should not impair health and future effectiveness by taking unnecessary risks about food and water. One should take reasonable precautions when living in a native household, but nothing is more rewarding than living with a native family if one really wants to learn to speak a language. In many circumstances, however, it is not expedient to live and eat with native families,[31] but it is often possible to construct one's home in the native pattern and to live in a village. One missionary in West Africa has lived in various villages of his tribe by procuring a cluster of native huts (each family unit usually has two or three huts) from the chief. There have been a number of inconveniences, but such inconveniences have been insignificant as compared with the advantages of being right with the people, constantly hearing the language, and being in so far as possible an integral part of the village life. The missionary who lives in the comparative isolation of a hill-top will find that it takes much longer to acquire a language. Where the circumstances prevent living in a village, one can make it a practice to itinerate frequently, for camping out or staying in so-called "rest houses" (as for example in central Africa) is more like village life than living on the mission compound.

The use of mechanical recorders (wire, tape, and disc) have been very widely recommended. These can prove very valuable, if properly employed, but their helpfulness has often been exaggerated. The primary difficulty with learning a foreign language through recordings such as Linguaphone is that there is usually no one around to correct one's pronunciation. Our pronunciations may sound all right to us, but our ears have ways of deceiving us. We think that we are reproducing the sounds that we hear when in reality we miss them badly. However, recordings can be used to very good advantage. Their principal uses are three:

   a. Getting practice in listening to the language. It is very helpful to listen over and over again to native stories, legends, or sermons by native pastors. The repetition of the same material assists us in isolating a high percentage of the meaningful units.

   b. Studying the intonation of the sentences. In order to study the natural rise and fall of sentences and phrases, there is nothing better than a mechanical recording. So

---

[31] This is generally true for languages considered under this third general procedure, but, of course, would not apply to most European and to some Oriental situations.

many times we miss the proper transcription if we must have the informant repeat an expression several times, for the intonations may change greatly in the artificial process of dictating slowly.

    c. Making a recording of one's own speech for comparison. One may profitably recite a number of memorized expressions or read some native text and then have it played back. One will usually be shocked by one's "terrible accent." Such a procedure will point out the gross errors, and accordingly one can concentrate on eliminating them. A series of such recordings made each successive month will indicate whether or not one is improving. One of the best types of recordings is of a conversation between a native speaker and the student. Differences of pronunciation, intonation, speed of utterance, and facility in handling the grammatical frames of the language will be evident immediately.

Mechanical recordings are very useful tools in language learning, but they cannot substitute for putting forms down on paper.

3.2.3.2.15 Using the Language at Every Opportunity

Using a language often means forcing oneself to use it and planning one's work and activities in such a way as to give the best practice. One of the most effective means is to go visiting. At first it is best to have one's informant go along, so that when one's vocabulary gives out, the informant may take over. However, one should not use such help too much or for too long a time. Sooner or later (and better, sooner) one must launch out alone. At the beginning a person feels terribly foolish, for the words seem to get stuck in one's throat and one's ears become filled with a meaningless assortment of sounds. But soon the phrases will begin to make sense. There are two important rules to remember when one begins to use the language without the help of some ready interpreter:

    a. Use the words, disregarding the fact that the forms may not be entirely right.
    b. Keep up to speed.

Some people do not wish to say a thing until they are sure that all the forms are perfectly correct. This is a great mistake. One should dive right in and begin using the words in order to convey one's meaning. The refinements of grammatical form will come, but first must come the broad sentence structures. There are those who never care to master the finer points of the language, and this is a great mistake. They continue to "bully" their way through the language without regard for the cultural niceties of expression. On the other hand, one must not remain tongue-tied for fear of using a wrong mode or tense, for one will not learn how to use any form without having some practice in using it. The man who never used an ungrammatical form never learned to speak a foreign language.

Using the native language in the home is a great advantage. English-speaking missionaries too often make a habit of speaking only English in their homes. Of course, it is one's easiest language, and it helps to give one a sense of "homeness," but constantly making use of English in a foreign language community frequently leads natives to be suspicious of what is being said, and sometimes they understand far more than the unsuspecting missionary guesses. In many cases the use of the native language can be a great spiritual blessing to those around. For example, one missionary family in Latin America used to make it their practice to pray in English during evening devotions. An Indian servant one time asked, "What are you doing?" The missionary endeavored to explain that he was "praying," but the poor native persisted in understanding it as "reciting," for the English sounded like the meaningless Latin liturgy which he had heard on rare occasions in the far-off cathedral. Finally, the missionary explained that he was just "talking to God." The astonished Indian then asked pleadingly, "Oh then, speak to God in my language so that I may listen in." Some of our most effective means of witnessing as to the reality of our religious experience comes from the constant use of the native language in all the circumstances of life.

3.2.3.2.16   <u>Making</u> <u>a</u> <u>Dictionary</u> <u>of</u> <u>the</u> <u>Language</u>

The missionary who finds a good dictionary of his language, for example, such as the Zulu-English Dictionary by

Doke and Vilakazi, is fortunate indeed. But even the process of making a dictionary can be profitable. Writing out a slip for each new word and filing it away helps one to remember the form. Being constantly on the alert for various meanings of the same word will also whet one's linguistic appetite, and quick reviews of vocabulary based upon one's dictionary can be very helpful. Sometimes a project which we have to develop ourselves has much more meaning than one already worked out, so even the necessity of making a dictionary for our own use and the assistance of others can be a blessing in disguise.

We should not restrict our dictionary, however, to the mere listing of words. All types of idioms must be included under the key word or words. For example, if the language of our dictionary were English, we would want to list in the dictionary such idioms as "give him the cold shoulder," "pick a lemon," and "I'll be switched." These idioms are not describable in terms of the regular meanings of all the constituent parts. They are special types of expressions, and corresponding specialized figures of speech exist in all languages. For example, in Miskito, a language of Honduras and Nicaragua, the phrase "to scrape off the lip" means "to whisper," and the expression "the moon has caught hold of his mother-in-law" means that "the moon is eclipsed." To say that one is under another's care, one must use the idiom "he is in the shelter of his armpit." No language is fully learned until all such idioms have been mastered.

3.2.3.2.17 Seeking Constant Correction from Native Speakers

It is not easy to get natives to correct a person. The prestige of being a missionary and a white foreigner makes people very reluctant to correct errors in pronunciation or grammatical forms. One British official in Africa complained bitterly that the natives would not correct his Arabic, and only by using extreme pressure on his servants could he induce them to correct him. It was only then that he found that he had been mixing up the phrases "Open the window!" and "Close the window!" When the servants heard him give an order concerning the window, they always looked at the window first and then proceeded to open it if it were closed or close it if it were open. For months the servants had played this little game, never presuming to correct the official.

Not only do some natives refuse to correct the white man, but some of them even imitate the white man's bad pronunciation of the native language. Just as some natives have thought that wearing shoes, shirts, shorts, and a tropical helmet would make them into new men and give them prestige, so some of them have even carried this imitative process to the point of mimicking the white man's errors in speech.

If one is going to be adequately corrected, a really determined effort must be made. One of the ways in which this can be done most easily is in the classroom. As the missionary is teaching, he should insist that the students stop him whenever he makes a grammatical mistake or pronounces words in such a way that they are difficult to understand. At first, students will be very reluctant to stop the teacher and correct him, but by highly praising the daring student who does interrupt, the teacher may induce the other students to participate in the process of correcting his speech. In the initial days and weeks, the instruction may be very slow indeed, for much of the time will be taken up with the corrections. However, over a period of months the missionary will undoubtedly put across much more because of the constant corrections than he would if he went bungling on, with the students actually missing much that he had to say. One guest professor in a university in Latin America followed this procedure in lecturing to his class in Spanish; and though the first few weeks were discouraging indeed, the results over the entire semester were much better than if he had gone blindly ahead using his imperfect Spanish.

Inducing people to correct one in conversation is not easy, but if one encourages corrections and takes time to express sincere thanks for help given, it is possible to make almost every conversation into a language-improving opportunity.

If there is no other way, one can hire informants to converse and correct mistakes. It is also possible to hire them to listen to one's sermons, lectures, and conversations, jotting down mistakes as they hear them, and then turning over such notes to the missionary. These notes should be carefully reviewed by the missionary at least three times. However, one should not review the mistake, but rather the correction of the mistake. Fixing a mistake in one's mind is a hazard. We must direct our attention toward the correct form.

One of the reasons why we do not insist on being corrected is that we tend to be satisfied with our ability. Natives may say that we speak even better than they do, but, of course, we must discount all such remarks. They may have reference to some public-speaking ability, or they may be referring to the extraordinary way in which we coin new words and phrases—most of which are just translationisms from English, and some of them may be very bad. For example, one missionary wanted a word for "grace" to use in John 1:14, where the Word is spoken of as "full of grace and truth." The missionary coined a compound "living gift," because he argued that "grace" was not only a "gift," but more than that, it was a "gift of life," or as he put it "a living gift." The natives never quite understood it, even though they were duly impressed by the missionary's ingenuity. What they actually understood by the phrase "living gift" was "chicken," for the only live gifts which they gave to one another were chickens. They accordingly understood the passage in John 1:14 to mean that the Word was "full of chicken and truth."

The only worth-while compliments about one's language ability are those accidental statements which actually reveal the native speaker's reactions. For example, a young missionary from Spanish-America was talking in Spanish with some foreign students who had recently come to one of the large universities of the United States. The topic of conversation was schools and methods for learning English. After a while, one of the Latin American students asked the missionary, "Well, where did you study English?" The fact that the missionary was not a native Spanish speaker was not detected, and such a question was a real compliment.

One British linguist working in the Sudan was so proficient in reproducing the difficult sounds that the natives exclaimed, "Surely his mother could not have been white!" The natives thought that anyone who could master such strange sounds and peculiar forms must have been born of a Negro mother. Such a statement is a compliment of the highest order.

Chapter 4

4. MASTERING THE SOUNDS

The mistakes which one can make in pronouncing the sounds of a foreign language are numerous, ridiculous, and serious. In preaching about the children of Israel crossing the Red Sea and following Moses, one missionary became so confused about the tones and the consonants of one Bantu language that he declared, "The children of Israel crossed the red mosquitoes and swallowed Moses." Such an illustration could be multiplied thousands of times. Some are just funny. For example, certain missionaries were always asking people what their "broom" was rather than what their "name" was. The difficulty was simply that the two words had the same consonants and vowels, but the word for "broom" was pronounced with a high tone followed by a low tone and the word for "name" was pronounced with two high tones. Some of the natives of one West African language thought that Lot's wife became a pillar of a "wall" rather than a pillar of "salt," since the two words differed only in the type of o sound; and until the missionary learned to distinguish clearly between the words, the natives naturally interpreted the form as meaning "wall" since it made much more sense to them to talk about a "pillar of a wall" than to speak of a "pillar of salt."

One of the serious errors in pronunciation was the confusion in one of the languages of central Africa between the words for "poison" and "blessing." The differences were only slight distinctions in tone, but the missionaries had never learned to distinguish them properly. As a result, in the celebration of the Lord's Supper they said, "This cup of poison we do bless," rather than saying, "This cup of blessing, we do bless." The native church had constructed an elaborate explanation when the problem was simply a mispronunciation. Since the native pagan practices included the drinking of the poison cup to prove innocence, they concluded that the missionaries concocted a poison brew and then blessed it. Because none of those who drank of it died as the result, the natives thought that this sacrament was a means of demonstrating the Christians' innocence of any major offense against the spirits. Most mistakes in pronunciation are, however, not so tragic, but it is amazing how unruffled some native congregations are when they hear a missionary make such a mistake as was made once in a language of central Congo: "The Lord will return in the glory of his Father, surrounded by <u>white pants</u>." Of course, the missionary had wanted to say "holy angels," but a little mispronunciation completely changed the meaning. Even though some congregations are surprisingly solemn at the time, the natives will often confess that they have no end of merriment among themselves mimicking the missionaries' errors and laughing uproariously about the mistakes in the recent sermon.

The sounds of a language are basic to everything else, and the sounds of every language are distinctive. Sometimes missionaries are confused by the similarity of the alphabet, and when they learn that Spanish has only five significant vowel sounds, they are delighted, for they know that English has many more such sounds. They imagine that they can just pick up the five closest English vowels and use them in Spanish. However, the Spanish vowels are not at all like English. Superficially, of course, there is a resemblance, but it does not take us long to recognize that a Spanish American who has just begun to learn English does not use English vowels. Exactly the same thing is true of the average English-speaking person learning Spanish.

One of the great difficulties is that native speakers of a language cannot tell us just how we should change our pronunciation to conform to theirs. They can easily detect that something is wrong, but they do not usually know how to help us correct the error. When we pronounce a Spanish <u>t</u> as we would an English <u>t</u>, it sounds queer to native speakers; but few teachers are sufficiently trained to tell us that we should put our tongue farther front in the mouth, in fact, right up against the upper teeth, and that we should eliminate the aspiration (the little puff of air) that follows the <u>t</u> when it is initial in the word. Because we cannot find native speakers who are able to give us the guidance we need in pronunciation, we should have some orientation in the study of phonetics (the science of sounds used in speech).

MASTERING THE SOUNDS

Some people think that the important thing is getting the words and grammar, and then gradually refining the pronunciation. As we have noted before, this is a false idea, for the early habits stick with us and soon become almost unbreakable. Some elementary phonetic training is usually invaluable. Of course, it is quite impossible to study all the sounds made by speakers of languages all over the world. But neither does the botanist undertake to study all the plants in the world before he begins to classify new specimens. He learns the fundamental characteristics and the way of going about his analysis, and then he is able to describe and identify forms that he has never studied before. The same is true with the student of phonetics.

One of the great difficulties in studying sounds from a textbook is that books cannot make noises. One needs a teacher who has heard such sounds and can reproduce them, or better still, a native speaker of a language which contains such sounds. However, a book can explain some of the problems and can make one aware of certain difficulties. If one learns to be a careful observer of sounds, at least half of the trouble is over.

4.1 Misconceptions about Phonetic Abilities

Some basic misconceptions about phonetic ability hamper some people's progress in a language. For example, there are those who claim that they have had no difficulty in learning the peculiar sounds of German because their ancestors came from Germany. This is nonsense. There are no hereditary gifts which enable one to acquire certain sounds and not others. In fact, any person of any race or tribe raised in any other part of the world can speak the language of that area without the slightest trace of "accent." Some people insist that the thick lips of Negroes account for some of the peculiar sounds in Africa and for their inability to acquire certain types of pronunciation of other languages. This is wholly untrue. There are Africans who speak French, Spanish, Portuguese, English, Arabic, and Afrikaans (a dialect of Dutch) in such a way that their speech cannot be distinguished from native speakers of these languages.

Certain tribes place disks in their lips and file their teeth or knock out certain teeth for the sake of adornment. One would think that such disfigurements would modify the speech appreciably, but that does not seem to be the case. The Ngbakas who have their two front upper teeth knocked out (the normal practice in the tribe) do not speak appreciably different from those who do not have such teeth removed.

4.2 What Makes the Sounds[1]

Most speech sounds are made by modifying the air stream which comes from the lungs. We may conceive of the air stream as being forced out by a bellows consisting of our lungs. It may be set in vibration by the vocal cords and is modified by the various articulators and cavities through which it passes. To identify the various mechanisms one should examine carefully the diagram on the following page.

There are two principal types of functional parts: movable and stationary. The movable parts are the lips, lower jaw, tongue, velum (the soft palate that hangs at the back of the mouth, including the uvula), and vocal cords. The stationary parts are the teeth, alveolar arch, hard palate, back wall of the pharynx, and the nasal cavity. By various combinations and placements of these parts all the multitude of speech sounds are produced. To describe these parts we need to make some more minute distinctions. For example, we

---

[1] The phonetic explanations in this chapter are very elementary; and some of the statements are slightly misleading because they do not attempt to cover all the possibilities. The student is advised to consult some of the following books on phonetics:

Henry Sweet, A Primer of Phonetics; Oxford, 1906.
Paul Passy, Petite Phonétique Comparée, Leipzig, 1912.
W. Rippmann, Elements of Phonetics, 2d edition; New York, 1903.
G. Noel-Armfield, General Phonetics, 4th edition; Cambridge, 1931.
Otto Jespersen, Lehrbuch der Phonetik, 2d edition; Leipzig, 1913.
Kenneth L. Pike, Phonetics; Ann Arbor, Michigan, 1943.
Diedrich Westermann and Ida C. Ward, Practical Phonetics for Students of African Languages; Oxford, 1933.

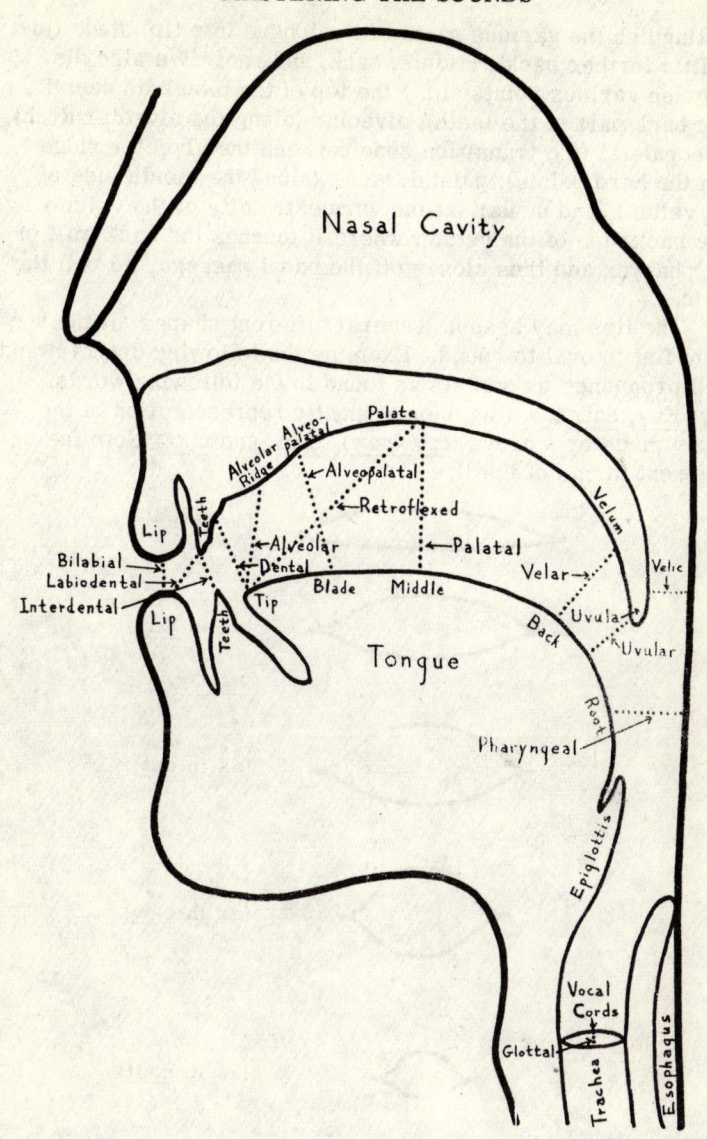

Figure 1. The Vocal Organs.

distinguish the various parts of the tongue into tip, blade (just a little further back), middle, back, and root. We also distinguish various points along the top of the mouth as dental (the back part of the teeth), alveolar (along the alveolar arch), alveopalatal (the transition zone between the alveolar ridge and the hard palate), palatal, velar (along the mouth side of the velum), and uvular (at the very extremity of the velum). The back side of the velum, where it touches the back wall of the pharynx and thus closes off the nasal passage, we call the velic.

The lips may assume several different shapes all the way from flat to oval to round. Examine the following diagram and then pronounce the vowels as found in the following words: key, Kay, cat, caw (the onomatopoetic representation of the sound made by a crow: caw-caw), coat, and coo. Note the different forms of the lips.

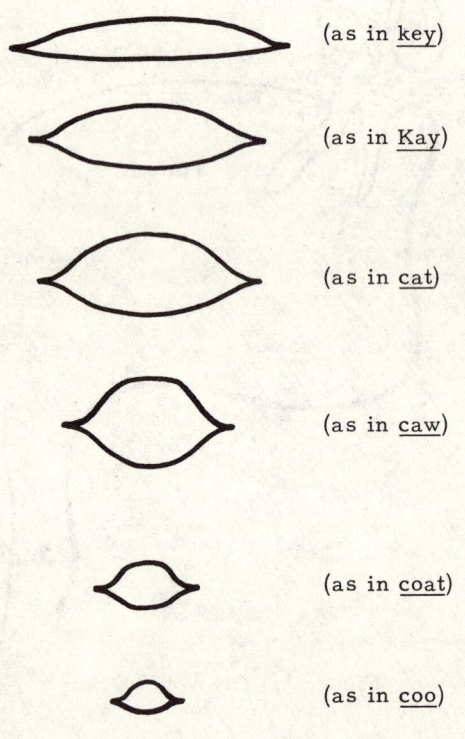

(as in key)

(as in Kay)

(as in cat)

(as in caw)

(as in coat)

(as in coo)

Figure 2. Degrees of Lip Rounding.

The tongue also may assume a great many different shapes. It may be flat as in the pronunciation of the exclamative Ah-ah!, deeply grooved as in the pronunciation of s, shallowly grooved as in the pronunciation of sh, "cupped" and drawn back (i.e., retroflexed) as in the pronunciation of r, humped up in the back in the pronunciation of coo. These are just a few of the tongue's possible positions, and our description of the form is somewhat inexact, for we are using words which are relative, and at the same time more or less nontechnical. We will note more of these shapes as we consider the ways in which various vowels and consonants are produced.

4.3 The Principal Types of Speech Sounds

For convenience we may divide sounds into their traditional classes of consonants and vowels.[2] This does not mean that some sounds which we list as consonants will not act like vowels, e.g., the r-sound in the Western American pronunciation of bird. In fact, we find all kinds of apparent exceptions in languages, but for the sake of describing the phonetic characteristics the usual distinction between consonants and vowels is helpful.

4.3.1 Consonants

Consonants (with the exception of certain clicks) interrupt the airstream coming from the lungs or materially affect its steady flow. The various results are called stops, fricatives, frictionless consonants (including nasals, laterals, and centrals), and vibrants.

4.3.1.1 Stops

Stops consist of a complete stoppage of the airstream at some point or points.[3] The diagram of the alveolar stop [t] would appear as on the following page.

---

[2] The distinction between contoids and vocoids is technically preferable (see K. L. Pike, op. cit.), but for our purposes the traditional distinction is more helpful.

[3] Clicks, as will be seen, are a type of minor exception to this statement.

Broken line indicates voicelessness

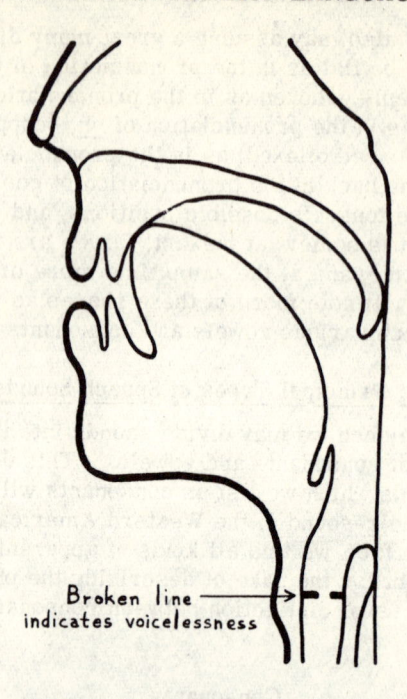

Figure 3. Production of [t].

 The types of stops are partially identifiable by the point in the mouth or throat where some articulator (movable part) stops off the air stream. A stop made by the lips is called bilabial (e.g., English p); one made by the tongue against the teeth is called dental (e.g., Spanish t); one made by the tongue against the alveolar ridge is called alveolar (e.g., English t); one made by the mid part of the tongue against the hard palate is called palatal (e.g., English k as in keen); one made by the back of the tongue against the soft palate (or velum) is called velar (e.g., English [k] as in caw-caw); and one made by completely closing the vocal cords is called glottal (e.g., the catch in the throat which occurs in the middle of the negative interjection huh-uh). If the vocal cords are vibrating during the time of a stop (this may occur except in the case of a glottal stop), we say that the sound is voiced. If the vocal cords are not vibrating, the sound is voiceless. We may chart the sounds which we have described as follows:

	Bilabial	Dental	Alveolar	Palatal	Velar	Glottal
Voiceless	p	t̪	t	k̟	k	ʔ
Voiced	b	d̪	d	g̟	g	

The traditional Roman alphabet does not provide us with enough symbols to designate the various principal sounds, and so we must use some diacritical marks and new symbols. The curve under a letter means that it is relatively farther front in point of articulation, and the top part of a question mark indicates a glottal stop.

As will be noted in the case of sounds for which the tongue is the principal agent, the front part of the tongue usually touches the front part of the mouth, the middle part of the tongue touches the middle part or the roof of the mouth (the hard palate), and the back part touches the velum. Sometimes, however, the tongue turns back (i.e., becomes retroflexed) and the tip touches the hard palate. This occurs in the so-called domal sounds that exist in some of the languages of India. To designate such a retroflexed sound we may use a dot beneath the letter, e.g. [ṭ] and [ḍ].

4.3.1.2   Double Stops

In some languages the sound is stopped at two points in the mouth at the same time, e.g., Ngbaka (a Sudanic language of northern Congo) gbɔ̀gbɔ̀ "lion" (cf. gɔ̀gɔ̀ "tooth"). (The vowel indicated by [ɔ] is like the vowel of English saw and the grave accent [ˋ] indicates that the tone of the syllable is low.) In the word gbɔ̀gbɔ̀ one does not pronounce [g] and then [b], as the orthography would seem to imply. The lips are closed, and the back part of the tongue is up against the velum at the same time. When the stop is released for the following vowel, the impression is just as though one had been saying a [g] and a [b] at the same time, which, of course, is precisely what does occur. The combination kp also exists in Ngbaka, e.g., in the word kpōkpò "mat."

4.3.1.3 Clicks

The clicks of South Africa are a very special kind of stop consonant. For a good description of these sounds one may read D. M. Beach, <u>The Phonetics of the Hottentot Language</u> (Cambridge, 1939) or C. M. Doke, <u>The Phonetics of the Zulu Language</u> (Johannesburg, 1926). Anyone who must learn a language containing clicks should by all means study such detailed descriptions. However, we may note briefly some of the principal facts about their formation. First, the back of the tongue is in contact with the velum and is drawn down and back rapidly while an anterior part of the tongue closes off the mouth at another point. The process of drawing the back part of the tongue down and back forms a vacuum, so that when the fore part of the tongue is released from the stop position, a little bit of air pops into the vacuum, making the click sound, just before the back part of the tongue is released for the following sound. All this sounds very complicated, but we are all able to make certain clicks. For example, a kiss is a type of bilabial click; the sound of admonition symbolized as <u>tsk tsk</u> is also a type of click; and the similar noise made by people driving horses is likewise a kind of click.

4.3.1.4 Aspirated Stops

In some ways it would be very nice if languages limited themselves to the basic, unmodified types of stop consonants which we have noted, namely, [p, t̪, t, k̪, k, ʔ, b, d̪, d, g, g].[4] What complicates the situation so greatly is the number of phonetic "additions" which these consonants may have. In the first place, these sounds may have little "puffs" of air added to them. In fact, in English all voiceless stop consonants which are initial in words have these puffs, which are called aspiration. (See section 3.2.2.1.) We are not aware of these aspirated consonants, for the occurrence or nonoccurrence of aspiration never makes differences in the meanings of words. But in some languages aspirated consonants contrast with unaspirated ones. Compare the aspirated and unaspirated consonants in the following words in Yipounou, a Bantu language

---

[4] In order to indicate purely phonetic values of symbols, they may be enclosed in brackets.

in the Gabon: kala "a long time ago" and kʰala "a crab," or tatila "to cry out" and tʰatila "to cry out to me."[5] In Mazatec, a language of Mexico, the contrast between aspirated and unaspirated consonants may be illustrated by kʰi^3 "it appears" and ki^3 "he went." (The raised numerals indicate tones from the highest, marked 1, to the lowest, marked 4.) There are also pre-aspirated consonants in Mazatec, cf. ʰti^4 "fish," ᵗhi^3 "round," and ti$^{3-4}$ "boy."[6] (Two raised numerals joined by a hyphen indicate a glide from one tone level to another.) These three words have differences of tone as well as differences of aspiration, but in order to be understood in Mazatec one must be exceedingly careful about such aspirations. To carry over one's habits from English would be disastrous. In some of the languages of India the voiced stops occur with aspiration, e.g., [bʱ, dʱ, gʱ]. (The symbol [ɦ] indicates a voiced h.)

Aspiration may also occur with click consonants. Compare, for example, the Zulu words tsà·tsá "to scrape a wound" and tsʰa·tsʰā "to shell beans." (The wedge indicates a click sound, and the combination [ts] means that the click sound has an s-quality. The marks over the vowels indicate tonal differences, and the raised dot denotes a long vowel.)

4.3.1.5   Affricated Stops

In addition to being aspirated, stop consonants can be affricated. This means that following the stop there is a friction sound[7] made at approximately the same point of articulation and as a kind of off-glide from the stop position. The common affricates are as follows:

[pf], as in German Pferd "horse."
[bv]
[ts], also symbolized as [c] and [ȼ], as in German Zeit "time."

---

[5] Tones are not marked on these words.

[6] Kenneth L. Pike and Eunice Victoria Pike, "Immediate Constituents of Mazatec Syllables," *International Journal of American Linguistics*, Vol. 13, No. 2, pp. 78-91.

[7] Affricated stops are combinations of stops plus fricatives (see section 4.3.1.7) made at the same general point of articulation. Students should read section 4.3.1.7 and then return to this description of affricates.

[dz], also symbolized as [ʒ].
[tθ], a combination of [t] as in tin with [θ], the initial sound of thin.
[dđ], a combination of [d] as in den with [đ], the initial sound of then.
[tš], also symbolized as [č], the initial sound of chin.
[dž], also symbolized as [ǰ], the initial sound of gin.
[tł], also symbolized as [ƛ], a combination of [t] plus a voiceless [ł]. This sounds like tl to English ears, but the l is "breathy" and without any accompanying vibration of the vocal cords.
[dl], also symbolized as [λ]. The sounds [tł] and [dl] are called lateral affricates because the off-glide is a lateral. (For a discussion of laterals see below.)
[kx], a combination of [k] plus a voiceless fricative [x]. (See section 4.3.1.7)
[gġ], a combination of [g] plus a voiced fricative [ġ]. (See section 4.3.1.7)

4.3.1.6 Glottalized Stops

In addition to aspirated and affricated consonants,[8] we also find glottalized consonants.[9] In the production of such consonants the glottis (i.e., the vocal cords) is closed during part or all of the time that the stop closure occurs. The glottis may be released simultaneously with the release of the stop or it may be released just after the stop is released. This glottalization tends to give a very throaty quality to the sound. Sometimes the larynx (i.e., the voice box, popularly called the "Adam's apple") remains relatively stationary, so that the resultant sound seems just a little emphatic, e.g., as in the Ngbaka words d'ànî "sore" and b'àná "will remain." In some instances, however, the larynx is raised, and this compresses the air between the stop closure and the closed glottis, so that when the consonant is released there is a noticeable

---

[8] There are also some other "added" characteristics, for example, palatalization, nasalization, and pharyngealization, but these are beyond the scope of this elementary discussion.

[9] Glottalization may also occur with continuants, but it is predominantly associated with stops and affricates.

pop of air coming out of the mouth, but it is much shorter and more abrupt than occurs with aspirated consonants. This contrast may be seen in the Zulu words k'á·k'á "to encircle" and kʰá·kʰá "to be acrid." It is also possible to lower the larynx, and in that case a rarifaction of air occurs in the mouth so that when the stop is released the air first pops in and then the following sound comes out. If we need to distinguish between a glottalized sound in which the air pops out in contrast with one in which it pops in, we may write the former as [kʔ] and the latter as [kꜗ].

In some instances there is a strange kind of two-way movement in the glottis. For example, the larynx may be drawn down, thus forming a partial vacuum in the mouth, but at the same time a little air may be going past the vocal cords, thus setting them in motion. The result is a glottalized, implosive (meaning that the air pops in after the release), voiced stop. Stops of this type occur in some of the Mayan languages of Mexico and Guatemala and in certain Bantu languages.

4.3.1.7   Fricatives

Fricatives are continuant sounds which occur with varying degrees of friction. This friction is produced by obstructing the oral passage in such a way that only a relatively small amount of air can pass. This air is set into a very irregular series of vibrations which are best described as just plain "noise." These fricatives may be made at many different points, and the quality of the sound differs depending upon the precise kind of channel through which the air escapes. For example, the initial sounds of sin and shin both have an s-like quality, but we sometimes describe the first as sharper and the second as flatter. By these terms we are describing in general acoustic terms what is physiologically a difference in the channel through which the air escapes. These differences may be diagramed as on the following page.

We cannot go into a complete description of all the fricative sounds, but the following are the most common:

[ɸ], an f-like sound, but with the air escaping between the two lips.

[β], a v-like sound, but with the air escaping between the two lips.

98   LEARNING A FOREIGN LANGUAGE

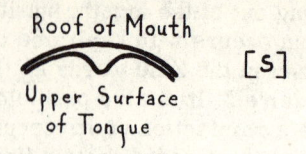

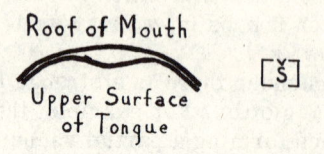

Figure 4. Channels for Production
of [s] and [š] (front view).

[f], the initial sound of English fine.
[v], the initial sound of English vine.
[W], the initial sound of English wheat. The capital letter indicates a voiceless sound. The principal difference between [W] and [ʙ] is that the first is made with rounded lips and the second with unrounded lips.
[w], the initial sound of English weep. Compare [ʙ], made with unrounded lips.
[θ], the initial sound of English thin.
[ð], the initial sound of English then.
[s], the initial sound of English sin.
[z], the initial sound of English zip.
[š], the initial sound of English shin.
[ž], the final sound of English rouge.
[Y], the initial sound of English huge. This is a regular [y], but without any vibration of the vocal cords.
[y], the initial sound of English yes.
[x], a "scraping" sound made by placing the middle or back part of the tongue against the hard palate or velum. This occurs in German and is written as ch, e.g., ich "I," acht "eight," and Buch "book." If we need to distinguish a front from a back variety, we may place a curve beneath the palatal fricative, e.g., [x̮].

[g], the same basic type of sound as [x], but with the vocal cords vibrating.

[h], the initial sound of English him. This is a glottal fricative.

[ɦ], a glottal fricative like [h], but with the vocal cords vibrating. Compare the Zulu hē·há "to entice" and ɦē·ɦá· "to split open someone's head."

Having examined these fricative sounds, it becomes much more evident what the affricates are, namely, combinations of stops plus fricatives made at approximately the same points of articulation.

4.3.1.8 Frictionless Consonants

There are three types of frictionless consonant sounds: nasals, laterals, and centrals. The nasals, e.g., m and n, are common to us. The laterals are l-like sounds, and the centrals are r-like sounds.

4.3.1.8.1 Nasal Consonants

Nasal consonants result from a closure at some point in the oral passage and an opening at the velic (the passage behind the velum leading out through the nose). The various points at which the oral passage is stopped off provide the characteristic distinctions between the various nasals. The principal differences are symbolized as follows:

[m], the first sound of English meet.

[n], the first sound of English neat.

[ñ], the second nasal sound in Spanish mañana "tomorrow." In the production of this nasal the tongue is in the alveopalatal position. It sounds to English ears like the [ny] cluster in canyon, but it is much more of a unit sound than the English sequence [ny].

[ŋ], the final sound in English sing. Compare English sin.

These same nasals also occur without voicing and may be symbolized as [M], [N], [Ñ], and [Ŋ]. The acoustic effect is like an h coming out of the nose followed by a very short voiced nasal.

4.3.1.8.2 Laterals

Laterals are made with the tongue touching the roof of the mouth (either the front or the middle part) and with the air flowing past one or both sides of the tongue. When the sound is voiced we write it with [l] and when voiceless with [ɫ]. This voiceless [ɫ] is frequently called the Welsh l and is written in Welsh as ll.

A palatal l, e.g., as occurs in the Italian word figlio "son," may be written as [ḷ].

4.3.1.8.3 Centrals

Central frictionless consonants are r-like sounds such as occur in English. These may be voiced (as they occur in English) or voiceless, in which case we may symbolize the sound as [R]. Note that these central frictionless consonants are quite different from the flap r sounds which are discussed in the following section.

4.3.1.9 Vibrants

Vibrants consist of flapped and trilled consonants.

4.3.1.9.1 Flaps

In the production of most flapped consonants the tip of the tongue flips up against or in passing quickly by some point in the front of the mouth, touches it. If the tongue is grooved, the sound resembles r. If the tongue is arched, the resultant sound resembles l. In many Bantu languages of Africa there is just one flap consonant, and sometimes it sounds like l and at other times like r. In such cases it would make no difference how it is written, for the different acoustic effect (i.e., the audibly perceptible differences) never distinguishes words.

We may symbolize flaps by placing a wedge over the symbol, e.g., [ř] and [ľ]. Sometimes the tongue is perfectly flat in the production of a flap consonant, and the acoustic effect is like a [d]. Some missionaries have been very concerned because the speakers of a language seem to mix up r, l, and d indiscriminately, while in actuality the difficulty was not with the natives at all, but with the hearing of the missionary. Rather than noting the significant feature of the sound,

MASTERING THE SOUNDS

namely, the flap, the missionaries were interpreting the various unessential characteristics in terms of the nearest English equivalents.

A labial flap occurs in Ngbaka. In the production of this sound the lower lip is first drawn in behind the upper teeth and upper lip. It is then drawn out rapidly past the upper lip against which it flaps. The sound occurs in the word kàkábà "crow."

4.3.1.9.2 Trills

Trills may be regarded as multiple flaps, that is, one flap after another in rapid succession. There are three principal types: bilabial [p̃] and [b̃], (cf. m̃bunga "odor" in Yipounou, a Bantu language of the Gabon), alveolar [R̃] and [r̃] (cf. Spanish pero [péro] "but" and perro [pér̃o] "dog"), and uvular [R̃] and [r̃]. The uvular trill may be practiced by imitating gargling and then cupping the tongue to give the r quality. The uvular trill occurs in many languages, including French, German, and Dutch.

4.3.1.10 A Chart of Consonants

As a summary to our analysis of some of the more common consonants, we may examine a chart of their phonetic types:

Type of Consonant[10]	Bilabial	Labio-Dental	Inter-Dental	Alveolar	Alveo-Palatal	Palatal	Velar	Uvular	Glottal
Stops									
Simple vl.	p			t		ḵ	k		
vd.	b			d		g̱	g		
Aspirated vl.	pʰ			tʰ			kʰ		
vd.	bʰ			dʰ			gʰ		
Affricated									
Centrally									
Released vl.	pf[11]		tθ	ts(c)	tš(č)		kx		h
vd.	bv[11]		dđ	dz(z̧)	dž(ǰ)		gġ		ɦ

[10]This chart does not include clicks, double consonants, and glottalized consonants. Glottalization may occur with all types of simple stops, affricates, and continuants, though it occurs less frequently with the last. The abbreviation vl. stands for "voiceless" and vd. for "voiced."

[11]These affricates are actually combinations of bilabial stops plus labiodental fricatives. The strictly bilabial affricates would be [pɸ] and [bβ].

LEARNING A FOREIGN LANGUAGE

Type of Consonant

	Bilabial	Labio-Dental	Inter-Dental	Alveolar	Alveo-Palatal	Palatal	Velar	Uvular	Glottal
Laterally									
Released vl.				tł(ƛ)					
vd.				dl(λ)					
Fricatives									
Central Flat vl.	p	f	θ		Y	ẋ	x		
vd.	ƀ	v	d		y	ġ	g		
Grooved vl.				s	š				
vd.				z	ž				
Rounded vl.	W								
vd.	w								
Frictionless									
Nasal vl.	M			N	Ñ		Ŋ		
vd.	m			n	ñ		ŋ		
Lateral vl.				Ł			Ł		
vd.				l			ḷ		
Central vl.				R					
vd.				r					
Vibrants									
Flapped vl.				Ř					
vd.				ř,ĭ					
Trilled vl.	p̃			R̃				R̄	
vd.	b̃			r̃				r̄	

   This chart does not attempt to be exhaustive. For a more exhaustive and slightly different type of classification see Kenneth L. Pike, <u>Phonemics</u> (Ann Arbor, Michigan: University of Michigan Press, 1947).

   The International Phonetic System is considerably more complicated in the types of symbols employed. These symbols have been chosen because they are more simply written and more easily reproduced on the typewriter.

4.3.2 <u>Vowels</u>

   Consonants are complicated enough, but vowels are even more so. We can usually detect rather easily what is happening in the production of consonants, for the movements of the organs are more evident and more easily described. In the production of vowels there are so many fine shades of distinction and so much depends upon relative position and shape rather than upon definite stopping, subsequent puffs of air, popping noises, and distinctly audible frictions.

   The description of vowels is most generally made on the basis of three types of factors: (1) the front, central, or back position of the tongue, (2) the high, mid, and low position of the tongue, and (3) the rounded or unrounded position of the lips. For example, in the production of the vowel sound of English beat, the tongue is described as front (i.e., the narrowest stricture through which the air passes is made by the front of the tongue near the alveolar arch), and high (i.e., the tip of the tongue is relatively close to the alveolar arch), and unrounded (i.e., the lips are relatively flat). The following is a diagram of the production of such a vowel:

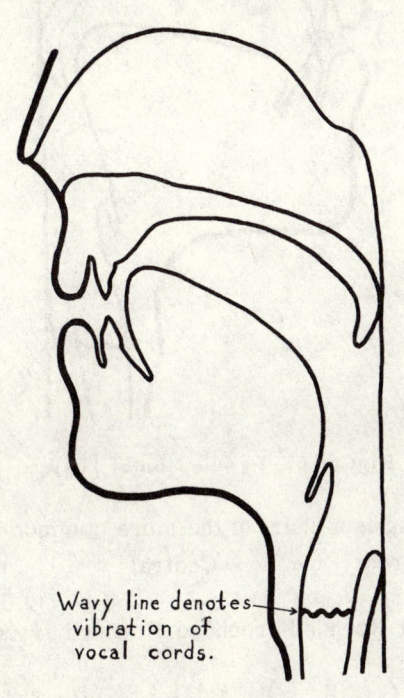

Wavy line denotes vibration of vocal cords.

Figure 5. Production of [i].

In the vowel sound of English boot we say that the tongue is back, and high, and that the lips are rounded. The production of this vowel would be diagramed as on the following page.

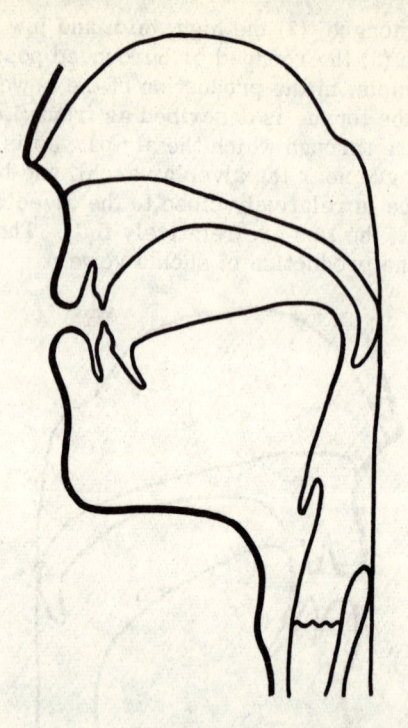

Figure 6. Production of [u].

The following is a chart of the more common vowels:

		Front		Central		Back	
		Un-rounded	Rounded	Un-rounded	Rounded	Un-rounded	Rounded
High	Close	i	ü	ɨ		ï	u
	Open	ɪ					ᴜ
Mid	Close	e	ö	ə			o
	Open	ɛ		ʌ			
Low	Close	æ	ɔ̈				ɔ
	Open	a		ɑ			ɒ

MASTERING THE SOUNDS 105

The basis for this type of chart may be seen in the following diagram:

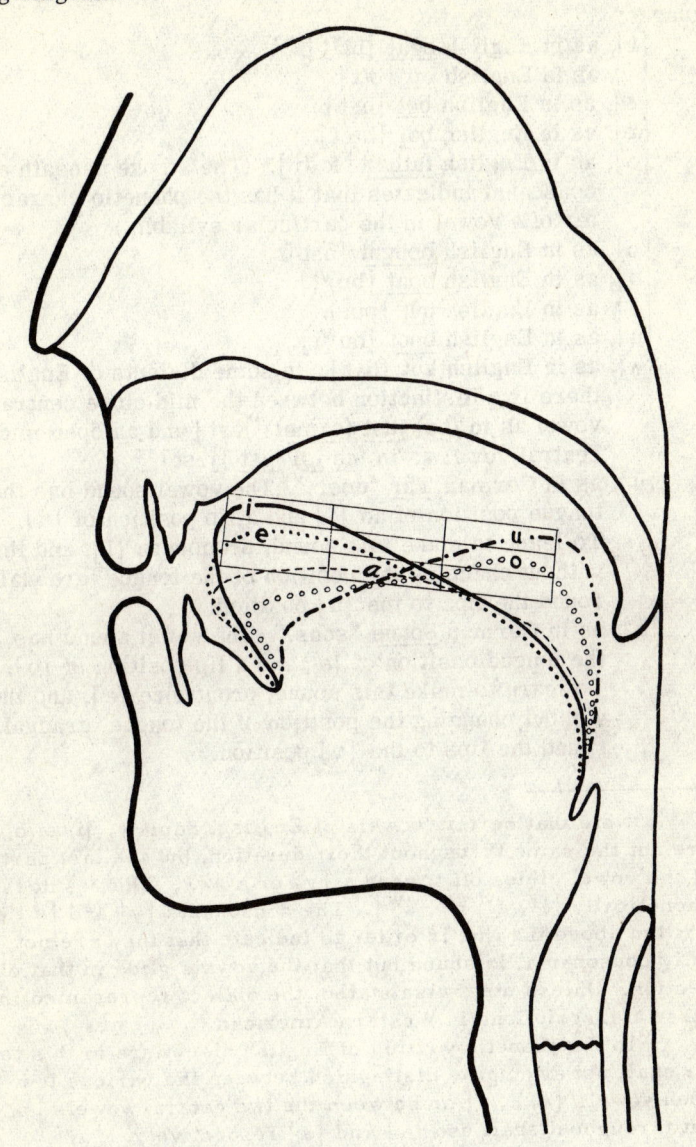

Figure 7. Basis of the Vowel Chart.

We may illustrate the values of the more common symbols by some sounds from English or other relatively familiar languages:

[i], as in English beat [bi^{y}t].[12]
[ɩ], as in English bit [bɩt].
[ɛ], as in English bet [bɛt].
[æ], as in English bat [bæt].
[ɑ], as in English father [fɑdr̩]. (The stroke beneath a consonant indicates that it has the phonetic character of a vowel in the particular syllable.)
[ɔ], as in English bought [bɔt].
[o], as in English boat [bo^{w}t].
[ʊ], as in English put [pʊt].
[u], as in English boot [bu^{w}t].
[ʌ], as in English but [bʌt]. In some dialects of English there is a distinction between the mid close central vowel as in (he) just (came) [jəst] and an open mid central vowel as in (he is) just [jʌst].[13]
[ü], as in German Tür "door." The vowel sound has the tongue position of an [i] and a lip position of [u]. To learn to make this sound, pronounce [i], and then, without changing the position of the tongue, gradually round the lips to the [u] position.
[ö], as in German Söhne "sons." The vowel sound has the tongue position of [e] and a lip position of [o]. To learn to make this sound, pronounce [e], and then, without changing the position of the tongue, gradually round the lips to the [o] position.

---

[12] Note that certain vowels of English, namely, [i, e, o, u], are not the same throughout their duration, but the last part of the vowel glides off toward a [y] or a [w]. The result is phonetically [i^y, e^y, o^w, u^w]. The consonants [y] and [w] are written above the line in order to indicate that they are not fully consonantal in sound but that the vowels glide in that direction. Unless otherwise stated, the dialect represented in these transcriptions is Western American.

[13] In the phonetic writing of English elsewhere in this text we shall not attempt to distinguish between the various low open vowels [a, ɑ, ɒ] or between the two central vowels [ə, ʌ,] but throughout shall use [a] and [ə] respectively.

With these readily identifiable points in the vowel chart one can distinguish various other types of vowel sounds. Of course, there are many more symbols which could be introduced, but these are the sounds which most commonly occur. If one is having difficulty assigning the phonetic value to a particular sound, and if the quality does not seem to be the same as indicated here, it is always possible to use certain extra symbols to assist in determining fine shades of phonetic distinction. For example, if the vowel appears to be more or less like [ö], but a little higher and slightly more central, one may indicate this fact by two extra wedges pointing in the direction of this positional difference, e.g., [ö$\check{>}$]. Such symbols are, of course, never to be used in a practical orthography of a language. They would only be of use to a missionary attempting to indicate minute phonetic distinctions.

4.3.2.1   Nasalized Vowels

One of the most common modifications of vowels is nasalization. We are accustomed to hearing that French has such nasal vowels, but there are many other languages which make distinctions between words on the basis of nasal and nonnasal vowels. For example, in Navaho ší "I" and šį́ "summer" are distinguished only by the nasal quality of the vowel. (Nasalization may be indicated by a wavy line over the vowel (as in Portuguese) or by a hook beneath the vowel (as in Navaho and in most scientific analyses). In Mazatec there are four unnasalized vowels and four nasalized vowels. Compare the following words: kh_i^3 "it appears," kh_i^2 "far," $c\text{?}e^4$ "his," $c\text{?}\underset{\sim}{e}^4$ "bad," $\check{s}a^{1-3}$ "work," $\check{s}\underset{\sim}{a}^{1-3}$ "liquor," $\check{c}h_o^3$ "you (pl.) write," and $\check{c}h\underset{\sim}{o}^{4-2}$ "woman."[14]

Nasalized vowels differ from unnasalized ones in the fact that during the production of nasalized vowels the velic is open. This means that part of the air coming from the lungs goes through the nose. Whether a vowel is nasal or not may usually be detected by pinching the nose shut and then listening to the vowel. A nasal vowel has a distinct nasal "twang" to it.

---

[14]Kenneth L. Pike and Eunice Victoria Pike, op. cit.

108   LEARNING A FOREIGN LANGUAGE

4.3.2.2   Glottalized Vowels

Sometimes vowels are pronounced with simultaneous stricture in the glottis. Frequently, the vowel is interrupted for a moment by a complete but light glottal stop. This may be symbolized as VʔV, in which V stands for any vowel. In other instances the second syllabic element is very weak, sounding as though it were an "echo" vowel. We may sumbolize this as Vʔᵛ. In still other cases the glottal quality continues almost evenly throughout the length of the vowel. This type of glottalized vowel occurs in Totonac, e.g., paša "he bathes" and pášá "you (sg.) bathe." In Maya, words with glottalized long vowels are written as VʔV, e.g., haʔas "banana," noʔoč "chin," and kuʔuk "squirrel," but in some dialects of Maya that which we write as a glottal stop is not a complete stop, but rather a glottal quality of the vowel. Such glottalized vowels occur in many languages and are very difficult to detect accurately since they may sound quite different in various combinations.

4.3.2.3   Long Vowels

When traditional dictionaries and grammars speak of long vowels in English, they usually have reference to different qualities. For example, they say that a long a sounds like [eʸ] as in fate, and a short a is like [ə] as in sofa. When, however, we speak of long vowels in phonetic terminology, we have reference only to their duration. A short vowel we say consists of one unit of length, called a "mora." A long vowel consists of two moras, and an extra-long vowel may have three moras. Employing different lengths of vowels to distinguish different meanings is very common in languages. For example, in Kissi, a Sudanic language of French Guinea, the difference between "to weave" and "to hit" in certain tense forms is just a matter of length, e.g., à lɔ̀ ndū sísà "you (sg.) weave it now" and à lɔ̀· ndū sísà "you (sg.) hit it now."

In Navaho length of vowels also distinguishes meaning. Compare bìtàʔ "between them" with bìtà·ʔ "his father," and bìtìn "his ice" with bìtì·n "his tracks," and ʔàcʔòs "feather, downy" with ʔàcʔò·s "vein, artery."

In Zulu the ideophones (little particles that symbolize different kinds of actions and states of being) exhibit four

MASTERING THE SOUNDS

different lengths. Compare bò "of a strike in the small of the back," bê· "of the roaring of a grass-fire," jâ: "of lying down," and wî:· "of a big noise." (The marks over the vowels indicate different tones, and the dots after the vowels indicate the number of additional moras, not denoted by the writing of the vowel itself.) Even in the plural of some Zulu nouns there are vowels of three moras, e.g., î·mp'í "army" and î:mp'í "armies," î·njá "dog" and î:njá "dogs," î·mbvú "sheep" and î:mbvú "sheep (pl.)."

Pairs of words that differ in meaning just on the basis of long or short vowels may be difficult to distinguish at times, but they are far less troublesome than the complex sequences of long and short vowel syllables. Note the following sentence from Zinza, a Bantu language of Tanganyika: ba·hoya izo·ba rya·ba rya·gwa ba·ragira "they chatted until the sun went down and then ate supper." (Tonal distinctions are purposely not written on these Zinza forms.) A syllable with a long vowel takes approximately twice as long to pronounce as a syllable with a short vowel. One should practice reading such a sentence, first slowly, and then more rapidly, preserving the proper length of syllables. The chances are that the average beginner will have difficulty. To help correct one's difficulties, one may construct the following exercise, based upon the same syllabic sequence:

ba·baba aba·ba ba·ba ba·ba ba·bababa

One should tap the time out either with the finger or with the aid of a metronome so that one can get into the swing of the sequences. If a person has trouble with matters of syllabic timing, he should construct a number of phonetic exercises, first using just one consonant and vowel, and then gradually using more and more complicated syllabic patterns. One should mark the length in these exercises of nonsense syllables and then attempt to read them correctly. Later, one may have a friend mark and read some. The student can then try to write down just what has been said. The following are illustrative:

tata· ta·tata tata·ta tatata· ta·ta·tata ta·ta·ta·
di·di di·di·di· dididi· di· didi didi· di·didi·di·
zozo· zo·zo· zozo zozo zo· zo·zo zozo·zo zo·zo· zo
pula· bitu· pu·wa·ri somu·la gu·hipo sisi·sa· tua·

English-speaking persons must be cautioned against substituting stress (i.e., emphatic pronunciation) for length. Long vowels do sound louder to us as English-speaking people, so that we must be sure whether in another language it is actually a long vowel or a stressed vowel which is prominent in the word or phrase. To confuse these two will result in a very bad pronunciation of a foreign language.

4.3.2.4 Voiceless Vowels

We are so accustomed to thinking that vowels are the conspicuously loud part of any syllable that we overlook the fact that vowels can be voiceless. For example, the only differences between some words in Comanche are the voiceless vowels. Compare 'tï·pE "mouth" and 'tï·pI "stone." (The voiceless vowels are written as caps, and the upright raised bar marks the onset of stress.) Such voiceless vowels are usually final in the word, but not always, e.g., 'surïkï̈se? "he."

4.3.2.5 Breathy Vowels[15]

Breathy vowels must be distinguished from voiceless vowels. Breathy vowels are voiced, but at the same time there is an accompanying breathy quality. The result is similar to a so-called "stage whisper." In the Abwong dialect of Dinka, a language of the Anglo-Egyptian Sudan, there are breathy counterparts to all the fourteen qualitatively distinct vowels, and sometimes this breathy quality is very difficult to hear without considerable practice and careful attention to distinctions. The words rṉn "meat" and rᴜn "run," and wṵt "ostrich" and wᴜt "village" differ in the occurrence or non-occurrence of breathy vowels.[16] (The subscript dots indicate breathy quality.)

---

[15] There are two other types of vowels which could be distinguished, namely, (1) pharyngealized vowels, resulting from the tensing and narrowing of the pharynx and faucal pillars, and (2) tense and lax vowels, resulting from the general tenseness or laxness of the vocal organs during the production of a sound.

[16] There are also differences in tonal classes, but these need not concern us here.

4.3.3 Prosodic Features

Up to this point we have discussed the various segments which comprise speech, i.e., the sequences of consonants and vowels. There are three prosodic (literally "singing") features which occur together with these consonants and vowels. These are length, tone, and stress. Length may affect both consonants and vowels of a syllable, but since length is generally associated with vowels, this problem has already been discussed above. In the following sections we shall consider only pitch (including tone and intonation) and stress.

4.3.3.1 Tone

Tonal languages are those which make distinctions in the meaning of words by employing pitch contrasts.[17] All languages, however, make some use of pitch contrasts since no language is spoken on a complete monotone. In English, for example, we may make distinctions between declarative and interrogative sentences by differences in the pitch of the final syllable or syllables of the sentence, e.g., John went home. (with falling intonation) vs. John went home? (with rising intonation). These differences in pitch do not make English a tone language, for the tones belong to the entire phrase or sentence, while in tone languages each syllable tends to have its own characteristic tone. For example, in Ngbaka, a Sudanic language of northern Congo, there are three words: lí "face" (with high tone), lī "name" (with mid tone) and lì "water" (with low tone). The only differences between these words are the different tones.

To an extent tonal languages are like music, but there are some very important distinctions. For example, the high, mid, and low tones in the Ngbaka words lí, lī, lì are not always on the same musical pitch. Women's voices are, of course, higher than men's voices, and the voices of individuals, both men and women, differ greatly in their range. What counts in tone languages is not the absolute pitch but the relative pitch. A word with a high tone is relatively higher than surrounding words with mid or low tones. Similarly, a word with a low

---

[17] Any student who expects to encounter a tone language should by all means consult Kenneth L. Pike, Tone Languages (Ann Arbor, Michigan: University of Michigan Press, 1948). This is a comprehensive and fully authoritative work.

tone is relatively lower than surrounding words with mid or high tones. Even in tone languages the whole pitch of the sentence (the intonation) may go up or down, and the relative tones on the syllables follow these rises and falls. Furthermore, we cannot predict just how far apart these tone levels will be in any language or in any particular situation. When, for example, a Ngbaka speaker is talking in normal conversational style, the differences between high and mid and between mid and low may not be much more than a single note on the musical scale. However, in the animated speech of argument or discussion the tonal differences may be three or four notes.

There are two principal types of tone languages:[18] contour tone languages and register tone languages. The contour languages are characterized by having pitch differences that for the most part consist of glides, e.g., long, short, gradual, abrupt, rising, falling, rising and falling, falling and rising. Furthermore, the end points of these glides (i.e., the beginnings and the ends) cannot be described as starting and ending at certain relatively fixed points. Register tone languages, however, have tones on certain levels, either two, three, or four,[19] and they may have all different types of glides between these levels. We may liken contour tone languages to a roller coaster, where the glides are long, short, abrupt, falling, rising, etc., but where the top and the bottom points of the glides are not describable as related to certain fixed levels. The register tone languages are like stairsteps, with two, three, or four basic steps, and with glides (usually on long vowels) extending from one step to another.

4.3.3.1.1   <u>Contour</u> <u>Tone</u> <u>Languages</u>

Contour tone languages occur in Asia. These include such languages as Chinese, Burmese, Siamese, and Annamese.

---

[18] There are some intermediate types, but these are not considered here.

[19] Languages with more than four distinctive tone levels have not been found. Some African languages have been described with five levels (e.g., Ibo), but these five levels take into consideration the sentence intonation. Doke has described Zulu with nine tones, but these nine tones reflect certain nondistinctive variations. Both Ibo and Zulu appear to have only three basic registers.

MASTERING THE SOUNDS

Black Thai,[20] spoken in Indo-China, is a typical contour tone language. The following tones are arranged in a line to show their relative positions and the extent and direction of the glides:

```
                 ╲or╱
   ╲    ╱    ╱   . . . . . . . . . . . normal pitch level
   1.   2.   3.  4.   ╲    ╲?
                      5.   6.
```

Every syllable in Black Thai occurs with one or another of these tones. Sometimes the same combination of consonant and vowel occurs with all six, e.g., ma[1] "dog," ma[2] "to soak," ma[3] "profit," ma[4] "to come," ma[5] the name of a particular river, ma[6] "horse." Tone 6 ends in a glottal stop, and in some dialects tone 4 may occur with glottalization of the vowel and with a slight rise before the fall.

In Burmese there are only four basic tones: (1) low, level, and long; (2) high, long, and falling toward the end; (3) high, short, and falling, with a slow glottal closure; and (4) high, extremely short, with a sharp glottal closure.[21]

Mandarin Chinese also has four basic tones, with a fifth neutral tone, but the contours of Mandarin Chinese are different from Burmese. Certain other dialects of Chinese, e.g., Cantonese, have several more tones.

In learning a language with contour tones, one must be sure to note the tone on every syllable. Furthermore, some of the tones may change when words come together in various combinations. For example, the Mandarin Chinese word bu "not" occurs with the fourth tone when it precedes words with first, second, or third tone, but when it precedes a word which has a fourth tone, then the word bu has a second tone.[22] Tone languages constantly exhibit these arbitrary kinds of changes.

---

[20] These data are supplied by M. Jean Funé, a missionary translator in Black Thai.

[21] William Cornyn, Outline of Burmese Grammar (Baltimore: Linguistic Society of America, 1944), p. 9. Cornyn also distinguishes a neutral tone, which may constitute a kind of fifth tone.

[22] C. F. Hockett and Cheoying Fang, Spoken Chinese (New York: Henry Holt and Co., 1945), p. 8.

4.3.3.1.2 Register Tone Languages

All the tonal languages of Africa (with the possible exception of Bushman and Hottentot) and the Western Hemisphere appear to be register tone languages. Such languages are much more numerous than some people have thought, for fully ninety percent of all the languages of Africa south of the Sahara are tonal languages. There are dozens of tonal languages in the Western Hemisphere, including for example, Apache, Navaho, Chipewyan, Yellow-Knife, Mixteco, Mazatec, Cuicatec, Zapotec, Chatino, and Chinantec.

A typical register-tone language is Mbanza, a Sudanic language of northern Congo. It possesses three registers, and the following words illustrate these differences: dùdù "mortar," dūdū "spear," and dúdú "hole (for animals to fall into)." When a person hears these words for the first time, he will not find that the two syllables of dùdù "mortar" are pronounced on exactly the same pitch when the word is spoken in isolation or final to the phrase. It so happens in Mbanza (as well as in most register tone languages) that in isolation (a type of phrase-final position) the tones fall off, thus marking the end of an utterance. Actually the second syllable of dùdù "mortar" is noticeably lower than the first, but this is true of all phrase-final syllables. Similarly, in dūdū "spear" the second syllable is lower than the first, but it is not as low as a low tone would be in that position. Also, the second syllable of dúdú "hole" is lower than the first, but it is not as low as a mid-tone syllable would be. This falling off of the second syllable occurs with all final tones of all words, and hence it is not distinctive in making differences in meaning.

Ngbaka, a Sudanic language of northern Congo, is also a register tone language.[23] All the verbs have four principal forms. Verbs with low tones may indicate present time, e.g., sà "is calling," gbɔ̀tɔ̀ "is pulling," with mid tones past time, e.g., sā "called," gbɔ̄tɔ̄ "pulled," with high tones imperative, e.g., sá "call!" gbɔ́tɔ́ "pull!" and with a low tone followed by a high tone future time, e.g., sǎ· "will call" and gbɔ̀tɔ́ "will pull." Notice that verbs consisting of a single syllable have a rising glide on a long vowel, but verbs of two syllables have a low tone on the first syllable and a high tone on the second.

---

[23] Note the illustrative data cited above in section 4.3.3.1.

MASTERING THE SOUNDS

Most Bantu languages have two-register systems.[24] The following examples from Chiluba (also called Luba-Lulua) are typical contrasts between words: dî·ná "name" and dí·nà "hole"; dyû·lú "nose" and dyú·lú "heaven"; mpàtá "a five franc note," mpátá "doubt," and mpàtá "plains"; mâ·ñì "a lot of something," má·ñì "palm oil," and mâ·ñí "leaves." There are not only these types of minimally different pairs,[25] but a difference in tone goes all the way through the verb system and in most cases is the only means of distinguishing the second person singular from the third person singular, e.g.,

1. údí úsùmá   "you (sg.) are biting"[26]
2. ùdí ùsùmá   "he is biting"
3. wâ·kúsùmá   "you (sg.) bit (past indefinite)"
4. wà·kúsùmá   "he bit (past indefinite)"
5. účìdí úsùmá "you (sg.) are now biting"
6. učìdí ùsùmá "he is now biting"
7. wá·sùmá   "you (sg.) kept biting"
8. wà·sùmá   "he kept biting"

Register-tone languages may have two, three, or four registers.[27] Two-register tone languages include Navaho, most central Bantu languages, and such Sudanic languages as

---

[24] Some in South Africa, e.g., Zulu, have three-register systems.

[25] Words that differ only in one feature.

[26] The tone marks which we write here do not distinguish the absolute phonetic pitches, but the distinctive differences of tone. A final high tone following a low tone does not have as high a pitch as a preceding high tone. Phonetically we could diagram form (1) as ⁻ ⁻ ⁻ — . Note that the three highs in a row tend to fall off in the phrase. If, however, instead of a final high we had a final low, the phonetic relationships between the forms would be approximately as follows: ⁻ ⁻ _
A final low would be much lower than a final high. The tone marks which we write only indicate the distinctive differences, not the ones that are conditioned by where they occur in the phrase. See the discussion below on phonemics, section 4.6.2.

[27] The following lists are by no means complete, and some of the languages included in the general language classifications have not been fully investigated. Accordingly, there may prove to be some inaccuracies.

Maninka-Bambara (French West Africa), Loma (Liberia), and Zande (French Equatorial Africa and the Belgian Congo). Three-register languages include certain Mexican Indian languages, e.g., Mixteco, Cuicatec, and Chinantec; most Sudanic languages; the Nilotic languages; certain Nilo-Hamitic languages, e.g., Masai and Kipsigis, spoken in Kenya; and some Bantu languages of South Africa, e.g., Zulu. Four-register tone languages include Mazatec, spoken in southern Mexico, and Gweabo (Jabo), spoken in Liberia.[28]

Two-register languages have four important tone possibilities: high, low, low to high, and high to low. In extra-long vowels, one may find low-high-low and high-low-high. But in general, we are confronted with only four types of tonal distinctions on individual syllables. In three-register systems there are nine possibilities. These may be diagramed as follows:

$$\begin{array}{c} C\acute{V} \\ C\bar{V} \\ C\grave{V} \end{array}$$

In four-register systems there are sixteen possibilities:

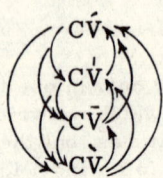

$$\begin{array}{c} C\acute{V} \\ C\acute{V} \\ C\bar{V} \\ C\grave{V} \end{array}$$

Fortunately, not all such level tones and glides occur on any one syllable, but in Mazatec there are five different words, distinguished only by tonal differences: te^1 "he will dance," te^2 "he dances," $\underline{te}^{2\text{-}3}$ "I dance," $\underline{te}^{4\text{-}3}$ "wide," and $\underline{te}^3$ "ten." Of the sixteen theoretical possibilities in Mazatec for level tones and one-direction glides, only twelve actually occur. The nonoccurring glides are 1-2, 2-1, 3-1, and 4-1. Of course, there is no special reason why these glides are missing. It just happens that way. However, Mazatec makes up for this

---

[28]See E. Sapir, "Notes on the Gweabo (Jabo) Language of Liberia," Language, Vol. 7, No. 1 (1931), pp. 30-41.

slight simplification by having two two-directional glides on single syllables. These are 4-2-4, e.g., vha³ntiai⁴⁻²⁻⁴ "we (exclusive) travel," and 4-2-3, e.g., va⁴⁻³ntia⁴⁻²⁻³ "I travel."[29]

Missionaries must give the greatest of care to mastering tonal languages, for mistakes can be made so easily. For example, in one language the only difference between "chief" or "boss" and "devil" is the matter of a glide. Naī with a level tone means "boss" and naī with a rising glide means "devil." The missionaries told the natives about the director of the mission, using what they thought was the term for "boss," but they discovered that they had been talking about the director as "their devil." Of course, such statements from the missionaries' own lips only added confirmation to what the local priests had already said, namely, that the missionaries were out there under the auspices of Satan himself.

Sometimes missionaries do not get tangled up in such obvious errors, but they so fail to get the proper tones that the people miss practically everything that is said. One group of missionaries working in a three-register tone language had so bungled the task of reducing a language to writing and of learning to speak it intelligibly that many of the boys attending their school for three years could not readily read a simple sentence of new material. These missionaries had never learned how to distinguish between "he" and "you (pl.)," forms that differed only in the matter of tone.

There are some Bantu languages of Africa which have lost their distinctive tonal contrasts. One of these is Swahili, which undoubtedly used to make differences between words on the basis of tone, but now there is no tonal distinction. The only prosodic feature is a stress on the next to the last syllable of each word. Because of this observed fact in Swahili many missionaries have assumed that their languages also had this same type of stress, for there is a tendency in many Bantu languages to lengthen the next to the last syllable of each phrase. One must not, however, be deceived by this feature of length, and assume that it is automatically the kind of stress which we have in English.

---

[29] See Kenneth L. Pike and Eunice Victoria Pike, op. cit., p. 89.

In Zanaki, a Bantu language spoken on the east shores of Lake Victoria in Tanganyika, there is an amazing development of tone. The tonal patterns have been preserved somewhat, but they no longer distinguish the meanings of words. All words of the same length have identically the same tonal patterns. The following forms illustrate the patterns:

2-syllable words: CV́CV́[30]
3-syllable words: CV̀CV́CV́
4-syllable words: CV̀CV̀CV́CV́
5-syllable words: CV̀CV́CV̀CV́CV́
6-syllable words: CV̀CV́CV́CV̀CV́CV́
7-syllable words: CV̀CV́CV́CV̀CV̀CV́CV́
8-syllable words: CV̀CV́CV́CV̀CV́CV̀CV́CV́
9-syllable words: CV̀CV́CV́CV̀CV́CV́CV̀CV́CV́

Notice that a 6-syllable word is like two 3-syllable words, that a 7-syllable word is like a 3-syllable and a 4-syllable word, that an 8-syllable word is like a 3-syllable and a 5-syllable word, and that a 9-syllable word is like three 3-syllable words.

In learning a tone language one must be sure to learn the tones of words just as one would any consonant or vowel. It is quite impossible, however, to assume that the tones will always remain the same, for in the same way as consonants and vowels change when forms come together, so tones also change. This may appear very confusing, but we will consider such problems in the next chapter. (See section 5.6.)

4.3.3.2 <u>Intonation</u>

No language is spoken on a monotone. That means that there are always some "modulations" of the voice, and in all languages such modifications of the pitch of the phrase or sentence become more or less conventionalized, that is to say, they become standardized and acquire certain meanings. But we must never assume that the intonation of one language is like that of another. That was, however, precisely the mistake

---

[30] C stands for any consonant or consonant cluster and V for any vowel. A combination CV therefore stands in this case for a syllable. The final high tone always becomes low when the word ends a phrase.

which one missionary was making during her teaching of public speaking to some Bantu young women in Congo. She was insisting that all declarative sentences should fall at the end and that all questions should rise. The trouble was that the native language simply did not work that way. It was a tonal language, and whether the individual tones were high or low at the end depended upon the particular words. Almost all sentences, whether declarative or interrogative, tended to start high and gradually drift down. Of course, the missionary never succeeded in teaching her students to "intone" their sentences like English though she tried desperately hard to do so. When she finally realized that it was quite unnecessary—in fact, entirely wrong—to attempt to do such a thing, she was relieved; but the tragedy of her prolonged, frustrated attempts should have been avoided and could have been if she had had just a little introduction to some of the basic principles of language study.

Few of us are aware of how complicated the intonational patterns of English actually are, and one of the best ways of conditioning ourselves for the study of other intonational systems is to become somewhat familiar with the features of our own. For example, in English there are four basic intonational registers,[31] with many subtle differences depending upon the types of final glides. Compare some of the following more common patterns:

1. $^{3-}$I'm going to ^{0}2-4 go.   (the normal, declarative pattern)[32]
2. $^{3-}$I'm going to ^{0}1-4 go.   (emphatic declaration concerning the action)

---

[31] See Kenneth L. Pike, The Intonation of American English (Ann Arbor: University of Michigan Press, 1945).
[32] The superscript numerals mark the four intonation levels, with 1 marking the highest and 4 the lowest. The hyphens show the relationship of register-points to the contours. The degree sign [°] marks the onset of the sentence or phrase stress.

3. I'm going to go. (emphatic declaration concerning the subject)[33]
    ⁰1-   ⁰-4

4. I'm going to go. (pompous, oratorical style)
    ⁰2- ⁰2-   ⁰-2

5. I'm going to go? (normal, mild question)
    3-   ⁰3-1

6. I'm going to go? (question implying "Is that what you mean?")
    2-   ⁰2-1

7. I'm going to go. (petulant declaration)
    1-   ⁰1-4

8. I'm going to go... (implying that something else is to follow)
    3-   ⁰3-2

9. Am I going? (normal question)
    3- ⁰3-1

10. Am I going? (insistent question)
     2- ⁰2-4

11. Am I going? (sarcastic question)
     3- ⁰4-3

Tonal languages do not exhibit so many types of intonational contrasts as nontonal languages, but even tonal languages can be intonationally very complicated. For example, in many of the Sudanic languages which have three registers there is quite an abrupt falling off of phrases in normal discourse. For example, in Ngbaka the final mid tone in à tɛ̃ wà fɔ̃ē "he is weeding the garden" is actually lower phonetically than the initial low tone, for the entire sentence descends in pitch. e.g.,

Mastering the intonation of a language takes infinite patience and determination to mimic constantly and consciously. Until we have spoken a phrase with its proper intonation, we have not spoken it correctly. The intonation of a language is often one of the last features to be mastered; but in many ways it is the most important, for it is the one great distinguishing mark of language proficiency. If need be, it is better to

---

[33] The glide from 1- to -4 is spread over the entire sentence. It could also occur on a single word, e.g., Yes!. Sentence 3 differs from 2 primarily in the placement of the sentence stress.

sacrifice a few correct grammatical forms in order to acquire a naturalness of utterance. Proper intonation is not just a linguistic elegance. It is a basic part of making oneself understood. How often we have had the experience of hearing some foreigner speak English with perfectly intelligible consonants and vowels and with standard grammatical forms; and yet we have had the greatest of difficulty in understanding because the intonational patterns were entirely unnatural and strange to us. The very same thing is true of our learning to speak a foreign language. Proper intonation contributes a high percentage to the total intelligibility of speech.

4.3.3.3 Stress

We as English-speaking people rarely have difficulty with languages which exhibit distinctive stresses, for such stresses occur in English. For example, compare the following nouns and verbs:

Nouns	Verbs
rébel	rebél
ímpact	impáct
íncrease	incréase
ínsult	insúlt
ínsert	insért
cóntest	contést
prótest	protést
cónvert	convért
próject	projéct

Of course, the difference in the stressed syllable is not the only distinguishing feature of these words. For example, there is a different vowel in the first syllable of the pair cóntest (n.) [kántɛst] vs. contést (v.) [kəntɛ́st]. However, the most obvious difference in these words is one of stress. Though we do not mark the stress when we write English, yet we must learn the syllable which carries the "accent," or the word is sometimes completely unintelligible. This arbitrariness about the placement of the stress in English proves very difficult to foreign speakers.

In Spanish the stress usually occurs on the next to the last syllable, called the penultimate syllable. When the stress is on some other syllable, it is usually marked. Compare carta "letter," and hablo "I speak," with papá "papa," interés "interest," ejército "army," and telégrafo "telegraph." This system of noting the stress in Spanish makes that feature of the language much easier to learn. The marking of stress also helps to distinguish words. For example, hablo (stressed on the first syllable) means "I speak" and habló (stressed on the second syllable) means "he spoke." Similarly, papá means "papa" and papa (stressed on the first syllable) means "potato" or "Pope."

In some languages definite stresses exist, but they never distinguish between words. Rather, the stresses serve to mark off words. For example, in Kekchi, a Mayan language of Guatemala, the stress falls on the last syllable of every word; and in Miskito, a language of Nicaragua and Honduras, it falls on the first. These features help in determining the length of the word units.

In the Isthmus dialect of Zapotec, a language of southern Mexico, there are high and low tones, with rising and falling glides. But in addition to these distinctive tones there are stresses, though the stresses never distinguish between words. Their position is determined by the phonetic nature of the word. For example, if there is a sequence in the word composed of V ʔ V (vowels with a glottal stop between), the first of these vowels has the stress. If there is no such V ʔ V combination, any long nonnasal vowel gets the stress; but if there are two such vowels, the first is stressed. If neither of these features (i.e., V ʔ V or V·) occurs in the word, the first syllable is stressed. There are certain other minor exceptions involving glottal stops. But with all these complex conditions which determine where the stress occurs, it is no wonder that learning to pronounce accurately a word having distinctive tones plus these nondistinctive stresses is no small task.

At times it is very difficult to know whether a particular prosodic feature is really tone or stress. In Pame-Chichimec, a language of Mexico, both tone and stress seem to be present as a kind of combined element, and this tone-stress distinctiveness must be marked on every syllable which has the higher tone and greater loudness. Compare such phonetically similar words as ndo ʔ wíugṇ "he gave" and ndo ʔ wíúgṇ "he swept."

MASTERING THE SOUNDS

In some languages there is no distinctive or fixed stress. For example, in the Barrow dialect of Eskimo the word tautugakṣigigiga "I ought to see him" would usually be stressed on the penultimate (next to the last syllable) or the antepenultimate (second from the last syllable). It would rarely, if ever, be stressed on the last syllable. But the stress is not necessarily restricted to the penultimate or antepenultimate syllable, for other syllables can also be stressed. Languages with such nondistinctive, movable stresses are not common.

4.4 Types of Phonetic Problems

We as English-speaking people have certain types of phonetic problems because of our particular language habits. It is only natural for us to carry over to another language those sounds which seem to approximate the foreign sounds, but in this we must be very careful. We are confronted with three types of phonetic problems: (1) sounds which are very similar to English and yet different, (2) sounds which have some resemblance to English sounds but which reflect an entirely different phonological system, and (3) sounds which are utterly different from those in English.

4.4.1 Similar Sounds

Some of the sounds of two different languages may be similar, but they are never completely identical. For example, such Spanish words as café "coffee," fácil "easy," médico "physician," and pluma "pen"[34] seem to some people to be very similar to English and to have almost identically the same vowel sounds as our corresponding words cafe, facil, medical, and plume. But this is by no means true. Our pronunciation of the word cafe is phonetically more or less like [kæféʸ]. The Spanish pronunciation may be symbolized as [kafé]. The Spanish vowels are level, clear vowels, and they lack the off glides toward [ʸ] and [ʷ]. The English pronunciation of plume usually has a definite postvocalic rounding of the lips and may be symbolized phonetically as [plúʷm], while Spanish pluma [plúma] lacks the [ʷ] offglide.

---

[34]Compare English plume, meaning "feather."

As English speakers we tend to substitute lax, lower vowels for unstressed tense vowels[35] in French. For example, in pronouncing the French word dicter [dikté][36] we substitute our [ɩ], as in bit [bɩt], for the French [i]. Since the phrase stress in French comes on the last syllable of [dikté] (i.e., when pronounced in isolation), we tend to hear the English lax vowel [ɩ] rather than the unstressed tense vowel of French. We also make the mistake of pronouncing the French final [e], with a [ʸ] off-glide. Our pronunciation of the French dicter [dikté] is thus approximately [dɩktéʸ]. This mispronunciation is encouraged by the fact that we have a similar word dictate. But even where there is no such cognate word, we tend to substitute our lax vowels for French unstressed tense vowels. When the French vowel [i] is stressed, e.g., in vous avez dit "you have said" [vuzavedí],[37] then English-speaking people frequently substitute the high front vowel English equivalent with the [ʸ] off-glide, the type of vowel which occurs in beat [bíʸt]. Such details of pronunciation may seem rather small and insignificant, but they are tell-tale features of foreigners' speech and often hinder our being intelligible.

In English we tend to slight the voicing of the voiced stops b, d, and g. For example, in our pronunciation of robe we pronounce a longer vowel than in rope, but the final b is sometimes entirely voiceless. We can test this voicelessness of b by pronouncing the word while having our fingers in our ears. It will then become obvious that the voicing stops sometimes in the middle of the lip closure and sometimes even before the lip closure. The voicing practically never continues throughout the lip closure. In the French pronunciation of robe [r̃ɔb][38] the [b] is voiced throughout. To our English ears this word sounds as though a final, short, mid central vowel [ə] were added, e.g., [r̃ɔbə]. In some dialects there

---

[35] Tense vowels are made with relatively tensed vocal organs, and lax vowels are made with relatively relaxed vocal organs.

[36] The acute accent indicates the placement of the phrase stress. French has no distinctive stress for individual words.

[37] Such a phrase is pronounced as though it were a single word.

[38] Notice that in French there is a different vowel, and the initial consonant is a velar trill or fricative.

is such a final vowel, but in others it is just the full voicing of the [b] which gives us this impression. If we pronounce a partially or completely unvoiced final stop, the impression to French ears is often as though we were pronouncing [p].

One of the most obvious difficulties which we as English speakers have with French and Spanish is our tendency to aspirate all the initial voiceless stops. In English such words as peak, take, and kill have strong puffs of air after them.[39] In French and Spanish such initial stops do not have aspirations. The English word pan is pronounced as [p^{h}æn], but the Spanish word pan "bread" is pronounced as [pan].[40] To our ears this initial unaspirated stop sounds almost like [b]. To speak either French or Spanish decently we must eliminate the aspirations after voiceless stops, or we shall be accused of "puffing" at people all the time. In fact, when Latin Americans try to mimic Americans one of the usual devices is putting in frequent strong puffs of air to imitate the sounds which we so frequently make in speaking Spanish.

Some languages have stops which are sometimes voiced and other times voiceless. For example, in Kipsigis, a Nilo-Hamitic language of Kenya, there are no contrasts between p and b, t and d, č and ǰ, and k and g. Sometimes, for example, one seems to hear [k] and at other times [g]. In word-initial and word-final positions and juxtaposed to a voiceless continuant, the voiceless varieties of stops tend to occur. In other positions the voiced consonants occur, but never does the contrast between voiced and voiceless consonants make a difference in meaning. We must therefore make certain that in such a language we do not introduce our English aspirated

---

[39] To test this, place a small piece of paper in front of the mouth and watch it move as the result of the aspiration, or pronounce the words against the back of the hand and feel the air as it comes out. The aspiration will be very easily noted, particularly if one compares the words speak, steak, and skill, which have no such aspirations following the stops.

[40] In some dialects it is pronounced as [paŋ] when phrase-final.

consonants and thus attempt to introduce differences which are completely nondistinctive in the native language.[41]

Another common habit which we have as English speakers is the reduction of unstressed vowels to [ə]. For example, our pronunciation of Spanish semana "week" is often approximately [səmánə]. The first and last vowels are reduced to [ə] because they are unaccented. The result is that the word is practically unintelligible. In Spanish it is extremely important that each vowel be pronounced with its full qualitative value. There is no "neutralizing" of vowels in Spanish as there is in English.

One of our great difficulties as English speakers is in the pronunciation of nasal vowels. The trouble is that we introduce a nasal consonant when we should have a pure nasal vowel, and then we nasalize vowels when they should not be nasalized. For example, in pronouncing French enchanté [ǫšǫte] "delighted,"[42] we tend to say [ǫⁿšǫⁿteʸ]. We insert a little [ⁿ] following the nasalized vowel. We also add the [ʸ] offglide. On the other hand, practically all vowels in English which are contiguous to nasal consonants tend to be nasalized. Such nasalization is stronger in some dialects than in others, but it can be readily noticed if one pinches his nose while pronouncing the word enemy. We do not have three nonnasal vowels and two nasal consonants. Rather, we partially nasalize all of the vowels. On the other hand, French ennemi [ɛnmi] "enemy" has two nonnasalized vowels. Our tendency to pronounce this French word as [ɛ̨nmį] gives the impression to

---

[41] In the orthographies of Nandi and Kipsigis (closely related languages) missionaries have tried to distinguish voiced and voiceless consonants, with the result that the spelling is very inconsistent and the native speakers are completely unable to follow any system for distinguishing p and b, t and d, ch and j, and k and g- Accordingly, such words as tukat "store" (borrowed from Swahili duka) is written in every way, e.g., dugad, dugat, dukat, tukat, tugad, tukad, dukad, and tugat. Where there is no phonemic basis of distinction (i.e., meaningful contrast) in the native language, it is practically impossible to teach a consistent spelling.

[42] The phrase stress is not marked, but would, of course, occur on the last vowel.

French persons that English people speak through their noses, while that is precisely what we conclude about the French. The trouble is that what is distinctive in French, the difference between nasal and nonnasal vowels, is not distinctive in English. As a result nasalized vowels sound like vowel-plus-n to us, and we pass over our own nasalized vowels, being quite unaware of them. These are the very types of problems which will concern us in the next section.

4.4.2 Similar Sounds but with Different Values in Other Languages

As we have noted above (section 3.2.2.1) both aspirated and unaspirated consonants occur in English, but we never distinguish words by means of such differences. In Yipounou, a Bantu language of the Gabon, the occurrence or nonoccurrence of the aspiration does make a difference in words. Compare the following forms: punga[43] "wind" and p^{h}unga "fibre"; tatila "to cry out" and t^{h}atila "to cry out to me"; kala "a long time ago" and k^{h}ala "crab" (cited in section 4.3.1.4). We have already pointed out other contrasts in Zulu and Mazatec (see section 4.3.1.4). The difficulty which we have as English speakers is in hearing these differences accurately. Frequently missionaries have spoken a language for years and never noticed such differences as kala "a long time ago" and k^{h}ala "crab." We tend to hear only those distinctions which we make in our own language. If the distinctions are noted, they are sometimes confused. For example, kala would sound almost like gala, but -gala is the stem of the verb "to deny." In English we have three different sounds: [g], as in gill, [k], as in skill, and [k^h] as in kill. However, the last two never distinguish between words, for their occurrence is "conditioned" by the surrounding sounds, in this case by the preceding [s]. In Yipounou, however, there are three types of sounds and all are distinctive: -gala "to deny," kala "a long time ago," and k^{h}ala "crab."

In some instances English makes more distinctions than other languages. For example, in Spanish there is no

---

[43] Tonal differences are not written. The first pair are not minimal, since there is also a difference in length of vowel.

distinction between [s] and [z]. The word mismo "same, self" may be pronounced [mísmo] or [mízmo]. The word means exactly the same thing whether it is pronounced with an [s] or a [z]. This change from [s] to [z] may also occur when words are pronounced as a single unit. For example, eres bueno "you are good" may be pronounced [érezbuéno].[44]

One of our linguistic "besetting sins" is to substitute stress for tone. The stressed syllables of English are ordinarily on a higher pitch than the unstressed syllables. Hence, when we hear syllables which are higher than other syllables, we immediately interpret this distinction as one of stress. For example, in listening to Mongbandi, a Sudanic language of northern Congo, we might assume that gbiŋga "to translate" is accented on the first syllable when the subject is mbí "I," but accented on the second syllable when the subject is ʔè "we." A native speaker might understand us, but he would undoubtedly be confused, for Mongbandi does not have such stressed syllables. The distinctions are ones of tone, and they are quite complicated. The following illustrate some of the forms:

1. mbî gbíŋgà "I translated"
2. ʔè gbīŋgá "we translated"
3. mbī gbìŋgā "I am translating"
4. ʔē gbìŋgā "we are translating"
5. mbí gbīŋgā "I will translate"
6. ʔé gbíŋgà "we will translate"
7. mbí gbīŋgà "I would translate"
8. ʔé gbīŋgá "we would translate"

The pronouns change their tones to indicate different tenses; past (1-2), present (3-4), and future (5-8). The verbs change their tones to agree with singular and plural subjects and to indicate differences in tense and aspect: completive (1-2, 7-8), continuative (3-4), and future (5-6). If we combine a future tense form of the pronouns (7-8) with the completive form of the verb (1-2, 7-8), we obtain a potential form of the verb, translated "would..." To try to explain all these differences as merely stressed and unstressed syllables would be hopeless. We must not confuse our stress distinctions, which

---

[44] No attempt has been made to distinguish between different qualities of vowels when stressed and unstressed.

include some tonal differences, with tonal languages, in which the distinguishing features are differences in pitch, and stress may be quite irrelevant. That is to say, just as in English pitch is irrelevant in distinguishing words (though pitch does occur in the intonation), so in Mongbandi (and similar tonal languages) stress is irrelevant in distinguishing words. The two languages possess a degree of phonetic overlapping, in that stress syllables in English tend to be higher in pitch and high-tone syllables in Mongbandi tend to be uttered with slightly greater stress (at least they are more perceptible to our ears). But we must not mistake the overlapping of pitch and stress features for identity, since the two languages have utterly different basic systems.

When a language possesses the same types of sounds but makes more distinctions than we do in English, we are usually in for trouble unless we give very close attention to details. For example, in Shilluk, a Nilotic language spoken in the Anglo-Egyptian Sudan, there are five different nasal continuants. The following are the combinative forms of nouns before the adjective ñàn "new": kwām[45] "chair," yíṇ "ear," pyén "bed," wáñ "house," and pūŋ "jar." The nasals are successively bilabial, interdental, alveolar, alveopalatal, and velar. We may detect the alveopalatal sound, for it strikes us as being like English [ny], but in this position it is very difficult to hear. The interdental nasal continuant usually escapes the notice of English-speaking persons at first. What we "hear" is just a simple alveolar n.

Sometimes the "extra" distinctions (i.e., ones which English does not have) so affect the surrounding sounds that they are more easily detected. For example, in Quechua there are two types of back stops: palatal and velar. English possesses both palatal and velar stops, in fact, several different back stops, extending from the palatal to the velar position. The [k] of beak [biᵞk], following a front vowel, is palatal; and the [k] of balk [bɔk], following a back vowel, is velar. Compare the k's in the following words: beak, bake, back, Bach, balk. There are several different points of articulation depending upon the preceding vowel. In Bolivian Quechua there are two principal positions: palatal and velar. Minimal

---

[45]Vowels with dots are "breathy."

contrasts may be illustrated by the words kaka "dirty" and qaqa "cliff."[46] The velar stops, however, considerably modify the contiguous vowels, even as in English the contiguous vowels modify the back consonants. In Quechua the high vowel sounds [i] and [u] become [e] and [o] respectively when they are juxtaposed to back consonants. Compare, for example, the following sets of forms: [k'usu] "wrinkle" and [q'osu] "animal which is finicky about its food," [k^{h}uya] "to have pity" and [q^{h}oya] "(a) mine," [kil^{y}a] "moon" and [q^{h}el^{y}a] "lazy."[47] In writing Quechua it would be perfectly proper to employ only three vowels i, a, u, for the vowel sounds e and o are always conditioned in occurrence by the presence of a contiguous velar consonant. However, at present Spanish words are sometimes borrowed with their vowel values intact. That means that Quechua is adding to its vowel inventory the mid vowels e and o of Spanish, and thus it is acquiring a five-vowel system. With some missionaries, however, there is a tendency to pronounce a word such as [q^{h}el^{y}a] "lazy" as [k^{h}ela]. The velar consonant, which is "foreign" to English usage, is changed to the more familiar [k], but the [e] is retained since that corresponds to an English phoneme. Such a pronunciation makes the form [k^{h}ela] different from [kil^{y}a] "moon," but it misses the mark in reproducing the Quechua sounds. The persistent tendencies for us to carry over our English habits of speech must be constantly combatted.

One error which we as English-speaking people frequently make and which causes us no end of trouble in being understood, is the tendency to use our intonational patterns when speaking a tone language. When we are somewhat in doubt about a word, we tend to raise the final intonation, and that just makes matters worse. For example, in Habbe, a Sudanic language of French West Africa, if we question the word for "mud" (which is pɔ́nū), the chances are that we will say something which will be interpreted as pɔ́nú, which means "pants." We unconsciously superimpose our intonational pattern for interrogation and end up by changing the word completely. We

---

[46] Stops occur in three series: unaspirated, aspirated, and glottalized, e.g., tanta "equal," t^{h}anta "rag," and t'anta "bread."

[47] L. M. Shedd, Quechua Grammar (New York: Bolivian Indian Mission, 1931).

can also make mistakes in languages which have entirely different intonational patterns. For example, in Futa-Fula, a language of French Guinea, the expression <u>gertogal</u> <u>moʔd'yàl</u> with falling intonation (marked by grave accent on the last syllable) means "a good chicken." The same expression with a high tone on the last syllable means "not a good chicken," i.e., "a bad chicken." The only distinction between many positive and negative expressions is just a difference in the pitch of the final syllable.

We have syllabic nasals in English, even as many Bantu languages have, but our syllabic nasals are never initial to a word or phrase, while most Bantu syllabic nasals are. We have no difficulty in pronouncing a syllabic nasal [m̩] in <u>trip</u> <u>'em</u> [trɩpm̩], and [n̩] in <u>button</u> [bə́tn̩][48] However, in pronouncing such Chichewa words as <u>mbó·mba</u> "judge" and m̩ná·si "friend, neighbor,"[49] English-speaking people tend to say [əmbó·mba, əmná·si] or [ɩmbó·mba, ɩmná·si]. What we can pronounce in a noninitial syllable seems very difficult for us in an initial syllable, and hence we introduce a short [ə] or [ɩ].

Sometimes one encounters a medial syllabic consonant in Bantu languages. For example, in the Zulu word úmm̀·bá "beast given to the bride's mother" the medial <u>m</u> is long and has a low tone. In every way it acts just like a vowel. There is no need of marking the syllabic character of the nasal by a bar beneath the letter since the grave accent denotes that it is syllabic. Unless we are careful, we either overlook such syllabic nasals, and accordingly shorten the word until it is unrecognizable, or we tend to put in a little [ə] just before the syllabic consonant.

4.4.3 Strikingly Different Sounds

Strangely enough we do not seem to have as much difficulty with the strikingly different sounds as with those which

---

[48] The nasal continuants [m̩] and [n̩] act just like vowels. We can make certain that there are actually no vowels in the second syllables of these words since the lips do not normally open between the [p] and [m] and the tongue is not drawn away from the top of the mouth between the [t] and the [n].

[49] Mark Hanna Watkins, <u>A Grammar of Chichewa</u> (Baltimore: Linguistic Society of America, 1937), p. 25-26.

are deceptively similar to English. However, some of the "exotic" sounds (i.e., exotic from our viewpoint) do cause us trouble. For example, in Kekchi, a Mayan language of Guatemala, there are not only front and back k's, but there are two types of such k's, glottalized and nonglottalized. The palatal glottalized stop is explosive, i.e., the air between the glottis and the palatal closure is compressed. Accordingly, in the word cik' "bird" the air pops out after the release of the k. However, in the word k'ak' "fire" the air between the velum and the glottis is rarified by drawing the larynx down, and as a result the air pops into the throat immediately upon the release of the stop consonants. It is quite necessary to distinguish between glottalized and nonglottalized forms, for kak means "our pig" and k'ak' means "fire."

In Kekchi there are three other glottalized consonants: č' as in č'oč' "ground," t' as in t'ant'o "fallen" and p' as in kap'. The glottalized č' and t' are definitely explosive, but what we write as a glottalized p' is actually implosive and sounds very much like [ʔb] in certain positions.

Sometimes the distinctions in sounds are exceedingly subtle. For example, in Futa-Fula there are many glottalized consonants and glottal stops which occur frequently. The results are sometimes very confusing when we begin to listen to a language. Compare the following three verbs: hab'uʔgol "to fight," haʔb'uʔgol "to tie," and habbuʔgol "to wait."[50]

We have already mentioned the double consonants that occur in many of the Sudanic languages. At first, they tend to sound like glottalized consonants, or just emphatic consonants, but a little experimenting and practice will soon enable one to detect the distinctive quality.

The clicks are the most famous "queer" sounds. Perhaps it would not be so bad if there were only three of them: (1) with dental articulation and sibilant off-glide, (2) with lateral release, and (3) cerebral, with the tip of tongue against front part of palate. The difficulty in Zulu is that these three basic varieties have four subtypes: (a) nasalized, with the velic open during the pronunciation, and voiced, (b) voiced and nonnasal, (c) voiceless, and (d) aspirated, with a puff of air

---

[50] The glottal stop before [g] is frequently lost in fast speech.

following the release of the click and before the subsequent vowel. This gives twelve possible types of clicks. In Bushman and Hottentot there is still another articulation, called denti-alveolar,[51] and there are five different types of release —making twenty clicks in all. The fifth type of release in Bushman and Hottentot is a glottalized variety.

Some missionaries have great difficulty with the "guttural" sounds of Arabic. One of these is the glottal stop, which should not give us trouble since we have it in such expressions as the English negation [hə̰ʔə̰]. However, we are not so accustomed to hearing glottal stops initially in words. In English, we normally begin vowel-initial words without a glottal stricture. In German, however, initial vowels do begin with a glottal stop. Compare the English <u>an</u> <u>arm</u> [æn arm] and German <u>ein</u> <u>Arm</u> [ʔain ʔarm]. Arabic has an h similar to the light English [h], but there is also a more fricative voiceless continuant which occurs with a certain amount of constriction of the pharynx. This is transcribed as [ħ]. Compare [ħabba] "like, love" and [habba] "blow."[52] There is a voiced counterpart of this [ħ], usually transcribed as [ʕ]. This sound often occurs with what is called a "glottal trill." Some have described the production of this sound as consisting of singing as low as one can, and then going a few notes further down the scale. This produces a voicing with a very rough, "strained" effect. It occurs in such words as [ʕadda] "count" and [ʕasal] "honey." The velar (or uvular) voiceless continuant [x] with strong friction is quite common and occurs in such words as [xaffa] "be light" and [xo·x] "peaches."

4.5 Mastering Foreign Sounds

We must first realize that every sound in every foreign language is a foreign sound and is different from English. This means that we cannot take any sound for granted, but must make sure that we are adequately reproducing it.

---

[51] D. M. Beach, <u>The Phonetics of the Hottentot language</u>, (Cambridge: W. Heffer and Sons, 1938).
[52] These transcriptions are from Sudan Colloquial Arabic. See J. Spencer Trimingham, <u>Sudan Colloquial Arabic</u> (Oxford University Press, 1946).

Our first method for attaining a mastery of foreign-language sounds is to observe carefully and constantly the manner in which they are produced. For example, we must note precisely the kind and degree of lip rounding employed in the production of various vowels. Then to check our own pronunciation, we should have a hand mirror with which we may observe our own lip placements.

To determine whether a sound is interdental, alveolar, or velar, we may have to look inside the informant's mouth while he is making it. A flashlight may be required, and sometimes the informant may have to be coaxed to open his jaw slightly so that we can look inside. Usually, however, if everything is done in a good-humored way and with a real desire to learn, an informant is glad to cooperate.

To determine whether or not a sound is strongly aspirated, we can use a slip of paper which is not too thin and observe the fluttering of the paper when words are pronounced. By placing the back of one's hand in front of the informant's mouth, one can also judge the relative amount of aspiration.

In order to detect some instances of nasalization it is necessary to have the informant pinch his nose while pronouncing certain words. This is particularly true if the words have nasal consonants, for often the nasal consonants deceive us, and we think that we are hearing nasalized vowels as well. If the nose is held, a nasalized vowel is quite easily distinguished from a nonnasalized one.

In the case of glottalized consonants, we can often observe the constriction and time of release by placing two or three fingers on the informant's larynx during the utterance of a sound. The extra little "bang" which occurs in most instances of glottalization will be immediately perceptible.

One of the best ways of observing the production of sounds is the careful investigation of what one does oneself in attempting to reproduce a sound. If one's informant is encouraged to be strict and not to agree to a pronunciation until it is perfectly intelligible, the student may note such features as where his own tongue is in the mouth, just how his own lips are rounded (by using a mirror), and whether or not his vocal organs are tense or lax. At first it may be difficult to tell precisely what is going on inside of one's mouth, for we normally speak without any conscious effort or knowledge about the mechanics of the task. However, by careful application we can train ourselves to be very sensitive to the position and form of our vocal organs.

The most important thing which we may do in learning to master the sounds of any language is to encourage people to correct us. They do not normally do this, either because of respect for us or because it is just too much trouble. Only constant encouragement will induce them to help us.

Almost all sounds can be mastered if we will just stick at the task long enough. Sometimes, however, we do need assistance in the way of helpful hints and exercises. Many valuable suggestions are made by Kenneth L. Pike in his book <u>Phonemics</u>.[53] There he discusses very briefly in the first section how many of the difficult sounds may be produced and practiced.

Sometimes we can employ nursery ditties and similar phrases as aids to the mastery of certain types of sound. For example, if we find that the language we are learning has no initial aspirated stops, e.g., as in French and Spanish, then we may practice the following sentences until we can say them without any aspiration:

> Peter Piper picked a peck of pickle peppers; a peck of pickle peppers Peter Piper picked.

> If a Hottentot tot taught a Hottentot tot to talk, ere the tot could totter, should the Hottentot tot be taught to say ought, or nought, or what ought to be taught her?

> Can cool cunning cowboys keep cows cantering?

By saying these expressions without the slightest aspirations after the stops, one can obtain practice in a different type of articulation. If, on the other hand, one wants to practice glottalized stops, the same sentences can be used, e.g.,

> P ʔet ʔer P ʔip ʔer p ʔick ʔed ʔ...

For practicing different types of guttural sounds, we can use the sentence

> How has Hank handed Henry his heavy hooks?

For the initial light aspirations, we may substitute glottal stops, heavy aspirates (voiced and voiceless), and velar

---

[53]Kenneth L. Pike, <u>Phonemics</u> (Ann Arbor, Michigan: University of Michigan, 1947).

continuants. The value of such exercises based upon English words is that we can concentrate upon the particular foreign sounds while at the same time pronouncing them in combination with other sounds. Just to repeat a glottalized stop over and over again is often not as valuable as including it in a regular flow of speech sounds, even though the surrounding sounds happen to be English.

Another way to practice the sounds of a language is to imitate the way in which native speakers of such a language speak English. By this process one will discover rapidly some of the major differences between the two languages. One must then learn to carry over these distinctions into the foreign language.

Sometimes students at first seem to get along rather well with the sounds of a language; but after they begin to speak more, they appear to lose some of their initial proficiency. The reason for this is that after beginning to make oneself understood by means of a more extensive vocabulary and greater familiarity with the grammatical forms, the student often relaxes his attention on the sounds. Such a situation is unfortunate, for no amount of grammatical correctness can make up for murdering the sounds.

Some people manage rather well in the pronunciation of words and phrases provided they speak very slowly. Such people seem to stall in their language learning and always give the impression of picking their way carefully through a sentence. This painful procedure—for it is painful to listeners—must be overcome. Three processes will enable one to break the bondage of tiresome limping in the language: (1) a determination to speak rapidly, regardless of whether grammatical forms are correct or incorrect, (2) practice in reading the language aloud and up to speed (if possible, an informant should be on hand to jot down mistakes), and (3) reciting of memorized materials faster and faster until one is actually speaking at an abnormally fast rate. In other words, we must overdo the matter of speed in order to be able to come up to the right speed. A pianist often practices playing difficult scores much faster than the correct speed in order that when he plays them at their proper speed he may not be "pressed." Similarly, the learner of a foreign language must practice speaking at faster than normal speed, in order that he may have proper facility in regular utterance.

We are often so chained to the book form of a language that we have the impression that sentences consist of words which are phonetically isolated from each other by tiny pauses. This is, of course, not true in English or any other language. In fact, in rapid speech we would pronounce the first part of the preceding sentence something as follows:

[dɪssfkɔ́rs natruʷnɪŋglɪš] This is of course not true in English.

It would be wrong to assume that this rapid type of pronunciation is the only one to be learned, but at the same time it would be more wrong to teach a person to place a phonetic pause between each word of the sentence. The former would be perfectly intelligible at its proper rate of utterance and would seem completely natural, but the latter would be artificial and certainly would bore the listeners if continued for any length of time. Such hesitating speech might actually result in misunderstanding.

Spanish is often taught as though each word is a separate and inviolate unit in the sentence. Actually there is a great deal of "running together" in the pronunciation of Spanish. Kahane and Beym[54] have listed a number of the more common changes in pronunciation resulting from the normal joining of words together. These will be listed under six different types, with traditional spelling for all but the changed portion. Underlining indicates the sounds which (1) undergo phonetic change, (2) are syllabified differently, or (3) result from a loss of a vowel.

1. lazmandan (las mandan) "they send them"[55]
   hijazmías (hijas mías) "my daughters"
2. tedijo (te dijo) "he told you"
   hoybendrá (hoy vendrá) "he'll come today"

---

[54] Henry R. Kahane and Richard Beym "Syntactical Juncture in Colloquial Mexican Spanish" Language, Vol. 24, No. 4, 388-96.

[55] The first form shows the change. The second is the form in its fully traditional writing. Following these is the meaning in English.

3. eṇque (en que) "in which"
   inclinaciómpor ellos (inclinación por ellos) "affection for them"
4. lo̱sombres (los hombres) "the men"
   se viero̱nellas (se vieron ellas) "they looked at each other"
5. hasta̱hora (hasta ahora) "till now"
   que̱ra (que era) "that it was"
6. y̱alto (y [i] alto) "and tall"[5][6]
   voy̱al jardín (voy al jardín) "I'm going to the garden"

These six types of changes include: (1) the change of a voiceless sound to a voiced one, (2) the change of a stop sound to a continuant sound (the Spanish letter v stands for the sound [b] in Mexican Spanish), (3) the change of nasals to agree with the articulation of the following stop consonants, (4) the syllabification of consonants with following vowels rather than with preceding vowels, (5) the loss of one of two identical vowels, and (6) the change of a sound from a vowel (syllabic) function to a consonantal one. These changes in Mexican Spanish are not simply rare changes that occur in very rapid speech; they are the perfectly normal types of pronunciation which characterize the speech of educated people.

French is noted for its elisions and coalescing of forms. Sometimes, however, we are not fully aware of all that does happen. Note the following sentences:[5][7]

1. /žvudrɛdlasúp/[5][8] Je voudrais de la soupe "I would like some soup"
2. /žənvṗpɑtpwasɔ̃/ Je ne veux pas de poisson "I do not like fish"
3. /kɛskəsɛkselümyɛrlá/ Qu'est-ce que c'est que ces lumières-là? "What are those lights?"

There are no phonetic breaks in these sentences. Of course, they could be pronounced very slowly, and certain phonetic breaks and more vowels would occur, e.g., /žəvudrɛ́ dəlasúp/.

---

[56]The conjunction y is normally syllabic, pronounced as [i], but in this instance it has become fully consonantal and begins the following syllable.

[57]See Francois Denoeu and Robert A. Hall, Jr., Spoken and Written French (Boston: D. C. Heath and Co., 1946).

[58]Slant lines indicate phonemic writing. See section 4.6.2. The final acute accents mark the sentence stress.

However, the normal pronunciation is as we have written it in a single phonetic unit. To pronounce the words as separate units is intolerably awkward. One of the most important phases of learning any language is mastering the pronunciation of phrases at normal speed of utterance. This is equally important to getting a satisfactory rendering of separate sounds.

4.6 A Usable Alphabet

If one anticipates the task of learning a language which has never been reduced to writing, one should by all means have some technical training in linguistics and make a thorough study of phonemics, which provides techniques for determining a scientific alphabet for any type of language. The most satisfactory text on this subject is Phonemics by Kenneth L. Pike.[59]

There are at least 1000 languages in the world which have not been reduced to writing. Without some basic understanding of the problems one can waste a great deal of time and in many instances come out with rather unsatisfactory results. One missionary who constructed an alphabet for an Indian language in the southwest United States failed to recognize or wrongly interpreted at least one-third of the sounds of the language. The result has been that practically no one has succeeded in learning to read this extremely complicated and incorrect transcription. However, most of the languages in which missionaries work have been reduced to writing, and some of them have long traditions of written form.

4.6.1 The Usual Situation in a Written Language

For a language which has a non-Roman alphabet or a syllabary,[60] the missionary should employ some type of Roman alphabet with certain phonetic symbols or diacritical marks during the process of learning to speak. It is unwise

---

[59] Kenneth L. Pike, Phonemics (Ann Arbor, Michigan: University of Michigan Press, 1947).

[60] A syllabary is a system of writing which employs a different symbol for each syllable. For example, each CV sequence is treated as a unit, rather than as two units, as it would be in an alphabetic system of writing.

to attempt to learn Arabic, for example, purely from the written form of Arabic. To try to master a strange orthography and new forms at the same time is confusing and involves needless delay. One should use some such transcription as occurs in J. Trimingham's book on Sudan Colloquial Arabic.[61] For most of the languages with non-Roman alphabets, there are keys to the sound values in the average grammar designed for foreigners. On the basis of these, the missionary can construct his own system of transcription.

A few languages use symbols which have no relationship to the sounds. This is true in Chinese. In such situations one must have some sort of phonetic alphabet with which to record the sounds. There are a number of possible systems of transcription.

We are concerned here for the most part with those "missionary" languages which do have a Roman alphabet, but for which the alphabet is usually deficient in one or more items. Very frequently there are more vowels in the language than are distinguished by the orthography. A number of Bantu languages have seven vowels, but in a number of these missionaries have written only five vowels, either because they had difficulty in distinguishing the seven vowels or because they simply thought that it was not necessary. Since English is so notoriously inconsistent, people have often assumed that extra symbols would have no value anyway. In Dinka the standard orthography indicates seven vowels, but in addition to the seven basic vowels, there are seven so-called centralized vowels. Furthermore, all fourteen of these vowels may apparently be breathy or nonbreathy. Of these twenty-eight possibilities the present orthography only indicates seven, but for a long time some missionaries wanted to use only five vowels.

For the most part the orthographies of Bantu and Sudanic languages do not indicate tones. In certain instances there are so many closely similar forms which differ only by tone and which the context cannot possibly resolve that it is imperative to indicate the tones. But usually missionaries have been content to omit all indication of tone. The reasons for this are that many missionaries have been totally unaware of

---

[61] J. Trimingham, op. cit.

the tonal differences and that in certain languages the context enables natives to read their languages rather well without the aid of such tone marks. We cannot here discuss all the problems concerning the construction of practical alphabets for native readers.[62] What we are concerned with is an adequate alphabet for the missionary learning the language.

Other frequent omissions in traditional alphabets include distinctions between certain kinds of consonants. In some instances aspirated and unaspirated consonants are not distinguished. This is true in many African languages. Glottalized consonants are often not distinguished from nonglottalized ones. In certain cases traditional alphabets have made unnecessary distinctions. For example, in Spanish b and v are generally pronounced exactly alike. Certain speakers try to insist on a difference, but it is very artificial and usually not made except when the speaker is consciously thinking of the orthographic contrast.

Missionaries have frequently introduced contrasts which occur in English but which are not significant in a native language. For example, in Jita, a Bantu language spoken in Tanganyika, the missionaries had great difficulty determining just which words should be written with l and which with r. In reality, there is no valid distinction, for the language has only one flap consonant, which sometimes sounds like l and other times like r. One could write it with one symbol almost as well as with the other, but to use two symbols is quite confusing to a native reader.

4.6.2 A Phonemic Alphabet

The ideal alphabet for any one learning to speak a language is a phonemic alphabet. Such an alphabet would represent each distinctive sound by one symbol. By a distinctive sound we mean one which makes a difference in meaning. All languages have hundreds of phonetically distinguishable sounds, but in each language there are limited groups of related sounds which contrast with each other. For example, in English there

---

[62] For further discussion of these problems see Eugene A. Nida, Bible Translating (New York: American Bible Society, 1947), pp. 100-129, and Kenneth L. Pike, Phonemics, especially pp. 208-227.

are a number of k's: aspirated as in kill, unaspirated as in skill, unreleased as in the first [k] of lick candy, inaudibly released as in licked (the [t] comes into position before the [k] is released), articulated at different points as in seek, sick, sake, sack, suck, sock, soak. A strictly phonetic alphabet would indicate all these minute distinctions, and many more. However, the important thing about this group of phonetically related sounds is that they contrast with the various varieties of [g]. Out of all the different sounds related to [k] and those related to [g] we discover that there is no overlapping and that [k] and [g] do distinguish words, e.g., kill and gill.[63] We must conclude that these two classes of sounds constitute two phonemes, which we may write with slant lines to distinguish them from their purely phonetic values, e.g., /k/ and /g/. Out of the hundreds of phonetically different sounds which any one language has, there are usually somewhere between a dozen and sixty phonetically related classes of sounds which turn out to be structurally significant.

In order to understand just a little better what is meant by a phonemic alphabet, we need to consider briefly two fundamental features: free and conditioned variation of sounds.

No two pronunciations of a sound are ever completely identical in every detail. This we may learn from examining recordings of such sounds by means of various electrical instruments. As far as our ears are concerned, however, there are many pronunciations which appear to be identical. Sometimes natives seem to us to be pronouncing a word quite differently on two occasions, and yet they may insist that the two utterances sound exactly alike to them. For example, Jita natives use an [r] or an [l] (see data cited in section 4.6.1), and they declare that the sounds are identical, unless, of course, they have learned some English in which such a distinction does contrast words. The Jita language does not train the native speaker to distinguish between these two phonetically different sounds. The reason is that [r] and [l] never dis-

---

[63] It is not necessary to discover two words which differ in only the one particular distinction, i.e., constitute minimal pairs. We may determine that two types of sounds are distinct phonemes if they show contrast in analogous phonetic environments. Such problems are, however, beyond the scope of this text.

tinguish two different words. This type of variation in sounds is free variation.

In Barrow Eskimo there are only three vowels: the front high vowel (which we write as i) sometimes sounds like [i], at other times like [ɪ], or even like [e]. The high back vowel u has a similar range of variation [u, ʋ, o]. The mid low vowel a also varies greatly. For a person who is listening to Eskimo with purely "English ears," there are all sorts of confusing differences, for a native speaker will declare that two pronunciations of a word are the same even though we as English speakers hear what seem to be utterly different vowels. This is because in Eskimo there are only three vowels which actually distinguish between words. That is to say, there are only three vowel phonemes. Much of the fluctuation which one hears between vowels is just free variation. Such problems of free variation exist in all languages. To speak a language well we must become phonetically conscious of such differences, but we must also understand that such differences do not distinguish forms.

Many phonetic differences which we hear are conditioned variations. We cannot consider all the various phonetic features which "condition" these variations, but we must be on the alert for some of the more common ones.. The reason for these conditioned variations is that sounds influence each other. For example, as noted above, in English the aspirated stops occur initially as in peak, take, and kill, but the unaspirated stops occur in speak, steak, and skill. The occurrence of the initial s conditions the unaspirated stop variety. We cannot say precisely "why" this type of situation exists, and in fact, we do not need to know. What we are concerned with is the fact that such a change does occur. While the fluctuation between [l] and [r] in Jita is primarily a matter of free variation, it is not so in Ilamba, another Bantu language of Tanganyika. In Ilamba the l-like variety of the flap occurs when preceded or followed by high vowels such as i or u. With other vowels the r-like flap occurs. In Quechua there are only three basic vowel phonemes i, u, and a.[64] When, however, the high vowels i and u are juxtaposed to a velar consonant, they sound

---

[64]Because of Spanish borrowed words there is developing in some dialects the basis of a five vowel system.

like e̱ and o̱ respectively (see section 4.4.2). That means that the variants e̱ and o̱ are conditioned by the occurrence of the velar sounds.

We have already mentioned in section 4.3.3.1.2 the fact that tones are often conditioned by where they occur in the phrase. A high tone at the end of a phrase may be considerably lower than a high tone at the beginning of the phrase. In fact, in some languages, e.g., Dinka and Shilluk, one may hear a high tone at the end of a phrase lower than a low tone at the beginning of a phrase. In treating tonal languages we must always bear in mind the conditioning of tones.

A phonetic alphabet attempts to indicate all these free and conditioned variants. A phonemic alphabet, however, only indicates those sounds (actually, classes of sounds) which contrast with one another in that they provide the basis for distinctions in meaning.

4.6.3   Practical Solutions to the Alphabet Problem

The new missionary should not attempt to insist on an orthographic reform just in order to take care of his own needs in learning to speak the language in question. Accordingly, he must learn how to make up for any deficiencies in the existing system by notations designed for his own benefit. It is quite unnecessary to attempt to use only the symbols of the International Phonetic System. These symbols are very complicated; and though they are technically accurate, they are often of little practical value to the average missionary. He must learn to use the traditional form of writing the language, but he must devise some sort of diacritical marks to indicate significant contrasts omitted in the original method of spelling the words. There are two types of problems: (1) how many distinctions should be marked and (2) how should one mark the existing orthography.

As a basic minimum one should mark all the differences which are phonemic, i.e., distinguish meanings. Whether these are aspirated consonants, glottalized vowels, tones, intonation, nasalization, or stress, they should all be indicated if they are phonemic. At first, one may even want to mark certain phonetic distinctions which are not phonemic. For example, if initial stops are aspirated and medial consonants are not aspirated, it might be well to indicate this on some of the first transcriptions of words. But in order to learn a language well, one must thoroughly master all the types of free and conditioned variations so that they become second nature. This usually cannot be done without conscious effort. In most instances, however, these problems of variation are taken care of through the process of conscious mimicry, rather than as the result of having analyzed the various individual phonetic distinctions.

Symbols for marking phonemic distinctions which are omitted from traditional alphabets should be such that they can be readily identified and easily added to typed or printed materials. The following are some of the suggested forms:

1. Aspiration may be indicated by a raised [ʰ] or by a reversed apostrophe [ʻ]. (This latter symbol will be readily recognized as the Greek sign for rough breathing.)
2. Back consonants may be indicated by a dot beneath the letter, e.g., /ṭ/.
3. Front consonants may be indicated by a curved line beneath the letter, e.g., /t̯/.
4. Extra vowel phonemes may be indicated by diaereses, e.g., /ä/, by a dot over the letter, e.g., /ė/, by a wavy line, e.g., /õ/, by accent marks, e.g., /ò/ or /ó/, or by underlining, e.g., /e̱/. One should make sure, however, that distinctions are marked systematically and economically. For example, if there are seven vowels in the language and the traditional orthography distinguishes only five, then two vowels must be marked, but they should be marked in accordance with a consistent system. If, for example, a language uses the symbols e̱ and o̱ to mark the four vowel phonemes /e, ɩ, o, ʋ/, one must decide whether to mark the /e/ and /o/ varieties or the /ɩ/ and /ʋ/ varieties. This depends upon the frequency. If the phonemes /ɩ/ and /ʋ/ are more frequent, one should retain the symbols e̱ and o̱ for these higher phonemes, and just mark the /e/ and /o/ phonemes. This is purely a matter of economy of effort. On the other hand, one should attempt to mark the same types of vowels in the same way. Sometimes, however, the orthographic system in

use is very arbitrary. One may find that the symbol e stands for the phonemes /e/ and /ɩ/, but the symbol o marks only a single phoneme, while the symbol u stands for the phonemes /u/ and /ʋ/. In order not to depart too far from the traditional form of writing the language, one must place a mark over some of the e symbols in order to distinguish the less frequently occurring phoneme, and a mark over the u symbol to distinguish the less frequently occurring phoneme. It really does not matter what device one ultimately chooses. The important thing is to be consistent.

5. Nasalization may be indicated by a hook under the vowel, e.g., /ę/, or by a tilde over the vowel /ẽ/.
6. Breathy vowels may be indicated by underlining, e.g., /e̱/, by a tilde over the vowel, e.g., /ẽ/, or by a dot beneath the vowel, e.g., /ẹ/.
7. Tones in a register system may be indicated as follows: high tone /á/, low tone /à/, mid tone /ā/, a mid-high tone (a fourth tone) /a̍/. Note, however, that if there are only two registers, one needs to mark only one, either the high or the low, depending upon which is less frequent. If the language has three registers, one needs to mark only two, for the one which is left unmarked will be distinctive by virtue of the fact that it has no mark. Similarly, in a four register system one may omit marking one of the registers. If long vowels are indicated by writing the vowel twice, glides which occur on such long vowels may be marked as follows: high-low /áà/, low-high /àá/, low-mid /àa/, mid-high /aá/, etc. If, however, the long vowels are not marked by writing two vowels, glides which occur on such long vowels or those which occur on short vowels may be indicated as follows: high-low /â/, low-high /ǎ/, low-mid /à̄/, and mid-high /ā́/, etc.
8. Tones in a contour tone language may be indicated by certain approximate symbols, e.g., a high tone /á/, a rising glide /á̂/, a rising-falling glide /â/, a falling rising glide /ǎ/, a low tone /à/, and a falling glide /a͡/. One may also use numerals over the vowels to indicate the number of distinctive glides, e.g., ba̍¹, ba̍², ba̍³, etc.

MASTERING THE SOUNDS

    In some ways it is better to use lines which will suggest the type of contour or relative pitch than to employ numbers.

9. Length of vowel may be noted by a dot placed after the vowel, e.g., /a·/, by a long mark (a macron) over the vowel, e.g., /ā/, or by doubling a vowel, e.g., /aa/. In using two vowels to mark a long vowel one must make certain that this does not conflict with the writing of possible rearticulated vowels (these are juxtaposed, identical vowels, but with each vowel distinctly pronounced).

It is not at all necessary to restrict oneself to these marks or to use them to indicate the values assigned to them here. One can use a tilde to mark a mid tone or a diaeresis to indicate glottalization. The important thing is that the markings be consistent. This does not mean, however, that all types of diacritical marks are equally useful for a native reader. We are simply suggesting here certain symbols which the missionary may use to mark materials written in the traditional orthography. There are two principles which should be noted as applicable to the missionary's use of diacritics as well as to the natives' possible adoption of them. First, markings over letters are more easily seen than those beneath letters.[65] Secondly, markings should not be crowded. For example, if one must mark nasalization, length, and high tones, it would be unwise to choose the symbols /ã/, /ā/, and /á/. In the case of a long, high, nasalized vowel there would be an excess of symbols above the letter, e.g., /ā̃́/. In a situation like this one should use such symbols as /ą/ for nasalization, /a·/ for length, and /á/ for high tone. The result of all three on one vowel would be /ą́·/, and the combination would be much easier to distinguish.

Sometimes missionaries have great difficulty in working out the system of tone in the language, and as a result they may give up making any kind of marks, assuming that they will naturally acquire the right pronunciation through practice.

---

[65] One may test this by placing a blank sheet of paper over the top half of a line of print and then over the bottom half of the line. It will be readily noted that one can read much much more easily by means of the tops of the letters than by seeing only the bottom portions.

This is quite deceiving. One missionary who gave a great deal of attention to the tone problem in a two-register tone language, but who had never considered it necessary to mark the tones, even in a more or less crude way, found that she was mispronouncing almost fifty percent of the tones. If she had begun to mark even the more conspicuous syllables, gradually the more subtle distinctions would have become more obvious. Though her markings might not have been one hundred percent correct, she surely would have been able to attain eighty to ninety percent correctness. If one can make only general approximations to the tone of a phrase, one should mark through the phrase in order to remember accurately its pitch form. For example, one may not be able to determine all the phonemic levels of such a language as Kissi, a Sudanic language of French Guinea, and write the following phrase as vɛ̀ yá gbéŋgbélá yɛ̀ ndū sísà nē· "How do I send him now?" Nevertheless, one could at least mark through the transcription of this phrase so as to indicate the general rise and fall of the sentence, e.g.,

vɛ ya gbɛŋgbela yɛ ndu sisa nɛ·

Most missionaries have difficulty with tone languages because they expect tones to have definitely fixed pitches and never to vary, either because of the intonation of the sentence or because of the surrounding tones. We have already pointed out the tendency for tones to differ because of the general intonation of the phrases, and in the next two chapters we shall discuss the ways in which phonemically different tones act to modify one another. We cannot consider the many intricate techniques which must be employed in properly analyzing a tonal language,[66] but we must mention two important features of analysis and proper identification. First, we must identify the tones of words from their occurrence in tone frames (see below), and not as isolated words; and secondly, we should start with the extreme pitch points (the highest and the lowest) and then identify the pitches which lie between the extremes.

We may illustrate some of the problems from Ngbaka, a Sudanic language of northern Congo. For example, if we should

---

[66]See Kenneth L. Pike, Tone Languages (Ann Arbor, Michigan: University of Michigan Press, 1947).

have an informant give us the following words as separate
items in a list or in response to requests for individual words,
we would be unable to distinguish the differences of pitch without having listened to the language for a long time: fàlà
"place," kòlā "chicken," ndìmbó "ball," tūlū "piece of cloth,"
kpōkpò "shoe," línzá "sky," sélè "spear," and yélē "buffalo."
The only way we can determine the pitches of these words is
to discover some relatively stable tone with which these various words may go. After trying several possibilities, we
find that the word d'á· "bad" always appears to be high—at
least there is no other word which is ever higher than this in
a short phrase consisting of nouns and words which are attributive to nouns. If we place d'á· before all the nouns which
we have listed, we obtain the following series:

    d'á fàlà "bad place"   d'á· kpōkpò "bad show"
    d'á kòlā "bad chicken"   d'á· línzá "bad sky"
    d'á· ndìmbó "bad ball"   d'á· sélè "bad spear"
    d'á· tūlū "bad piece of cloth" d'á· yélē "bad buffalo"

However, as we obtain this series of words, we are frequently
in doubt as to the correct tones, for we do not know just how
low the final syllable is. Furthermore, a phrase such as
d'á· línzá "bad sky" gradually falls off in tone rather than being perfectly level, for the intonation of the phrase "pulls"
the tones down. Even if we got a final low tone word such as
gè "this,"[67] we would not be absolutely certain of the relative
tones because of the intonational patterns which would call for
a descending tonal pattern anyway. What we need is a frame
which will have a pitch pattern opposite to the intonation one,
and in this way we can determine much more easily just what
the relationships of tones are. There is one perfect frame in
Ngbaka for these noun expressions. It consists of a low-tone
word mbè "other" and a final high-tone word kpó "one." To
determine the basic tones of the Ngbaka nouns, all we do is to
place them in the frame mbè ... kpó, meaning "other ... one"
i.e., "another." Our forms then appear as:
    mbè fàlà kpó "another place"
    mbè kòlā kpó "another chicken"

---

[67]Furthermore, this word gè is always preceded by a suffix which undergoes various changes and makes the analysis
quite complicated. See section 5.6 for a discussion of this
problem.

mbè ndìmbó kpó "another ball"
etc.

In this Ngbaka material we are fortunate, for the nouns and attributives do not constantly change, depending upon the various classes of words. In some languages we find that nouns may have one tone following a high tone adjective and other tones following a low tone adjective. In some instances, adjectives differ in tone depending upon the tones of the nouns with which they occur. Despite all these complications, however, we must still employ frames in analyzing tones. In isolation we are practically helpless to identify the tones, for tone is not a matter of absolute pitch but of relative pitch. In the data above we have also illustrated the fact that in determining the tones of words we attempt to find relatively fixed high or low tones to serve as guides, and that in so far as possible we try to overcome any possible effects of the intonation, or at least we attempt to reckon with any changes that may be caused by intonational contours.

4.7 <u>Writing Down Sentences as the Native Informant Speaks</u>

Some missionaries seem to succeed rather well as long as informants are giving them single words or very short phrases, but they become hopelessly lost with longer expressions, and especially in writing down texts. One reason for this is that they often try to write texts too soon, that is, before they have become sufficiently familiar with the sounds and many of the meaningful parts of words. Even a highly skilled linguist would not presume that his transcriptions of a language were phonemically accurate until he had studied it intensely for at least a month or so. And even after that there are many problems which trouble the analyst for many months. Part of the solution to our difficulty is becoming more familiar with the language. However, apart from these factors, there are some details of procedure which should be noted:

1. Do not try to get every single detail the first time the native speaks a sentence. In going back over the sentence or at a later repetition, one can detect many of the mistakes made in the first transcription.

MASTERING THE SOUNDS

2. Attempt to write down the forms heard at the normal speed of utterance. It is very valuable to have an informant repeat some expressions quite slowly in order to identify all the segments (i.e., the consonants and the vowels), but our transcription should not be of the abnormally slow speech, but of the normal utterance. To write down only the very slowly uttered forms would result in our introducing many inaccuracies: transition vowels, glides, and open breaks between sounds.
3. Always print the symbols. By printing each symbol separately as we write we are much better able to identify the form. To write letters together, particularly if they include some strange phonetic symbols, may result in a great deal of ambiguity.
4. Transcribe short-hand symbols immediately. We often fall into the habit of indicating certain recurring endings and short words by some short-hand symbols. But to leave these forms untranscribed may give us some texts which are difficult to read and understand after the writing has gotten cold.
5. Practice writing down the language. As one has occasion to listen to people speak, it is a very good practice to take notes in the language. This is a means of giving us practice in writing the language and at the same time further help us in remembering and analyzing.

4.8 <u>Appropriate Gestures</u>

We are often inclined to forget that gestures (connotatively meaningful movements of arms, hands, head, and face) are very highly conventional types of expression and that almost every language community has its own special variety. It is usually easy enough to distinguish an Englishman and a Frenchman speaking together in French even when we cannot hear a thing they are saying, since their mannerisms are so different. To master a language fully means employing all the accompanying forms. In the same way that we do not consider that the extravagant gestures of some Italians are befitting American English, so the matter-of-factness of our gestures seems quite out of place in speaking Italian in many communities. The person who wants to learn Spanish really well must acquire the gestures employed in the various Spanish-speaking communities.

In some societies the use of gestures is quite different from our own. For example, among the Yaqui Indians of northern Mexico an official spokesman may be whipped by native chiefs if he pleads his cause with the gestures so customarily used by Spanish-speaking Mexicans. The Yaquis consider that the use of hands and arms in gesturing is very bad taste, and that to do so indicates that one's arguments are so weak that some such artificial devices must be employed to reenforce one's pleas.

Some missionaries have so endeared themselves to native speakers by their proficiency in using native gestures that they have elicited such comments as "Ah, you can see that he really speaks our language."

Chapter 5

5. FIGURING OUT THE FORMS

The function of a good grammar is to guide one in determining the way in which various types of forms [i.e., meaningful combinations of sounds] are used in words and sentences. The usual grammar is, however, merely an introduction to a language and treats only the more conspicuous features. It serves to guide and supplement one's own observation and learning, but it is never a substitute for one's own analysis. Of course, there are many people who speak English perfectly well and yet have never heard about a root, a suffix, a noun, or a predicate. Perhaps they are happier for the fact. But those of us who find it necessary to learn some strange language as an adult usually discover that a certain amount of critical observation and comparison (i.e., analysis) is very worth while. Rather than impairing our ability to speak the language, it may greatly aid us. However, we cannot substitute learning about a language for actual ability to use a language. Analysis then is not our goal as practical linguists but simply a very convenient tool for acquiring more rapid and accurate facility in speaking.

5.1 The Minimal Meaningful Parts of Languages

The minimal meaningful parts of languages are called "morphemes." They are the smallest elements of any utterance which have meaning. In English they may constitute words, e.g., boy, girl, cow, fish, hat, jump, or they may combine to form words, e.g., receive, deceive, boyish, fishy, hatful, jumper. The first group of words cannot be broken down into any smaller meaningful units, but the second group of words can be divided into such parts as re-, -ceive, de-, -ceive, boy, -ish, fish, -y, hat, -ful.[1] Each one of these elements is a minimal unit and hence a morpheme. Sometimes

---

[1] The hyphens indicate the points of attachment of morphemes. Forms which may occur as complete words are usually not written with hyphens.

we find a number of morphemes combined into a single word. For example, the word <u>formalizers</u> consists of five morphemes: <u>form</u>, <u>-al</u>, <u>-ize</u>, <u>-r</u>, <u>-s</u>.

5.2 Different Sizes of Words

A grammar of a language tells us how the various morphemes combine to form words and sentences. This is essentially all that a grammar consists of, but a comprehensive grammar of any language is very complicated. Naturally, some languages have more complex structures than others. For example, Navaho is much more complicated than Spanish, and Zulu is a great deal more complex than German. The Bantu languages have more extensive word-forming arrangements of morphemes than do the Sudanic languages, in which a high percentage of words are single morphemes. However, the arrangements of words into sentences in the Sudanic languages often involve many more complications than occur in most Bantu languages. Some missionaries have thought that the Bantu languages have a very complicated grammar and that the Sudanic languages have little or no grammar. This is a mistake, but their judgment is based on the fact that missionaries have automatically associated long words with complex grammar. In the practical analysis of languages we usually distinguish between the arrangements of morphemes in words, which we call "morphology," and the arrangements of words in sentences, which we call "syntax."[2] The difficulties which a language may lack by virtue of a simple morphology may often be compensated for by a complex syntax.

Languages differ greatly in the way in which they arrange and group morphemes. There are languages which we call "isolating." In these almost every morpheme constitutes a separate word.[3] Many of the Oriental languages occur in this

---

[2] In many language structures one cannot distinguish readily between morphology and syntax, as there are numerous instances of overlapping. See Eugene A. Nida, <u>Morphology</u> (Ann Arbor, University of Michigan, 1949). However, this basic division into morphology and syntax is valid for most languages and serves as a very practical guide for analysis and description.

[3] We are using "word" here in the usual traditional sense. Many of the "words" in isolating languages are phonologically dependent particles, called clitics (see section 5.8).

class, e.g., Chinese, Burmese, Black Thai, Lisu, and Nosu. Japanese and Korean, however, do not come under this classification. Many of the Sudanic languages are of the isolating language type, and among these Ngbaka, spoken in northern Congo, is rather representative. Note the following sentence:

dùŋgî tɔ̀ą̄ hą̄ą̀ na̅ ʔɛ́ kɔ̀ą̄ na̅ mò tɛ́.
"Bat said to-him that I desired that you come."

The meaning of this sentence is "The bat said to him, 'I desire you to come'." There are two morphemes in this sentence which are phonetically bound to other words: (1) -ą̄ which indicates completive action in the verbs and (2) -ą̄ which indicates a third person pronoun with certain preposition-like words.[4]

At the opposite end of the scale of languages there are those which combine many morphemes into single words. Eskimo, Quechua, and Navaho are typical examples. Note the following word in Barrow Eskimo igluḵpiyumalaaktuŋa "I am anxious to build a house for myself." This word is made up of the root iglu- "house" (cf. English borrowing igloo), -ḵpi "to cause something to be made," -yuma "to intend to do something," -laak "to be anxious about doing something," -tu "for oneself," -ŋa "I." Compare the Chanco Quechua word ñitirul^{y}awačkanña "it is indeed crushing me already," which consists of a root ñiti- "to crush," -ru an emphatic suffix, -l^{y}a "only," -wa "me," -čka continuous action, -n "it," and -ña "already."[5] In both of these languages the roots are always initial, and all the morphemes which are attached to the roots follow them. That is to say, all the bound morphemes are suffixes. In Navaho practically all the bound morphemes occurring with verbs are preposed to the roots, i.e., they are prefixes. In describing the verbs in Navaho we recognize twelve different positions. The last position is that of the root, and prefixes occur in the eleven preceding positions. The following is a list of positions, with some of the morphemes which occur in them:

---

[4]The morpheme -ą̄ indicates first person, so that hą̄ą̀ means "to me."

[5]The final particle -ña is a phonetically dependent element called a clitic.

1. Adverbial prefix: ʔá- "thus," ná- "back," naa- "around"
2. Theme prefix: dah- "to start off," ʔáłah- "together"
3. Iterative (repeated action) mode: ná- "again and again"
4. Number: da- distributive plural
5. Direct object: ši- "me," bi- third person[6] (when the subject is some other person), yi- third person (when the subject is also third person), ha-, ho- time, place
6. Deictic (pointing) prefix: ʔa- "someone, something," ǰi- third person
7. Adverbial prefix: ni- "completely," di- inceptive (i.e., beginning)
8. Tense: di- future
9. Mode: si- perfective, go- optative (i.e., hoped for), yi- progressive
10. Subject pronoun: š- "I," ni- "you (sg.)"
11. Classifiers:[7] d-, ł-, l-[8]
12. The stems, which may occur in a number of different forms, e.g., -ʔaah momentaneous imperfective (i.e., momentaneous action not completed), -ʔáh continuative imperfective (i.e., continuing action not completed), -ʔą́ perfective (completed action with regard to the present), ʔáál progressive (i.e., progressing action) and optative (i.e., hoped-for action), and ʔááh iterative (i.e., repeated action), of the stem meaning "to handle one round or bulky object."

Morphemes in all twelve positions never occur in any one word, but some words have morphemes in a number of these positions, and they combine in many very complicated ways. The following word will illustrate some of the reasons why Navaho is one of the most difficult languages in the world:

---

[6] Persons are listed as follows: first person denotes the speaker; second person, the ones spoken to; and third person, those spoken about. Some languages have a fourth person, i.e., the next third person who is spoken about.

[7] The classifiers are prefixes which arbitrarily go with various roots and which help to distinguish transitive and intransitive types of action. Transitive action is one in which the action extends to some object, and intransitive action is one in which there is no such object.

[8] There is a fourth classifier called "zero." This is a significant absence of one of the other classifiers.

FIGURING OUT THE FORMS

ńdadidoot'ááł "he will forgive you" is composed of the following forms:

1. ń- < ná- "back"[9] (position 1)
2. da- distributive plural (position 4)
3. di- inceptive (position 7)
4. doo- < di- future plus yi- progressive (positions 8, 9)
5. t' < d- classifier plus the initial glottal stop of the stem -ʔááł (position 11)
6. -ʔááł progressive stem of "to handle."

Most languages which have many bound morphemes are not restricted exclusively to suffixes or prefixes, but they usually have some of both. The Bantu languages are typical of such structures. Note the following word in Congo Swahili hatutakamupikizwa "we are not going to cause him to be hit." This consists of the following morphemes: ha- "not," tu- "we," taka- future, mu- "him," pik- stem of "to hit," -iz "to cause to,"[10] -w passive, and -a indicative mode.[11]

Just because languages are able to combine many morphemes into complex words does not mean that all their words are monstrously long. Some words are short and others long. It would be quite wrong for us to assume that we can easily classify languages into either of two categories: those with long words and those with short words, i.e., isolating or synthetic in their structure. Most languages have some characteristics of both. Eskimo and Quechua tend toward one end of the scale, and Ngbaka tends toward the other, but in between there are hundreds of different degrees of complexity in structure.

---

[9] The symbol < means "is derived from" or "comes from." The opposite symbol > means "becomes." The different forms are the result of changes which take place in morphemes. Such problems will be discussed below in section 5.6. The numbers over the morphemes indicate the relative positions 1-12.

[10] It is possible to consider the -i as a separate kind of stem-forming morpheme.

[11] This final morpheme is not quite so easily classified, but this is sufficient for our general purposes.

5.3 Discovering the Morphemes

It should be obvious to us that we cannot possibly identify all the parts of the Congo Swahili word hatutakamupikizwa "we are not going to cause him to be hit" by just looking at the one word. Furthermore, we cannot ask an informant for the meanings of the parts ha-, tu-, taka-, etc. He would be completely unable to answer such questions. The only way in which we can discover the bound morphemes of a language is to compare forms which have recurring partials, i.e., parts which are identical. To illustrate, let us examine the following list of Congo Swahili words:

1. ninasema "I speak"
2. ninapika "I hit"
3. tunapika "we hit"
4. tulipika "we have hit"
5. tutakapika "we will hit"
6. tutakapikiwa "we will be hit"
7. tutakamupika "we will hit him"
8. hatutakamupika "we will not hit him"
9. tutakapikizwa "we will cause being hit"
10. hatutakamupikizwa "we will not cause him to be hit"

By comparing the forms 1 and 2, we discover that -sem- must mean "speak" and -pik- must mean "hit."[12] What we have done is to isolate the differences in form and correlate these with the differences in meaning. Of course, we often run into difficulty, and most languages are not as easily analyzed as Congo Swahili, but the principles of procedure are essentially the same.[13] The basic part of our task is to continue comparing forms until we have discovered the minimal units which have any meaning of their own. By comparing forms 2 and 3 we discover that ni- must mean "I" and tu- "we." By comparing forms 3 and 4 we find that na- indicates present tense and li- indicates perfect tense. By comparing

---

[12] These data do not provide a way of determining the identity of the suffix -a. Some grammarians consider it a part of the stem when it is juxtaposed to the stem.

[13] For a comprehensive and detailed exposition of procedures in identifying morphemes, see Eugene A. Nida, Morphology (1949), pp. 6-60.

forms 4 and 5 we learn that taka- is the future tense morpheme. By this same procedure we go through the entire set of forms discovering the parts of words and their meanings.

The difficulty in any actual language situation is that one is not provided with a series of words so arranged that the morphemes are readily identified. Many times the morphemes change their forms, as for example, the English negative prefix which is im- when combined with possible (impossible), and in- when combined with tolerable (intolerable). We have a "feeling" that im- and in- are just the same, even though their forms are slightly different. In other cases, the morphemes are almost totally disguised in form, as in some of the Navaho morphemes cited in section 5.2.

To analyze a language in any systematic way, i.e., to observe it carefully and methodically, we need some way of sorting all the words that we get. Otherwise we are swamped with a great accumulation of details which we never seem able to understand or master. One of the best methods is to write out words on separate slips of paper for systematic filing. Such slips of paper are not only handy for memorizing and reviewing, but they can be sorted according to the various stems and according to the different prefixes and suffixes which seem to recur. We may wish to alphabetize the words, first from the beginning of the word and then from the end of the word. This enables us to discover many morphemes, which might otherwise escape our attention.

If we discover that some one morpheme appears to recur many times and that its meaning is very difficult to ascertain, we can write out a slip for each word in which this form occurs. After we have collected thirty or forty such occurrences, we can generally discover what the meaning is; or if the meaning is still doubtful, we can at least be sure of recognizing and learning the words in which the morpheme occurs.

It is often very valuable to file in separate sections those words that act like nouns and those that act like verbs. We can also make distinctions for other classes, such as adjectives, pronouns, and particles. By systematically arranging the information which we collect from informants, we can learn it more readily; and our powers of observation will be greatly increased, for we will be gathering in a single place various related forms. Anyone who does this will be amazed at what he finds and at how much fun there is in finding it. To discover a usage for oneself rivets it in the memory and makes language learning a fascinating series of discoveries about formerly strange and unusual phenomena.

Our analytical observations about some types of languages are very important, for they save us from the tedious method of memorizing paradigms. Anyone who has studied Greek or Latin remembers the boring practice of learning and reciting long sets of related forms. Of course, it was not too bad, for a Greek verb does not have much over 600 different forms, even counting the participles. But almost any Congo Swahili verb could occur in at least 5,000 different forms, and many languages have several times that many possible combinations of prefixes and suffixes with stems. If we should try to memorize paradigms consisting of thousands of forms, we would be hopelessly lost. What we need to observe are the patterns upon which the language is constructed. On the basis of these we can often construct new forms that we have never heard of before, simply by observing the way in which morphemes go together. Let us suppose, for example, that we should hear the Congo Swahili form ninalomba and learn that it means "I ask." Without much hesitation we ought to be able to construct on the basis of the forms which we have examined above the word nilimulomba, meaning "I have asked him." We would do this by noting that the subject occurs first, except where the negative prefix ha- is used. After the subject comes the tense form, and we may find li- in form 4. The object pronoun mu- occurs next to the verb stem and is found in forms 7, 8, and 10. Of course, there are possibilities that our form would be wrong; but more often than not, if we use care in following the patterns which are revealed by the language structure, we can form new expressions. In fact, our capacity to say things that we have never heard before is absolutely essential, for that is the very essence of language use, namely, employing the framework of signs (all morphemes are types of signs) to say things that we have never heard before. Only when we can do that, can we be said to be actually speaking the language.

In order to know what to look for, we need to examine briefly the various principal types of morphemes. This may be done best by noting (1) the kinds of phonemes that may make up morphemes and (2) the ways in which morphemes are related to each other. We must, however, also consider the different forms which a single morpheme may have.

5.4 The Types of Phonemes that Make up Morphemes

Morphemes are made up of segmental phonemes, suprasegmental phonemes, and combinations of segmental and suprasegmental phonemes. The segmental phonemes are the consonants and vowels of the language, i.e., the segments into which the continuum (the flow) of speech may be divided. The suprasegmental phonemes are ones which occur simultaneously with one or more segmental phonemes. Tones and stresses are suprasegmental phonemes since they do not have an independent existence apart from the segmental units with which they are combined. The intonational patterns likewise consist of suprasegmental phonemes.

Morphemes consisting of segmental phonemes are the most common. We have already examined some of these in Quechua, Eskimo, and Congo Swahili. What we are usually not so aware of are the morphemes consisting of suprasegmental phonemes. In Ngbaka the noun morphemes consist of segmental phonemes (i.e., consonants and vowels) and certain tones (see section 4.3.3.1). The verbs, however, are quite different in their structure. They are completely neutral as far as tones are concerned, for all the verbs occur with the same tones, and the tones distinguish four basic tenses or modes of action. Examine the following sets of verbs:

Present Tense	Past Tense	Future Tense	Imperative	Meaning
1. à	1a. ā	1b. ǎ·	1c. á	"to put (many things)"
2. wà	2a. wā	2b. wǎ·	2c. wá	"to clean"
3. sà	3a. sā	3b. sǎ·	3c. sá	"to call"
4. b'ĩlĩ	4a. b'ĩlĩ	4b. b'ĩlí	4c. b'ĩlí	"to cut"
5. ñɔ̀nɔ̀	5a. ñɔ̄nɔ̄	5b. ñɔ̀nɔ́	5c. ñɔ́nɔ́	"to eat"
6. yòlò	6a. yōlō	6b. yòló	6c. yóló	"to stand"

What we have in these Ngbaka verbs are six different morphemes consisting of segmental phonemes and meaning "to put, to clean, to call, to cut, to eat, to stand," and four different morphemes indicating differences of tense and mode. These are ˋ or ˋ ˋ present tense, ˉ or ˉ ˉ past tense, ˇ or ˋ ˊ

future tense, ´ or ´ ´ imperative.[14] We have combined two different tonal forms, e.g., ` and ` `, into a single morpheme because it is perfectly obvious that the differences are dependent upon whether the verbs consist of one syllable or two syllables; and since the meaning is identical in either case, we more or less instinctively unite these similar tone forms.[15]

This situation in Ngbaka is, however, not widespread. In most Sudanic languages the verbs fall into various classes, depending upon their own characteristic tones; but their tones are often modified to indicate differences of tense or differences of subject. Note the following forms in Mongbandi:

Completive Forms
with Singular Subjects

1. ŋgbò "to swim"
2. mā "to hear"
3. yó "to carry"
4. hùlù "to jump"
5. hākà "to teach"
6. sīgí "to go out"
7. dîkò "to read"

Continuative Forms
with Singular Subjects

1a. ŋgbō
2a. mā
3a. yō
4a. hùlū
5a. hàkā
6a. sìgī
7a. dìkō

The forms 1-7 are illustrative examples of seven different classes of verbs, each with its own distinctive tone. However, in the continuative forms all these verbs have identically the same tones regardless of the tones they have in the completive forms. The verbs become mid if the word is monosyllabic (one-syllable) and low-mid if the word is bisyllabic (two-syllable). We describe the morphemes 1-7 as consisting of segmental and suprasegmental phonemes. The forms 1a-7a consist of two kinds of morphemes: (1) the segmental phonemes (i.e., the consonants and the vowels) and (2) the tones, either mid or low-mid. These tones on forms 1a-7a are, however, different from the tones of the Ngbaka verbs, for the Mongbandi verb tones actually "replace" the basic tones of the verbs.

---

[14] The meanings of the four tonal morphemes are somewhat simplified but are based upon the most common usage of these verb forms.
[15] In the following section we shall discuss the scientific basis for this type of procedure.

In some languages the tonal changes are very complex, and a number of minimal tone contrasts may occur. For example, in Kpelle, a three-register tone language of Liberia, one encounters the following series of forms containing the second person pronoun ka and the verb stem pa:
 ká pá "and you (pl.) come"   ká pā "you (pl.) came"
 kā pá "come!"   kā pā "you (pl.) come"
 kà pá "you (pl.) have come" kà pà "if you (pl.) come"

In English morphemes such as man, boy, girl, go, and jump consist of segmental phonemes and also a suprasegmental phoneme of stress. The constituent parts of such a morpheme as man /mǽn/ are the consonants and vowels /mæn/ and the primary stress /´/. Some morphemes in English have a secondary stress, e.g., the re- /rìy-/ in recover, meaning "to put a cover on again." This re- differs from the re- /riy-/ in recover, meaning "to get well." In English we may distinguish four different degrees of stress which may involve particular morphemes: primary stress /´/, secondary stress /ˋ/, zero (a significant absence of) stress / / (unmarked), and contrastive stress, e.g., the typical contrast on the first syllables of the nouns in the expression "emigration not immigration." This contrastive stress may be marked as /´´/, but both this stress and the phrase stress, mentioned in section 4.3.3.2, must be considered primarily as intonational.

5.5   Different Forms of Single Morphemes

We have already mentioned how morphemes do not always have the same form. For example, as we noted, one negative prefix in English occurs as im- in impossible, but as in- in intolerable. We rather assume that this is the same minimal element in English though we may not at first be able to explain just how this is so. A little observation, however, soon reveals that the im- form, ending in a bilabial nasal, occurs before the bilabial consonant p of possible, and the in- form, ending in an alveolar nasal, occurs before the alveolar stop t of tolerable. After having discovered the conditions which "govern" the differences between im- and -in, the formal discrepancies do not seem to be significant.

We use as a definition of a morpheme the statement formulated by Bloomfield, "A linguistic form which bears no partial phonetic-semantic resemblance to any other form is ...a morpheme."[16] This is a kind of negative definition, but it enables us to group together under a single morpheme different, but related forms. Of course, where a morpheme has the same form in every occurrence and always has the same meaning, e.g., the suffix -er: player, walker, runner, dancer, jumper, there is no difficulty. But sometimes we encounter wide differences of form. For example, in English the unstressed indefinite article, which we write either as a or an, has the phonemic forms /ə/ and /æn/. However, the form a /ə/ occurs only before words beginning with a consonant, e.g., a man, and the form an /æn/ occurs only before words beginning with a vowel, e.g., an ape. Nevertheless, we consider that the two forms /ə/ and /æn/ belong to the same morpheme, for the distribution of these different forms (i.e., their occurrence with other morphemes) can be described in terms of the phonological surroundings, in this case, the type of following phonemes. When there is more than one form of a morpheme, we may call each form an allomorph.[17]

Morphemes are very frequently "conditioned" by the phonological forms of the morphemes which surround them. This occurs in the following words of Tepehua, a language of central Mexico:

ki·mpay "my father"
ki·ŋkin "my aunt"
ki·ntukay "my namesake"
ki·šapu "my soap"

The allomorph ki·m- occurs before words beginning with a bilabial stop consonant. The allomorph ki·ŋ- occurs before words beginning with a velar stop consonant. The allomorph ki·n- occurs before words beginning with a dental stop consonant, and the allomorph ki· occurs before words beginning with a continuant. We may describe the distribution of these

---

[16] Leonard Bloomfield, *Language* (New York: Henry Holt and Co., 1933), p. 161.

[17] The different sounds which combine to make up a phoneme are called allophones, and so by analogy, we use the term allomorph to designate the different forms which make up a single morpheme.

FIGURING OUT THE FORMS 165

four allomorphs purely on the basis of their phonological surroundings. In such instances, we may write such a morpheme as /ki·m- ~ ki·ŋ- ~ ki·n- ~ ki·-/. The wavy lines symbolize the fact that the allomorphs have phonologically defined distributions.

In some instances forms seem to be exasperatingly complex and without rhyme or reason, while in reality there is some underlying regularity about them. Compare, for example, the following sets of forms in Ngbaka:

1. lì "water"
2. zɔ̰ "nose"
3. nṵ "world"
4. kò "money"
5. lī "name"
6. gā "boat"
7. zḛ̄ "smoke"
8. lē "village"
9. lí "face"
10. ŋgbá "slave"
11. tɔ̀kɔ́ "blood"
12. fàlà "place"
13. zɛ̀kɛ̀ "moon"
14. tūlū "piece of cloth"
15. mbē·tī "letter"
16. fɛ̄lɛ̄ "string"
17. kólò "rain"
18. yélè "buffalo"
19. kùtū "fog"
20. vǔ·và "mosquito"

1a. lì· gɛ̀ "this water"
2a. zɔ̰æ[18] gɛ̀ "this nose"
3a. nṵī gɛ̀ "this world"
4a. kòē gɛ̀ "this money"
5a. lī· gɛ̀ "this name"
6a. gǣ· gɛ̀ "this boat"
7a. zḛ̄· gɛ̀ "this smoke"
8a. lē· gɛ̀ "this village"
9a. lí· gɛ̀ "this face"
10a. ŋgbǽ· gɛ̀ "this slave"
11a. tɔ̀kɔ́æ gɛ̀ "this blood"
12a. fælǣ· gɛ̀ "this place"
13a. zɛ̄kɛ̄· gɛ̀ "this moon"
14a. túlí· gɛ̀ "this piece of cloth"
15a. mbé·tí· gɛ̀ "this letter"
16a. fɛ́lɛ́· gɛ̀ "this string"
17a. kólé· gɛ̀ "this rain"
18a. yélé· gɛ̀ "this buffalo"
19a. kùtí· gɛ̀ "this fog"
20a. vǔ·vǣ· gɛ̀ "this mosquito"

The form of the nouns which occur before gɛ̀ "this"[19] seem to be very highly irregular, and it might appear that each word would have to be memorized separately. That is to say, it would seem that we could not predict what the combining forms (1a-20a) would be from knowing the basic forms 1-20. However, these discrepancies are not as great as they

---

[18] The vowel æ is limited to certain Ngbaka dialects. The types of vowel reductions differ slightly from one dialect to another.

[19] The same forms occur before other attributives, including certain possessives.

might at first appear. If we examine what happens to the tones we will discover the following regular changes:

1. ˋ > ˍ
2. ‑ > ˊ
3. ˊ > ˊ
4. ˋˋ > ‑ ‑
5. ‑ ‑ > ˊˊ
6. ˊˋ > ˊˊ
7. ˋ‑ > ˋˊ
8. ˇˋ > ˇˊ [20]

Once we have gathered together all these tonal changes and listed them, they do not appear to be as "irrational" as we might have thought at first. The resultant tones are either higher or have a rising glide.

The changes which occur in the vowels are slightly more complicated, but still we can discover some parallelisms in the changes. Note the following:

1. i > i·
2. e > e·
3. ɛ > ɛ·
4. a > æ· (including a in the first syllable of bisyllabic words)
5. u > i· if a dissyllabic word, but > ui if a monosyllabic word.
6. o > e· if a dissyllabic word, but > oe if a monosyllabic word.
7. ɔ > ɔæ

There are certain important features about these changes:
1. The resultant vowels are all long or consist of two vowels (diphthongs).
2. The added element is a kind of front vowel. Note that æ is further front than a, and the o is fronted to e·.

We learn from another dialect that the basic form of the suffix is -e and the tone of the morpheme tends to be higher than the preceding word or to raise the tone of the preceding word. What at first may have appeared to be completely irrelevant and unrelated types of changes can be resolved into some rather simple rules. If we make such comprehensive

---

[20] Type 8 is like 6, with an extra initial low tone, which does not change.

FIGURING OUT THE FORMS

observations as these, we save ourselves a great deal of time in learning the language and improve our facility as well as our accuracy in speaking the language.

In this Ngbaka data we may say that the various allomorphs of the morpheme -e are phonologically defined. By that we mean that the particular ending which occurs on the word may be predicted on the basis of the basic form of the word. However, it is sometimes easier for us simply to list the various resultant forms than to attempt to describe all the various allomorphs. The important thing is to organize one's observations in an effort to describe whatever regular patterns the language may possess.

In many instances the distribution of the different allomorphs of a morpheme cannot be described in terms of phonological surroundings. For example, the plural of box is boxes /báksəz/ and the plural of ox is oxen /áksən/. There is nothing about the phonemes of box and ox which will give us any clue as to what plural ending to use. The only way to describe the distribution of these allomorphs /-əz/ and /-ən/ is to identify the morphemes with which they occur. There are some other words that have no suffix at all in the plural, e.g., sheep, trout, salmon. This significant absence of a suffix can be called a zero allomorph. The allomorphs, e.g., /-əz/, /-ən/, and zero (symbolized as -0), whose distribution is only definable in terms of the morphemes with which they occur, may be called morphologically defined allomorphs, and their relationship may be symbolized by the use of the infinity sign, e.g., /-əz ∞ -ən ∞ - 0/. The plural formations in English are complicated by the fact that some of the allomorphs have phonologically defined distributions (i.e., their occurrences are governed by the surrounding phonemes) and others have morphologically defined distributions (i.e., their occurrences are governed by the surrounding morphemes). For example, boxes /báksəz/ occurs with /-əz/, but deeds and bones have the forms /dídz/ and /bównz/,[21] and the words tops and bats have the forms /táps/ and /bæts/. If we examine all the words in English which occur with this s-plural suffix, we find that the allomorph /-əz/ occurs after phonemes which are sibilants

---

[21] In a phonemic transcription of English the phonetically consonantal off-glides [y] and [w] become full consonants.

(s-like sounds): /s, z, š, ž/, or have sibilant off-glides: /č, ǰ/; the allomorph /-z/ occurs after all nonsibilant voiced phonemes; and the allomorph /-s/ occurs after all nonsibilant voiceless phonemes. This means that some of the allomorphs, namely, /-əz, -z, -s/, have phonologically defined distributions, and their relationships may be symbolized as /-əz ~ -z ~ -s/. However, these allomorphs differ from the allomorph /-ən/ (as in oxen /áksən/) and from the zero allomorph /-0/ (as in sheep, trout, salmon). We may indicate all of these relationships as /(-əz ~ -z ~ -s) ∞ -ən ∞ -0/.

All this may seem unnecessarily complicated; and for us who speak English as a mother-tongue, such descriptions of minute details may appear to be quite irrelevant for the person who is learning to speak our language. In fact, one may contend that when we are speaking we have no time to think about such minutiae. That is all very true. Our use of a language must be automatic, but a little objective analysis may give us greater insight into a language and aid us immensely in understanding the real value of thorough study. For example, one missionary had translated a Gospel into a language and was reading it to the people for their approval. They seemed to understand the narrative satisfactorily, but some of the natives inquired as to why the disciples and Jesus swore at each other all of the time. The missionary assured the people that such was not the case, but the natives were unconvinced. The missionary had failed to observe the native language usage carefully and had not considered many troublesome little morphemes because he had regarded them as relatively unimportant. The truth was that he had failed to appreciate the use of certain so-called "honorific" morphemes, which were used to indicate that the speakers had respect for those to whom they spoke. Failing to use such forms gave the impression that the characters of the Gospel narrative were speaking disrespectfully to and of each other.

This book is not designed to introduce one to the techniques of critical analysis, but any student of a language will be helped if he realizes that different forms which appear to have the same meaning may be grouped together if the distribution of these different forms may be described on the basis of (1) the different kinds of phonemes in the environment or (2) the different morphemes with which they occur.

5.6 Types of Morphemes

There are many different ways in which we may classify morphemes. One of the most important is the distinction between roots, the basic cores of words, and the bound morphemes which are added to them. In a word such as formalizer there is a root form- and three nonroots. We usually find at least one root in each word, and we may encounter words that are made up of more than one root. For example, compounds are words containing more than one root, e.g., greenhouse, blackbird, he-goat, bittersweet, upstart, and breakwater.

We sometimes wish to distinguish between roots and stems. All roots when they occur in combination with nonroots (except the last structurally added nonroot) constitute stems, but stems may include more than just a simple root. For example, in the Congo Swahili words which we discussed in section 5.3, we would say that the roots were -sem- "to speak" and -pik- "to hit," but the word "stem" could be applied to any form containing the root but which was not a complete form, e.g., for the first word we could say that -sema, and -nasema were both stems. The form ninasema "I speak" is not a stem since other nonroots are not added to this combination.

In addition to the distinctions between roots and nonroots (primarily a matter of distribution), we need to recognize certain other differences between morphemes based upon the relationship of morphemes to each other. The principal distinctions are between additive, replacive, and subtractive morphemes.

Additive morphemes are the most common. These include roots, affixes, and reduplicatives. We call these morphemes "additive" because they are added to one another. For example, we have already noted in this section how roots may be added to roots, e.g., blackbird, kingfish, bellhop, and in the illustrative data from Eskimo and Quechua (see section 5.2) we indicated the way in which suffixes were added to roots. Congo Swahili illustrates how both prefixes and suffixes are added to roots. There are, however, more additive morphemes than just prefixes and suffixes. We also encounter infixes and suprafixes. Infixes are morphemes that are inserted within the root. For example, in Tzeltal, a Mayan language of southern Mexico, there is a morpheme -h- which is infixed in the root and which makes an intransitive verb out of a transitive one. Compare the following verbs: kuhč "to endure" < -kuč' "to carry," k'ehp "to clear (as of the weather)" <-k'ep "to clear away," wihk' "to awake" < -wik' "to open (the eye)."[22]

In the Semitic languages, infixes are very common. In Hebrew, for example, the roots usually consist of three consonants (called the "radicals"), and the vowels which are inserted are the infixes. Compare the following Egyptian Arabic words: katab "he wrote," ka·tib "writing (person)," and kita·b "book" from the stem *ktb,[23] and galas "he sat," ga·lis "sitting (person)" from the stem *gls.[24]

On the whole, infixes are much rarer than prefixes and suffixes, but they occur frequently enough to cause considerable trouble at times.

Suprafixes are morphemes which consist of suprasegmental phonemes and which are added to some root or stem. These were illustrated by the Ngbaka verbs cited in section 5.4. The intonational patterns of a language should also be regarded as made up of suprafixal morphemes.

Reduplicative morphemes are not readily illustrated in English though we do have some features which closely resemble them. For example, we often repeat a root, e.g., tut-tut, choo-choo, put-put. In some languages such roots may be repeated three or four times, e.g., in San Blas mu·a means "to rise and fall gradually," while mu·amu·amu·a means "to rise and fall rapidly," as of small ripples in the water. These types of words, however, can best be described as consisting of repetitions of the same root. In this sense they are special kinds of compounds. Reduplicatives may be illustrated by the following words in Hausa:[25]

---

[22] Marianna C. Slocum, "Tzeltal (Mayan) Noun and Verb Morphology," International Journal of American Linguistics, Vol. 14, No. 2, p. 83.

[23] A star indicates a nonexistent form in actual speech but one which we may abstract by the process of analysis.

[24] L. Bloomfield, Language (New York: Henry Holt and Co., 1933), p. 243.

[25] Carleton T. Hodge, Hausa (Baltimore: Linguistic Society of America 1947), p. 39.

FIGURING OUT THE FORMS

Reduplicated Stems	Simple Stems
1. gaggawsʔaa "a brittle one"	1a. gawčʔii "brittleness"
2. tàttawraa "a tough person"	2a. tawrii "toughness"
3. mùmmuunaa "an ugly person"	3a. muunìi "ugliness"

In these words we are not concerned with the suffixes -aa and -ii, which designate objects and qualities, but rather with the fact that the initial consonant and the following vowel of the root (as shown in 1a-3a) are repeated. We could say that the initial C_1V_2[26] cluster of the root becomes $C_1V_2C_1C_1V_2$ in the reduplicated portion.

In Tojolabal, a Mayan language of southern Mexico, the reduplication may occur at the end of the word. Compare -setet "to go around and around" with -set "to go around," and -timim "to lightning" with -tim "to spread out."

In some instances a reduplicated portion of the root or stem is repeated with some other characteristic phonemes. For example, in Greek the reduplicated verbs in the perfect tense occur with the vowel /e/. Compare the following:

Reduplicated Perfects	Basic Stems
1. leluka "I have loosed"	1a. lu·- "to loose"
2. bebouleuka "I have considered"	2a. bouleu- "to consider"
3. gegrapʰa "I have written"	3a. graphʰ- "to write"
4. dedu·ka "I have made enter"	4a. du·- "to make enter"

In some instances one encounters a very extensive reduplication designed to emphasize a word. For example, in Kipsigis, a Nilo-Hamitic language of Kenya, the word áčìčá "no" may be reduplicated with as many as five to ten different repetitions of the medial syllable čì, e.g., áčìčìčìčìčìčìčìčìčìča. In the medial reduplication of kàřàřàn "good" the syllables with flap /ř/ are modified to kàr̄::::àn, in which the trilled /r̄/ has the duration of several syllables.

Reduplicatives are very special types of additives in that they consist of adding to the stem a part of the stem, with or without some additional phonemes not included in the stem.

---

[26] The subscript numerals designate the phonemes in order.

Replacive morphemes, as their name implies, replace parts of other morphemes. These are abundantly illustrated in English. For example, the plural of tooth /túwθ/ is teeth /tíyθ/.[27] The pluralizing morpheme in this instance consists in replacing the syllabic part of tooth /túwθ/ with the replacive morpheme /iy/. We may symbolize this type of morpheme as /iy ← uw/. The arrow reads "replaces." We also have a rather common replacive morpheme in such verbs as sheathe, wreathe, teethe, save, strive, thieve, advise, and house, which we describe as derived from the nouns sheath, wreath, teeth, safe, strife, thief, advice, and house. Note that the nouns end in /θ, f, s/, but the verbs end in /d, v, z/. We may describe this kind of change as consisting of the replacive morpheme /(d←θ) ~ (v←f) ~ (z←s)/. The wavy symbol indicates that the particular change which takes place depends upon the phonological character of the forms.

Replacive morphemes may be very extensive in a language, and in many instances they are very irregular in formation. We have already noted some replacive morphemic changes involving suprasegmental phonemes in the Mongbandi verb forms (see section 5.4). We also find many replacive morphemes in the Nilotic languages. Examine the following three words of Shilluk:

Singular Forms   Plural Forms   Singular Combinative Forms[28]
1. wāt "house"   1a. wàt "houses"   1b. wán "... house"
2. yīt "ear"   2a. yìt "ears"   2b. yín "...ear"
3. tūk "chin"   3a. tùk "chins"   3b. túŋ "... chin"

Note that in the plural of these words the replacive morpheme is a tone lower than the tone on the singular stem. In the combinative forms, there are two replacives: (1) a high tone and (2) a replacement of the final stop consonant by a nasal continuant made at the same point of articulation. From other forms such as singular kwàm "chair" and combinative kwám, we learn that the replacive tone for the combinative is a tone higher than the singular tone, even as the replacive tone for the plural is a tone lower than the singular tone.

---

[27] We may also say that teeth has a zero suffixal plural in the same way that sheep, trout, and salmon do.

[28] These are special forms which occur in certain combinations with postposed modifiers.

FIGURING OUT THE FORMS 173

In the same way that the addition of elements to basic forms may denote some meaning, so the subtraction of some portion of the basic forms may be meaningful. A distinctive loss of this type is called a subtractive morpheme. We can best illustrate this by French. Compare the following words:

Feminine Forms	Masculine Forms (before consonants)	
1. /movɛz/ mauvaise	1a. /movɛ/ mauvais	"bad"
2. /ptit/ petite	2a. /pti/ petit	"little"
3. /grą̃d/ grande	3a. /grą̃/ grand	"big"
4. /fos/ fausse	4a. /fo/ faux	"false"
5. /sul/ soûle	5a. /su/ soûl	"drunk"
6. /frɛš/ fraîche	6a. /frɛ/ frais	"fresh"

If we describe the spelling of these words, we of course must discuss the addition of the -e to the feminine forms. But linguistic analysis is not concerned with spelling. If that were the case, we would be entangled in all kinds of contradictions. What we must describe are the actual pronunciations. To do this, we could assume that the masculine forms were the roots and that various consonants were added to them in order to form the feminine adjectives. This type of description would be very complicated, and the rules would be long and involved. We can simplify the description ever so much if we assume that the feminine forms represent the roots (or stems, as the case may be) and that a subtractive morpheme of the final consonant forms the masculine series.

5.7   Determining the Extent of Words

Determining just how much to write as a single word in a strange language is not as easy as it might appear. People do not speak in word units, but in phrase units; therefore we cannot depend upon the hesitations in the informant's speech to decide what is a word and what is less than a word. The ultimate solution to many of these difficulties of writing a language can only be found by a thorough scientific analysis,[29] but there are three "rules of thumb" which may help to guide our investigation and ultimate analysis.

---

[29]These problems are fully discussed in Eugene A. Nida, Morphology (Ann Arbor; University of Michigan Press, 1949).

1. A form which is used in isolation is likely to constitute a word and should be written as a separate item, unless, of course, it occurs as a part of a compound. We can not depend upon the meaning of a form in another language to give us any satisfactory clue. For example, carpenter is a single word in English, but the equivalent in some African languages is literally "he who builds houses." This phrase is syntactically just like any other so-called relative clause, and because it is translated by a single word in English is no guarantee that it should be written as a single word in another language.
2. A form for which informants can readily give the meaning when it is spoken in isolation is probably a word. For example, in Congo Swahili ninamupika "I hit him" would be found to be a word, for informants could not readily give the meanings of the parts ni-, na-, or mu-. They might be able to give the meaning of -pika because of its occurrence in many forms and because their attention would be drawn to this meaning by the discussion of the various combinations and elements. One convenient factor in Congo Swahili is that each word is accented on the next to the last syllable. This provides us with a very helpful phonetic rule. This is not true, however, of all Bantu languages, for the emphasized vowel (long and with stress) that occurs in many Bantu languages marks the next to the last vowel of a phrase and not necessarily the next to the last syllable of each word.
3. Forms that are freely movable tend to be words. For example, the English word of would rarely be spoken alone, and native speakers might have much difficulty in explaining its meaning, but of is freely movable. It occurs before all types of words, e.g., adverbs, of very poor people; adjectives, of fine garments; articles, of the people; nouns, of John; pronouns, of me. In addition it follows all types of words. Usually the word of is phonetically dependent upon the following word or words, but it may have its own stress, e.g., óf the people, bý the people, and fór the people. Though of is generally a clitic (see Chapter 6 for a discussion of such forms), it has the syntactic "movability" of a word and should

FIGURING OUT THE FORMS 175

be written as a separate item in a practical orthography.[30]

4. Phonologically bound forms which are syntactically equivalent to full words are clitics, and they should be written as full words unless they are phonologically syllabified as an integral portion of the preceding or following word or unless the placement of stress is dependent upon their incorporation in the "word." For example, the unstressed indefinite article a /ə/ is phonologically bound to the following word or words. Note that a board and aboard are phonologically identical /əbówrd/. However, the clitic a is syntactically equivalent[31] to words which may be pronounced in isolation. Compare the following series of forms: this man, that man, some man, one man, a man. The fact that a occurs in the same types of syntactic constructions in which words such as this, that, some, and one occur means that we should treat a as a syntactically significant form (a clitic), and should write it as a separate word in a practical orthography.

In some instances, we do not write clitics as separate words because they may be integrally syllabified with a preceding or following form. For example, in Maya there are three clitics -oʔ "that," -aʔ "this," and -eʔ "identified object," which occur final to noun phrases preceded by le. However, these clitics are always syllabified with the preceding words, which invariably

---

[30] In these features a practical orthography differs from a strictly scientific type of writing. In a scientific treatment we attempt to represent in so far as possible the basic phonological features of the language. That is to say, we are describing the speech patterns in terms of their fundamental acoustic-auditory contrasts. In writing a language, however, we must deal with visual factors, which are in many ways quite different. The ear takes in the entire stream of utterance and segments them automatically into meaningful components, but the eye is often assisted in selecting meaningful units (i.e., words and clitics) by having them isolated graphically on paper.

[31] By "syntactically equivalent" we mean that the word occurs in the same positions and with the same kinds of expressions.

end in a consonant, e.g., le ški ʔičpan šč'upa ʔ "this pretty woman" and le šk'aak'as šč'upo ʔ "that bad woman." Since the final clitics are never pronounced in isolation, and since they are always syllabified with the preceding consonants, it has been found practical to write them with the preceding words. In Quechua the postposed clitics (see section 6.1) are written as part of the preceding word, for the stress of the word as a whole occurs on the next to the last syllable of the full unit which includes these clitics.

At first the new missionary is almost always in a quandary as to just what to do about writing certain troublesome forms, but often such problems resolve themselves after one studies the language more. The problem may be very adequately solved by observing whether forms always go with just one set of words, for example, nouns or verbs, or whether they are freely movable in the sentence. Furthermore, one will find that natives who have been taught to write exhibit a great deal of similarity in the manner in which they combine or fail to combine morphemes. Of course, they tend to be somewhat inconsistent, but the primary distinctions between those forms which are words and those forms which are parts of words will usually be indicated by the manner in which native speakers tend to write their own language. Naturally, if they have been drilled in one particular manner of writing, they will reflect that system. To obtain any valid results from natives' writing habits, one must not be dogmatic during the process of teaching people to read and write.

5.8   The Parts of Speech

We are so accustomed to thinking of nouns, verbs, adjectives, pronouns, adverbs, conjunctions, prepositions, and interjections that we just assume that all languages have these types of words. Furthermore, we assume that if they have pronouns, they probably have relative, interrogative, adjectival, personal, and demonstrative pronouns. Such assumptions are very wrong indeed. The Indo-European languages, of which English is one, are unusual among languages for the relatively large number of different kinds of words, i.e., parts of speech. Many languages get along quite well with fewer.

FIGURING OUT THE FORMS

For example, Turkish has three principal types: nouns, verbs, and some dependent particles (clitics).[32] In most Bantu languages there are nouns, verbs, independent pronouns, attributives, and particles. The Mayan languages have substantially the same number of classes of words. In Marshallese there are three types of words: (1) possessed and possessible words, (2) unpossessible words, and (3) pronouns, which substitute for words of the first two classes.

Even the difference in the number of classes of words is not as great as the contrast in the ways in which such classes are used. For example, in the Mayan languages most of the words which we would think of as conjunctions and prepositions are actually possessed nouns. For example, in Maya Pedro yetel Juan[33] "Peter and John" means literally "Peter his-withness John." The word yetel consists of a noun stem -etel "withness" plus the third person singular possessive prefix y-. In Kekchi, a Mayan language of Guatemala, the word čigwu "before me" consists of a particle či- "at," plus the possessive pronoun gw- "my," plus the noun -u "face." In Marshallese a typical sentence such as e-bat am jerabal "you work slowly," literally means "it-is-slow property-your work."[34] This sentence consists of the pronoun e- "it," the unpossessible word bat "slow," a possessed stem a- "property," -m "your," and jerabal, an unpossessible word meaning "work."

In beginning to study another language we must not think of words in terms of their English or Latin formal equivalents. Each language has a system of its own, and we can learn to speak it best if we recognize this fact. What counts are the forms which the language actually exhibits.

5.9 The Categories Expressed by Bound Forms

It is utterly impossible in an introductory book of this nature to discuss all, or even the major, categories expressed

---

[32] C. F. Voegelin and M. E. Ellinghausen, "Turkish Structure," Journal of the American Oriental Society, Vol. 63, No. 1 (1943), pp. 34-65.

[33] The proper names are in their Spanish forms.

[34] Robert A. Hall, Jr., Leave Your Language Alone (Ithaca, New York: Modern Language Department, Cornell University, 1948), p. 63.

by bound forms in various languages. We must, however, point out some of the more common and also some of the unusual formations (i.e., strange to us as English speakers). Also we need to indicate some of the apparently contradictory features of some languages.

Categories are classificatory divisions indicated by various formations. We are accustomed to some of these in English, e.g., tenses in the verbs, number (singular vs. plural) in nouns, and case (subject vs. object) in six pronouns: I, we, she, he, they, who vs. me, us, her, him, them, whom. As long as languages have the same distinctions as we have, we do not have trouble; but when the categories are somewhat different, we may become badly confused. For example, in many languages there is a difference between an inclusive first person plural, which includes those spoken to, and an exclusive first person plural, which excludes those spoken to. One missionary was preaching in such a language on the theme, "We have all sinned and come short of the glory of God." However, he used the exclusive first person plural. What he was saying was simply that he and his friends, not including those he was speaking to, were all sinners. Since in that area white men had a reputation for lying and deceiving the people, the natives could well realize that such was true, but they could not understand why the missionary would go to such trouble to travel so far to tell the people that he and his associates were sinners. It all seemed entirely too evident.

In some instances certain categories are expressed by classes of words with which we do not normally associate such meanings. For example, in Mongbandi the tenses (times of action) are indicated by tones on the pronouns. The first person pronouns mbi "I" and ?e "we" have low tones in the past tense, mid tones in the present, and high tones in the future. In Hupa the nouns may indicate differences in tense:[35]

    xonta "house now existing" (present tense)
    xontaneen "house formerly existing (i.e., in ruins)" (past tense)
    xontate "house that will exist (i.e., not yet built)" (future tense)

---

[35] Robert A. Hall, Jr., Leave Your Language Alone, (Ithaca, New York: Modern Language Department, Cornell University, 1948), p. 154.

The following categories are some of the most common:[36]
1. Possession
2. Definite vs. indefinite
3. Number (singular, dual, plural).[37]
4. Person: first (the speaker), second (those spoken to), third (those spoken about).[38]
5. Location, e.g., near the speaker, near the one spoken to, remote from either.
6. Value, e.g., the forms in Korean which distinguish between words addressed to a superior, to an equal, or to an inferior.
7. Shape, the classification of objects as to "long and slender," "flat and round," "angular," "spherical," etc.[39]
8. Gender: masculine, feminine, and neuter.
9. Grammatical cases, e.g., subject forms, object forms, and attributive forms.
10. Tense, e.g., past, present, future, remote past, and remote future.
11. Aspect (the kind of action), e.g., momentaneous (action covering a short period of time), continuative (action which continues), repetitive (repeated action), habituative (habitual action), completive (completed action), and incompletive (uncompleted action).
12. Voice (the relationship of the participants to the action), e.g., active (the subject performing the action), passive (the subject being the goal of the action), reflexive (the subject acting upon himself), reciprocal (the subjects acting upon each other), transitive (an action involving an object), intransitive (an action not involv-

---

[36] For a fuller list, with some illustrative data, see Eugene A. Nida, Morphology (Ann Arbor, Michigan: University of Michigan, 1949).

[37] A few languages distinguish a trial, i.e., three objects.

[38] Some languages distinguish a fourth person, i.e., the second third person to be introduced into a context, e.g., in "John hit the man, and he hit him back," the subject he would be translated by a fourth person.

[39] Such classifications exist in Tarascan nouns and to an extent in verb forms of Navaho.

ing an object), and causative (the subject causing an action).
13. Mode (the psychological atmosphere of an action as interpreted by the speaker), e.g., indicative (indicating neutral attitudes), optative (indicating hope), desiderative (indicating desire), interrogative, negative, dubitative (indicating doubt), potential (indicating possibility), conditional (indicating a conditioned occurrence), and subjunctive (indicating the contingent character of the action).

Critical observations about morphemes and the ways in which they combine to form words can be very helpful to one learning a language. Such analyses are especially valuable to a person who wishes to translate anything into an aboriginal language. However, one must not substitute knowing about a language for actually knowing the language. Analytical procedures are basic helps, but for the missionary they are not ends in themselves. Nevertheless, they will enable a speaker to avoid many errors and make it possible for him to progress very rapidly in the mastery of otherwise troublesome formations.

Chapter 6

6. PUTTING WORDS TOGETHER

Many missionaries master the difficult forms of words, at least those which recur most frequently, but some never seem to learn how to put words together into natural phrases. They use the foreign words, but the syntax (i.e., the order and arrangement of words) is completely English. Even with a rather decent pronunciation we often betray our English background by the "translationisms" that crop out in our speech. These foreignisms are even more conspicuous in formal translations, and especially so in many missionary translations of the Bible. One always feels a certain reluctance about modifying the grammatical form of the Scriptures for fear of being guilty of interpretive renderings and paraphrases. As a result, some translators have been doggedly literal. In one instance the translators in an African language followed the King James Version with such word-for-word consistency that almost anyone could pick out the corresponding native words even though he did not know the native language. The translation was practically an interlinear rendition. However, to make things worse, other missionaries translating into the same language followed the French Segond Version with almost the same literalism when they were translating the Old Testament. No native language should ever be made to follow the literal wording of another language, for each language has its own distinct syntax, just as it has its own peculiar sounds and types of words.

It is true that wrong pronunciations tend to mark us most conspicuously as foreigners, but awkward word order and syntactically incorrect constructions can be even more irritating to the cultured native speaker. This is especially true in languages where the people take great pride in the literary or rhetorical capacities of their language. This is true, for example, in many parts of the Orient, but also among such historically nonliterate peoples as the Zulus of South Africa, the Zapotecs of the Isthmus of Tehuantepec, and the San Blas Indians of Panama.

6.1 Different Syntactic Systems

We must recognize that all languages have their own systems of putting words together. We may compare, for example, the literal translations of John 3:16 in German, Spanish, and Yipounou (a Bantu language of Gabon).

German (Luther's)

Also	hat	Gott	die	Welt	geliebt,	dass	er
Therefore	has	God	the	world	loved	that	he

seinen	eingeborenen	Sohn	gab,	auf	dass	alle,
his	one-born	Son	gave,	on	that	all

die	an	ihn	glauben,	nicht	verloren	werden,
who	on	him	believe,	not	lost	be

sondern	das	ewige	Leben	haben.
but	the	eternal	life	have.

Spanish (Hispano-Americana)

Porque	de	tal	manera	amó[1]	Dios	al[2]
For	of	such	manner	loved-he	God	to-the

mundo,	que	dió[1]	a[3]	su	Hijo	unigenito,	para
world,	that	gave-he	to	his	Son	one-born,	for

que	todo	aquel	que	en	él	cree,[1]	no
that	all	who	that	in	him	believe-he,	not

se[4]	pierda,	sino	que	tenga[1]	vida	eterna.
himself	lose-he,	but	that	have-he	life	eternal.

---

[1] The verbs contain in their endings a substitute for the subject pronoun.

[2] This is a contraction of *a* "to" and *el* "the." See footnote 3.

[3] This use of the preposition *a* "to" (see also the occurrence indicated in footnote 2) only marks the direct object of the verb when it is a person or a personalized object.

[4] The reflexive pronoun *se* in this type of construction is equivalent to a passive without an agent, e.g., "be lost."

Yipounou

Mu	mbari	Nzambi	amaronda	butamba	nana	rie
In	cause	God	he-loved	world	such	that

amavega	Muana	andi	divingu,	iri		wotsu
he-gave	Son	his	only	in order that		all

emuvayili		yitu	agobungu,			tumba
he-him-make-to		faith	he-not-destroyed-be,			but

oba	na	monyu	umutumbu	na	mutumbu.
he-be	with	life	ever	with	ever.

Even with this brief introduction to some of the differences in the way in which languages put words together, it should be obvious that learning the framework of sentences is every bit as important as learning the framework of words. In fact, in many ways sentence structure is much more important and more difficult to master. Native speakers can readily correct our mistakes in word forms, but they are often at a loss to know just how to help us untangle our awkward sentences. In no language are all the words rigidly restricted to just one possible order. It is this freedom of choice which is often our undoing, for we do not recognize the limits of choice; and since there is a measure of freedom, we begin to think that the natives put their words together in just any way. To illustrate some of the differences between languages with an isolating structure and those with very long involved words, we may note the contrasts which occur in the following texts, one from Ngbaka, a Sudanic language, and the other from the Chanco dialect of Quechua.

Ngbaka

dùŋgì	ʔɔ́[5]	ŋgɔ́	tè	nɛ̀	ʔà	kīfī	zūà
Bat	slept	up-in	tree	and	he	turned	head-his

dɛ́	nù	nɛ̀	tɔ̰̄ā̰	hā̰	dùŋgì	nā̰	ʔɛ́	kɔ̰̀ā̰
to	ground	and	said	to-him	bat	that	I	desired

---

[5] The tone of this verb is changed by the following word.

nā mò⁶ té.⁷ kó lē dé⁷ tòā dó·
that you (sg.) come. Thus we make house with

mɔ̄. kó dùŋgì tɔ̰̄ā̰ nā gɔ̄ ʔέ dὲ·⁸ sέ
you (sg.). Thus bat said that not I make will

tòā dó· mɔ̄.
house with you (sg.).

A free translation would be as follows: "A bat slept up in a tree and turned his head to the ground. The ground said to the bat, 'I wish you would come. Then we could make a home together.' Then the bat said, 'No, I will never make a home with you'."

Quechua (Chanca dialect)

učwilʸa, imatam wilʸawanki? xakučikyá
"Uchwilla, what tell-me-you? Come-we-then

ayqekunančikpaq čay mačay niwasqaykiman.
escape-our-for that cave tell-me-certainly-your-to"

xinaspansi risqaku utqaylʸaman.
Then-they-say went-certainly-they hurry-only-to.

čaypis učwilʸa yaykuračisqa
That-in-they-say Uchwilla enter-made-certainly

antoniuta mačay ukuman kaynata nispan,
Antonio cave inside-to thus saying-his,

qamqa xatunmi kanki.
"you-there large-indeed are-you."

A free translation would be as follows: "'Uchwilla, what are you telling me? Let's go in order to escape to the cave which you have told me about.' Then, it is said, they went hurrying there. Uchwilla, who kept saying, 'You are indeed big,' made Antonio enter the cave."

---

[6] The subject form of the second person pronoun is mò, and the object form is mɔ̄.

[7] After a verb of "desiring" the imperative verb forms are used (see section 5.4).

[8] There are several different past and future tenses. The future with sέ is used in answer to questions or requests.

PUTTING WORDS TOGETHER

In order to fully appreciate the type of syntactic constructions which are illustrated by these Quechua sentences we need to identify more fully the morphemes which go to make up the complex words, i.e., those consisting of more than one morpheme. These are listed below in the order of their occurrence in the text:

učwilʸa < učwi- "little one" and -lʸa "only, just."
imatam < ima- "what," -ta object indicator, and -m affirmative enclitic.
wilʸawanki < wilʸa- "to tell," -wa "me," and -nki "you (sg.)" subject.
xakučikyá < xaku- "to go," -čik "we (inclusive)," -yá "then."
ayqekunančikpaq < ayqe- "to escape," -kuna pluralizer, -nčik "our (inclusive)," and -paq "for."
niwasqaykiman < ni- "to say," -wa "me," -sqa definite past tense, -yki "your (sg.)," and -man "to."
xinaspansi < xina- "thus," -spa a noun-forming suffix of simultaneous action by someone other than the subject of the main verb, -n "his," and -si "they say" (a quotative particle).
risqaku < ri- "to go," -sqa definite past tense, and -ku "they."
utqaylʸaman < utqa- "to hurry," -y a noun-forming suffix, -lʸa "only," and -man "to."
čaypis < čay "that," -pi "in," and -s "they say" (a quotative particle).
yaykuračisqa < yayku- "to enter," -ra definite action, -či "to cause to," -sqa definite past tense.
antoniuta < antoniu "Anthony" and -ta object indicator.
ukuman < uku- "inside" and -man "to."
kaynata < kay- "that," -na a restricted noun-forming suffix, and -ta object indicator.
nispan < ni- "to say," -spa a noun-forming suffix of simultaneous action by someone other than the subject of the main verb, and -n "his."
qamqa < qam- "you (sg.)" and -qa indicating a definite object and frequently occurring in the same phrase with the enclitic -mi.
xatunmi < xatun "large" and -mi affirmative enclitic.
kanki < ka "to be" and -nki "you (sg.)."

The ways in which Ngbaka and Quechua combine words into phrases and sentences is manifestly different, but in each language there are very subtle distinctions. For example, in Ngbaka there are two forms of the second person singular pronoun, one for subject and one for object positions. There are also two forms of the first person pronoun: (1) ?é used in indirect discourse and (2) mí used in direct discourse. Note also that in Ngbaka one does not say "I with you" but "we with you." Quechua also has many minute distinctions in tense, inclusive and exclusive first person, and contrasts between actions performed by the same or by a different subject from that of the main verb. We cannot expect the distinctions of one language to be completely paralleled by those of another; in fact, relatively few such parallelisms actually occur since the different categories of languages are so numerous. Our task as practical linguists is to discover the types of distinctions which any language makes and to examine all the possibilities of employing such contrasts in our own speech.

Not only do languages differ in the average length of words, but they also differ in the average length of sentences. Of course, this does not mean that the sentences of some languages are restricted to just three or four words and that others normally have fifteen or twenty. It does mean, however, that in some languages there is a tendency to string many clauses together into single structural units, while in others the usual practice is to place several shorter and more independent utterances alongside of each other. Greek is the classic example of a language which permits the running together of many clauses, and the Apostle Paul is sometimes accused of exceeding all practical limitations of a sentence. However, Paul's sentences are by no means as long as some which are employed by other writers of Ancient Greek. In the Nilotic languages it is also possible to construct long sentences, but as a rule speakers avoid long, involved sentences. In Quechua one may encounter very long sentences provided the subjects of most of the verbs remain the same, but Quechua does not provide for the many complex types of subordinate clauses which are so common in Greek. Any student who has studied Greek and then takes up Hebrew is almost certainly impressed with the relatively simple sentence structure of the latter language. However, structural complexity is not primarily a matter of sentence length as such but of the manner in which the parts of sentences are bound together. For example, in Zinza, a Bantu language of Tanganyika, relatively independent verb phrases may be strung along in a single "breath group" (i.e., without any pause). The Zinza sentence izó·ba ryá·ba ryá·gwa ba·ragira, literally "sun it-was it-fell they-ate," consists of three formally independent expressions izó·ba ryá·ba "sun it-was," ryá·gwa "it-fell," ba·ragira "they-ate." Each one of these units is equivalent to an entire sentence, but they are all included in a single phonological phrase and must be treated as a formal unit. Furthermore, these three expressions do combine into a single meaningful sentence signifying "when the sun had set, they ate." This type of arrangement of clauses is called paratactic, i.e., arranged alongside of each other. The other type of arrangement, in which clauses are combined by means of conjunctions such as "when, as, because, if, though, while," is called hypotactic, i.e., one arranged beneath (or dependent upon) another.

6.2 The Arrangement of Words

It is impossible for us to discuss all or even the principal types of arrangements of words in phrases and clauses. We should, however, examine some of the typical differences which may be found. For example, in the Mayan languages many relationships between words are indicated by a kind of possessive construction. In Tsotsil, a Mayan language of southern Mexico, the equivalent of "the bridge over the river" or "the river's bridge" is sbak'oal uk'um, literally "its bridge, the river." The prefix s- is the third person singular possessive pronoun which refers to uk'um "river," and the suffix -al indicates that an inanimate object is the possessor. The phrase sp'inal panin, literally, "its pot, the corn" designates "the pot for the corn," while the phrase spaninal p'in, literally "its corn, the pot" denotes "the corn for the pot."

The Bantu languages are famous for the prefixal concords which show agreement of words. Compare the following two sentences in Chichewa,[9] one singular and the other plural:

---

[9] Mark Hanna Watkins, A Grammar of Chichewa (Baltimore: Linguistic Society of America, 1937), p. 28.

1. <u>namwáli</u>   <u>wáṁbáyɛ́</u>   <u>áṅámura</u>   <u>m̩cu·kɔ,</u>   <u>m̩balɛ́</u>
   girl   little   she-is-lifting   water-pot,   sister

   <u>wákɛ́</u>   <u>wábwínɔ</u>
   her   good

   <u>áṁsɛ́·za</u>   "The little girl is lifting the water-pot; her
   she-her-is-helping.   good sister is helping her."

2. <u>anamwáli</u>   <u>ƀá·ƀáyɛ́</u>   <u>ƀáṅámura</u>   <u>micu·kɔ,</u>
   girls   little   they-are-lifting   water-pots,

   <u>abalɛ́</u>   <u>ƀáwɔ́</u>   <u>ƀábwínɔ</u>
   sisters   their   good

   <u>ƀá·sɛ́za</u>   "The little girls are lifting water-pots; their
   they-them-are-helping.   good sisters are helping
                             them."

The formally principal words in these sentences are the nouns, for the adjectives agree with the nouns, and the verbs contain pronominal substitutes for all subjects and objects.[10] For example, the word <u>áṁsɛ́·za</u> contains a prefix <u>á</u>-, which indicates that the subject is a singular subject of the first class of nouns (in this instance <u>m̩balɛ́</u> "sister"), and a prefix <u>m̩</u>-, which indicates that the object is singular and belongs to the first class of nouns (in this instance <u>namwáli</u> "girl"). In the word <u>ƀá·sɛ́za</u> "they are helping them" there is a reduction of the fuller form *<u>ƀáƀásɛ́za</u>, in which the first <u>ƀá</u>- would indicate the plural subject and the second <u>ƀá</u>- the plural object.

Compare the following noun expressions in Ilamba, a Bantu language of Tanganyika:

1. <u>a·nto</u>   <u>a·koe</u>   <u>ako·lu</u>   <u>abele</u>[11]   "his two big men"
   men   his   big   two

2. <u>i·nto</u>   <u>ya·koe</u>   <u>iko·lu</u>   <u>ibele</u>   "his two big things"
   things   his   big   two

---

[10]Object pronouns within the verb are restricted to (1) nonpersonal objects for which there is no corresponding noun in the sentence and (2) personal objects with or without a corresponding noun in the same sentence. Bantu languages differ considerably in this detail.

[11]Tones are not written in this transcription.

3. mi·no   ma·koe   mako·lu   mabele   "his two big teeth"
   teeth   his   big   two

4. pizo·mba piakoe   piko·lu   pibele   "his two big huts"
   huts   his   big   two

These types of agreement in Bantu languages are not greatly different from what we find in many Indo-European languages, but in the latter the agreements are indicated by suffixes, not by prefixes, and they are by no means as extensive. Compare, however, the following expressions in Spanish:

una carta clara y exacta, escrita en inglés "a clear and
    exact letter, written in English."
un libro claro y exacto, escrito en inglés "a clear and
    exact book, written in English."

The word carta "letter," which is feminine in grammatical gender, occurs with attributives ending in -a, e.g., una, clara, exacta, and escrita. The word libro "book," which is masculine in grammatical gender, occurs with attributives ending in -o, e.g., claro, exacto, and escrito, or with attributives having no vowel ending, e.g., un.

The choice of these so-called masculine and feminine endings[12] is not dependent solely on the phonological forms of the noun endings. For example, the word dia "day" which ends in a is nevertheless masculine, e.g., un dia "a day," and the word mano which ends in o is nevertheless feminine, e.g., una mano "a hand."

The relationships between words may be formally indicated by differences of tone just as well as by contrasts in consonants and vowels. For example, in Ibo the words ényí "elephant" and òkē "rat" which are high-high and low-mid in their basic tones become high-mid and mid-mid respectively when they are possessive attributives, e.g., ísí ényī "elephant's head" and ísí ōkē "rat's head."[13]

---

[12] The terms "masculine" and "feminine" became associated with these classes of words in classical grammars of Greek and Latin. The reasons for this are that many words ending in -a designate female persons, and many ending in -o designate male persons. These biological distinctions are, however, very restricted, and there are many contradictions.

[13] Ida C. Ward, An Introduction to the Ibo Language (Cambridge: W. Heffer and Sons, 1936).

In Kipsigis, a Nilo-Hamitic language of Kenya, tonal differences are employed to distinguish between subjects and objects of the verb. For example, compare the following sentences: mí tàŋkì·t pé·k "the tank is in the water" and mí táŋkí·t pè·k "the water is in the tank." The verb mí "to be in a place" is followed by the nouns taŋki·t "tank" (a borrowing from English) and pe·k "water." As objects the nouns occur with a high tone and as subjects with a low tone. This type of pattern runs throughout the language, and disregarding such tonal distinctions results in constant misunderstanding.

In many tonal languages the combination of words into phrases changes the tones which occur on words in isolation. Compare the forms of the following expressions in Bambara, a Sudanic language of West Africa:

In Isolation	Following ó "that"	Preceding kélé "one"
kɔ̌nɔ̌ "stomach"	ó kɔ̌nɔ̌ "that stomach"	kɔ̌nɔ̌ kélé "one stomach"
kɔ̌nɔ̌ "bird"	ó kɔ̌nɔ̌ "that bird"	kɔ̌nɔ̌ kélé "one bird"
bɔ́kɔ́ "clay"	ó bɔ́kɔ́ "that clay"	bɔ́kɔ́ kélé "one clay"
bɔ̀kɔ́ "mud"	ó bɔ̀kɔ́ "that mud"	bɔ̀kɔ́ kélé "one mud"

In Turu, a Bantu language of Tanganyika, there is a complicated development which results in many tonal modifications, some of which seem to be without any rhyme or reason; and yet they are all perfectly regular, despite the many apparent exceptions. Before a noun object with a basic high tone in the first syllable, the last syllable of the preceding verb becomes high. For example, the combination of gòàhɔ·rìà "we despise" and kó·kò "grandfather" results in gòàhɔ·rìá kó·kò "we despise grandfather." However, if the object is a word such as mòntù "man" (a word with a basic low tone in the first syllable), the first syllable of the object becomes high, e.g., gòàhɔ·rìà móntù. This is not so complicated, but with the words ŋkɔ́· "spirit" and ŋkɔ̀· "sheep" there is a strange but regular development. Before ŋkɔ́· "spirit" the tone of the verb becomes high because the first mora of the word ŋkɔ́· "spirit" (this acts the same as a syllable) is high. Before the word ŋkɔ̀· "sheep" the preceding verb does not change because the noun begins with a low tone, but the tone of the noun is changed in accordance with the regular "rule." As a result the first mora becomes high. The word "sheep" in this construction is therefore ŋkɔ̂·. Compare the two expressions:

gòàhɔ̂·rĭá ŋkɔ̂· "we despise the spirit"
gòàhɔ̂·rĭà ŋkɔ̂· "we despise the sheep"

The two nouns are identical in form in this construction, and the difference in meaning is actually indicated by the contrastive tones on the verb forms. Tonal languages are simply full of these types of tonal perturbations. This means that we must be constantly on the alert for such changes and employ all types of frames in the learning of a language. To be successful in the mastery of a language, we must continually emphasize the necessity of learning words in combinations. This is precisely what makes a syntactic knowledge of a language so very necessary; and the keener our observations about such patterns of phrase construction are, the more readily and thoroughly will we be able to master some of the intricate and unusual formations.

In order to understand properly the different arrangements of words in syntactic constructions, we need to consider the significant features of such arrangements. These include (1) the order, (2) the juncture (the point of contact between the words), and (3) the forms which mark the inter-word relationships of concord, government, and cross reference.

6.2.1   Order

Order is one of the most important features of arrangement and is employed to mark many significant relationships. For example, in English we generally distinguish between subject and object elements by order alone, e.g., John hit Bill and Bill hit John. In Latin, however, the constituents of the sentence pater filium amat "the father loves the son" could be arranged in any order and the meaning would be substantially the same, though not all orders are equally common, e.g., filium amat pater, filium pater amat, amat filium pater, etc. Of course, there would be some differences in emphasis, even as there is in the English sentences John ran away, Away ran John, and Away John ran. But in Latin there is no way of mistaking the relationships of these words because the ending of the word pater "father" indicates that it is subject, and the ending of filium "son" indicates that it is object of the verb.

The form of the verb <u>amat</u> "he loves" indicates that the subject is third person and singular. All these words are formally marked, and the differences in order only serve to indicate different connotations but do not change the basic grammatical relationships.

In some cases the same word in a different order will have a different meaning. For example, in Spanish the word <u>pobre</u> may mean "unfortunate" when preceding a noun and "poverty-stricken" when following, e.g., <u>la pobre mujer</u> "the poor (unfortunate) woman" and <u>la mujer pobre</u> "the poor (poverty-stricken) woman." Compare also <u>mi caro amigo</u> "my dear friend" with <u>mi caballo caro</u> "my expensive horse" and <u>varios papeles</u> "several papers" with <u>papeles varios</u> "miscellaneous papers."

In many languages different classes of words have different positions in attributive (i.e., modifying) relationships. In Loma, a language of Liberia, attributive nouns precede the words they modify, e.g., <u>gálá pélé</u> literally "God house," i.e., "the church," and <u>gálá kɔ́lɔ́</u> literally "God book," i.e., "the Bible." Adjectives, however, follow the nouns which they modify, e.g., <u>dúu nɔwɔ</u> literally "child dirty," i.e., "dirty child" and <u>ziɛ lei</u> literally "water cold," i.e., "cold water."

Because we can be partially understood by natives even though we employ the wrong order of words, we sometimes relax our careful attention to the details of word order. This is a tragic mistake, for it not only impairs our mastery of the language, but keeps us from attaining proper fluency and prevents people from fully appreciating what we have to say. There is nothing that jars the listener as much as the wrong order of words.

6.2.2 Juncture[14]

When words come together, there are often important

---

[14] The word "juncture" is used here to distinguish two somewhat similar but functionally different features: (1) the phonemic junctures, i.e., audibly perceptible differences in transition (discussed in the second paragraph), and (2) structural junctures, i.e., points at which certain formal modifications occur. For a detailed discussion of these different types of junctures see Eugene A. Nida, <u>Morphology</u> (Ann Arbor, Michigan: University of Michigan, 1949), pp. 85, 86.

PUTTING WORDS TOGETHER

phonemic changes which take place. For example, in English we may say I will meet you or I'll meet yuh /áyl míyčə/. The alternative forms are optional, but in some languages similar types of changes may be obligatory. In English, however, we cannot change you /yúw/ to yuh /yə/ or /-ə/ in every situation. It is only in certain combinations that this alternant occurs. Modifications which take place between two words are called "sandhi" changes. The word sandhi has been borrowed from Sanskrit, in which it was used to identify the special forms used in combinations of words.

In certain instances there are no changes of segmental phonemes when words combine, but there may be important differences in the phonemic junctures. By phonemic junctures we mean distinctive pauses or points of transition from one intonational phrase to another. For example, in English we have two different types of junctures to distinguish restrictive from nonrestrictive relative clauses. In the expression the man who came to see us there is usually no pause between man and who. But in the sequence my father, who came to see us there is generally such a pause between father and who. This phonemic difference helps to set off two types of postposed modifying clauses. The first type of clause restricts the object which it modifies, and the second adds some supplementary information about the object. Distinctions of this type may be found in many languages.

In the preceding chapter we noted that morphemes often change their forms because of the preceding or the following phonemes. Very similar changes may take place between words, though such modifications between words are rarer in occurrence than those within words. In Mongondow, a language of northern Celebes, the word in "to, of" undergoes a number of such changes, e.g., im pajoi "of the rice," im baloi "of the house," iŋ Kota "to Kota," in tundi "of the stars," il lipu ? "of the village," ij Jakub "of Jacob," and ir roda "of the car." These changes of final n before other words does not, however, occur with every word-final n before other words. These modifications are restricted to just certain types of syntactic combinations, and as such we may say that they mark certain structural junctures.

In section 6.2 we noted the changes in tone which take place in Turu when verbs and noun objects are juxtaposed.

This type of modification is also a type of sandhi change and is very prevalent in tone languages.

6.2.3 Concord (Agreement)

The relationships between words are often formally marked by morphemes indicating the same categories. For example, in the Chichewa and Ilamba data cited in section 6.2, the prefixes of the related words indicate the same categories of singular and plural and identify classes of formally related words, i.e., words having these same types of prefixes. Such types of agreement are called concord. The data cited from Spanish (section 6.2) illustrates this same type of grammatical device to show the relationship of words. We are also familiar with this in Greek, where adjectives must show agreement with nouns in number, gender, and case. That is why we find such contrasts as ho agat^{h}ós ánt^{h}rɔ·pos "the good man" and hɛ· agat^{h}ɛ́· númp^{h}ɛ· "the good maiden." The forms -o and -os indicate masculine, singular, and nominative, and the form -ɛ· indicates feminine, singular, and nominative. One of the very important syntactic features of these phrases is the fact that each word indicates the same categories, i.e., gender (masculine or feminine), number (singular or plural), and case (nominative, genitive, dative, accusative, or vocative).

English used to exhibit a great deal more concord between forms than it does now. In Old English there were such forms as se· sta·n "the stone" (a masculine noun), se·o ġiefu "the gift" (a feminine noun), and dæt ba·n "the bone" (a neuter noun). All these gender distinctions have disappeared in the agreement of adjectives with nouns, and we are left with only two cases of agreement between singular and plural adjectives and nouns: this man, these men; that person, those persons. However, we still indicate some agreement of number and person between the subject and the verb, e.g., the man goes, the men go.

6.2.4 Government

Some constructions require particular forms of words. For example, in a subject-predicate construction in English the subject pronoun forms I, we, he, she, they, and who are used, e.g., I go, we run, he hits, she works, they follow, and who did. In a preposition-object construction the object forms of these words occur, e.g., for me, with us, to him, by her, without them, and through whom. We say that the preposition "governs" the object case. This situation occurs only with six words in English, for these are the only words which still exhibit contrastive subject and object forms. This type of government may be called primary, in that the restrictions as to form are imposed by the construction itself; that is to say, all words which occur in such constructions and which have different forms occur in the particular form depending entirely upon the construction in question.

In certain instances, however, there may be secondary restrictions as to form. For example, in German all nouns and pronouns which occur with prepositions occur in an oblique case (i.e., genitive, dative, or accusative). However, some prepositions occur with genitive forms, others with dative, and still others with accusative.[15]

With genitive case forms:
> während des Tages "during the day"

With dative forms:
> von dem Tage "from the day"

With accusative forms:
> für den Tag "for the day"

We may describe these differences of case forms by stating that there are certain secondary restrictions of "government," i.e., some prepositions require one case and others require another. We may, however, describe such differences simply as matters of distribution, saying that certain forms occur with certain prepositions.

Features of government may involve the objects of verbs. For example, in Latin all objects occur in some oblique case (i.e., genitive, dative, accusative, or ablative), but the particular case form which occurs is dependent upon the verb. Compare the following expressions:[16]

Genitive object:
> meminit bovis "he remembers the ox"

---

[15] There are also prepositions which occur with dative or accusative, with certain differences in meaning.

[16] L. Bloomfield, Language (New York: Henry Holt and Co., 1933), p. 192.

Dative object:
>   nocet bovi· "he harms the ox"

Accusative object:
>   videt bovem "he sees the ox"

Ablative object:
>   u·titur bove "he uses the ox"

In certain instances languages exhibit differences in form between principal and nonprincipal verbs in a sentence. This is a regular procedure in Comanche, where dependent verbs generally have distinguishing forms. In some languages not all dependent verbs have special forms, but the selection of one or another form is dependent upon the type of main verb. For example, in Spanish the verb dice "he says" normally requires an indicative form of the dependent verb, e.g., dice que es verdad "he says that it is true." But the verb niega "he denies" requires a subjunctive form, e.g., niega que sea verdad "he denies that it is true."

We are so accustomed to segmental phonemes indicating case distinctions that we may overlook the fact that tones can also distinguish restrictions of government. The illustrative dàta from Ibo, cited in section 6.2, indicates the way in which differences of tone may define relationships between words. In the Kipsigis data, also cited in section 6.2, the differences in tones likewise distinguish relationships between words as determined by the requirements of the construction. To this extent, therefore, they constitute primary restrictions. Some additional illustrative data from Kipsigis will indicate how extensive and complicated such patterns can be:

1. kîlè·nčí čè·sú pétèrò·   "Jesus said to Peter"
2. kîlè·nčí čé·sù pètèrō·   "Peter said to Jesus"
3. kîlè·nčí pètèrō· čé·sù   "Peter said to Jesus"
4. kîlè·nčí pétèrò· čè·sū   "Jesus said to Peter"
5. mí pè·k tèré·t   "the water is in the pot"
6. mí pé·k tèrè·t   "the pot is in the water"
7. mí tēré·t pè·k   "the water is in the pot"
8. mí tèrè·t pé·k   "the pot is in the water"

Note that petero· "Peter" occurs with two different tonal forms pétèrò· object and pètèrō· subject. However, the word čè·su "Jesus"[17] occurs in three tonal forms: čè·sú pre-object

---

[17] There are no phonemic voiced stops or affricates in Kipsigis.

subject, čè·sū post-object subject, and čé·sù object. Similarly pè·k "water" has two forms pè·k subject and pé·k object, and tere·t "pot" has three forms: tēré·t pre-subject object,[18] tèré·t post-subject object, and tèrè·t subject. The number of tonal irregularities in Kipsigis are great, and we cannot predict from one form of a word just what its object or subject tonal pattern will be. Compare the following expressions:

1. kîlè·nčí là·kwè·t čî·tó "the child said to the person"
2. kîlè·nčí là·kwé·t čî·tò "the person said to the child"
3. kîlè·nčí kēsò̀kōrōrè̂·t ké·čì·ryēt "the serval cat said to the sheep"
4. kîlè·nčí kēsókóróré̄·t kè·čí·ryēt "the sheep said to the serval cat"

The different tonal forms of the subjects and objects must be learned as a basic part of the words. They are just as essential as the different affixes employed by languages such as Greek and Latin.

6.2.5 Cross Reference

Words may be related to one another by means of pronominal elements which refer to certain classes of forms. For example, in Tsotsil the phrase sčoy šun "John's fish" consists of s- "his," čoy "fish," and šun "John." Literally, the phrase is "his-fish John." The pronominal prefix s- "his" indicates a cross reference to the possessor šun "John."

In French this type of cross reference may occur with noun and pronoun subjects. For example, in Jean, est-il venu? "Has John come?" the noun subject Jean "John" and the pronoun subject il "he" are related by cross reference. If the subject were Jeanne "Jean," the pronoun would be elle "she," e.g., Jeanne, est-elle venue?[19] "Has Jean come?" The pronouns il "he" and elle "she" refer to masculine and feminine persons respectively.

There are some instances of cross reference which appear to be very similar to agreement. For example, in

---
[18] This form, however, is automatically conditioned since the basic low tone on the first short syllable becomes mid between two high tones.

[19] The orthography indicates a subject agreement in the verb ending -e, but this is not reflected in the pronunciation of standard French.

Spanish one says la muchacha canta "the girl sings" and las muchachas cantan "the girls sing." The verb stem cant- occurs with a suffix -a after the singular subject and a suffix -an after the plural subject. These sentences would seem to be exactly parallel to the English equivalents the girl sings and the girls sing. However, there is a vast functional difference. The verb canta actually means "she sings" and is fully capable of constituting an entire sentence. However, the Engligh word sings could never stand alone. The Spanish canta contains a pronominal bound suffix -a, which is a functional substitute for a singular subject, not just a sign of agreement with such a subject, as is the case with the English verb suffix -s. Accordingly, the Spanish verbs indicate cross reference with their subjects, while the English verbs indicate agreement with their subjects.

A significant difference also exists in the Bantu languages. For example, the words which modify nouns show agreement with the nouns, but the verbs indicate cross reference. Note the following sentence from Luvale:[20]

litemo	lyami	lyamwaza	lyalinene
hoe	my	good	big

ngunaližihi[21]   "I have broken my good big hoe"
I-have-it-killed (i.e., broken)

The words lyami "my," lyamwaza "good," lyalinene "big" all indicate that they are in agreement with the noun litemo "hoe." The verb ngunaližihi "I have broken it" contains a pronominal element li- which constitutes a cross reference to the noun expression. The verb ngunaližihi is a completely independent type of expression and may constitute a complete sentence just as a verb in Spanish may. However, in Spanish only the subject is pronominally included within the verb, and in this Luvale verb both the subject and the object references are included by means of the pronominal prefixes ngu- "I" and li- "it."

---

[20] A. E. Horton, A Grammar of Luvale (Johannesburg: Witwatersrand University Press, 1949), p. 36.
[21] Tonal contrasts are not indicated.

6.3   Types of Syntactic Units

In examining the way in which words go together in a language and the functions which they perform in the syntax, we need to have some understanding of the types of words and the combinations of words. First of all, we should be aware of the "syntactic inventory," i.e., the various classes of words which may occupy various positions in the sentence. These classes of words are usually called the parts of speech, e.g., nouns, verbs, pronouns, prepositions, adjectives, adverbs, and interjections. As we noted in section 5.9 some languages formally distinguish a number of such classes, and others do not. In the syntactic inventory, however, we are not concerned wholly with the morphological forms of words but how they may function in syntactic combinations. For example, in English we have a large class of words which we would call "particles" as far as their morphology is concerned, for they do not exhibit any inflectional changes and very few derivational formations, i.e., they are principally just single morphemes. However, in the syntax we need to differentiate between them. For example, we classify some as prepositions, e.g., in, by, through, with, of; others as conjunctions introducing only postposed clauses, e.g., and, but, or, for; others as conjunctions introducing either preposed or postposed clauses, e.g., because, when, while, as, till; and others as interjections, e.g., ouch, oh, whew.[22] These classes are enough to indicate that in the syntax we must become aware of the types of constituents, i.e., the words and phrases which occur in the same types of constructions.

Our attention must also be directed toward the kinds of combinations which occur and how such combinations operate in the language, for each language has its own restrictions as to the types of words which can be used in any one construction. For example, in English we can place a number of different kinds of words in front of nouns, e.g., an adjective as in good man, a noun as in gold ring, and an adverb as in (the) above statement, but we cannot use a conjunction as a modifier

---

[22] There is, of course, some overlapping. For example, the words for and but occur as prepositions and as conjunctions.

of a noun, e.g., *whether thing. Every language is selective of the syntactic units which go together.

Various languages may permit the same types of modifiers but require that they occur in different relative positions. In English we may have both adjectives and verbal phrases modifying nouns, but adjectives normally precede and the verbal phrases follow. In Spanish, however, it is possible to have the very reverse of this situation. In the expression <u>las hasta ahora casi ignoradas pinturas búdicas</u>[23] literally, "the until now almost unknown paintings Buddist" (meaning "the Buddist paintings which until now have been almost unknown") the verbal phrase <u>hasta ahora casi ignoradas</u> "until now almost unknown"[24] precedes the noun, and the adjective <u>búdicas</u> "Buddist" follows the noun. The English equivalent completely reverses this arrangement of modifiers.

In order to understand more adequately just how words and phrases are combined and the ways in which they function[25] in languages, we should very briefly consider several features: (1) sentence-forming and non-sentence-forming constructions, (2) endocentric and exocentric constructions, (3) coordinate and subordinate constructions, (4) paratactic and hypotactic constructions, and (5) immediate constituents.

6.3.1   <u>Sentence-Forming and Non-Sentence-
           Forming Constructions</u>

Any expression which is a complete utterance is a sentence. Most languages exhibit at least two main types of sentences, principal and nonprincipal. In English the principal sentence type consists of a subject and predicate construction, e.g., <u>John went</u>; <u>The people refused to go</u>; <u>We were all disappointed when everyone pulled out</u>. The nonprincipal sentences in English include vocatives, e.g., <u>John</u>! <u>Police</u>!, exclamations, e.g., <u>Ouch</u>! <u>Whew</u>!, and such aphoristic expressions as <u>The more the better</u> and <u>First come first served</u>.

---

[23] <u>Hispano-Americano</u>, Vol. 14, No. 360 (March, 1949), p. 30.

[24] This verbal phrase contains a preposed prepositional phrase <u>hasta ahora</u> "until now."

[25] By function we mean (1) distribution, i.e., the positions of occurrence of forms and (2) the relationship of the parts of the constructions to the whole (cf. endocentric and exocentric).

We become so accustomed to thinking that every sentence must have a verb that we are shocked when we discover languages in which verbs are not always necessary. Even in Greek, however, it is not necessary to have a verb in every sentence. For example, one may employ ho anér·r agathós, literally "the man good," as a complete sentence meaning "the man is good."

In Ngbaka, a Sudanic language of northern Congo, the sentence à dò tūlū kọ̀à, literally "he with cloth hand-his" (meaning "he has cloth in his hand"), has absolutely no verb. Even in nonpresent tenses the tense particles occur, but there is no verb, e.g. à zí dò tūlū kọ̀à "he had cloth in his hand" and à zé dò tūlū kọ̀à "he had cloth in his hand a long time ago."[26]

Compare the Marshallese sentence cited in section 5.9. Such a sentence is quite different from what we are accustomed to in English.

The nonsentence-forming constructions are those which do not normally constitute sentences.[27] These are numerous in all types of languages. We may illustrate a few from English, e.g., prepositional phrase from the people, adjective-noun good man, pronoun-adverb those there, verb-adverb went quickly, verb-adjective felt good, adverb-adjective very fine, conjunction-noun (Peter) and John, and adverb-adverb very quickly.

6.3.2 Endocentric and Exocentric Constructions

Some combinations of words have substantially the same function in a sentence as the principal word or words of the construction, while others have quite different functions. For example, the expression poor man, consisting of an adjective and a noun, functions just like any noun, and the noun man is

---

[26] The tense particle zí denotes regular past and zé remote past time.

[27] It is possible for almost any type of expression to constitute a complete utterance if it is given in answer to a question. For example, in reply to the question "Where did he go?" one might answer "To the garage." In this very restricted context the phrase to the garage would constitute a type of sentence-forming construction.

the principal (or head) word of the expression. We may say that this type of combination is endocentric, i.e., its functional center is contained within the construction. On the other hand, the expression from father, consisting of a preposition and a noun, does not function like a noun. For one thing it cannot be a subject as a noun could, cf. the impossible expression *from father was there and the perfectly normal expression father was there. Furthermore, the phrase from father cannot itself act like a preposition. The function of from father is thus different from either constituent part, and hence we may call it exocentric, i.e., its functional center is not contained within the construction.

Endocentric constructions may have more than one head. For example, the expression John, Bill, and Mary may be said to have three coordinate heads, and since the head words consist of nouns and the expression as a whole functions substantially like a noun, it is endocentric.

On the whole, endocentric constructions are much more common than exocentric ones, for languages tend to build up sentences by adding words as modifiers to other words. Where simple modifiers occur, one is likely to find an endocentric construction.[28] In order to illustrate some of the different endocentric and exocentric constructions, we may list the following in English:[29]

    Endocentric
        Adjective-noun: good boy, fine water
        Adverb-adjective: very good, fully conscious
        Verb-adverb: ran quickly, fell slowly
        Noun—relative-clause:[30] people who came, things which we bought

---

[28] There are some few exceptions to this. For example, in the compound upset the adverb up modifies the verbal set, but the combination functions like a noun, and hence it is exocentric.

[29] These lists are quite incomplete, and they are purposely simplified to include as few constituents as possible. See section 6.3.5 for a discussion of immediate constituents and related problems.

[30] The longer hyphen marks the primary break in the naming of the construction.

Pronoun—prepositional-phrase: those in town, some with Jim
Verb-noun: hit Tom, saw cattle
Verb—adverbial-clause: came when he could, went where he was

Exocentric
Noun-verb: people left, snow fell
Preposition-noun: from John, for mother

6.3.3 Coordinate and Subordinate Constructions

Some combinations of words are coordinate and others subordinate. For example, in English the phrase John and Bill consists of coordinate items. In some instances, there are several coordinated items, usually with the last introduced by a conjunction, e.g., pens, pencils, papers, and books (were scattered everywhere). Each coordinated item may have its own coordinator, as in the expressions either Jim or Bill and neither father nor mother.

In subordinate constructions one element is functionally subordinated to another, e.g., good in good man and very in very fine. We usually describe this relationship as saying that good modifies man, and very modifies fine. There are certain subordinate elements which are not traditionally called modifiers but which are definitely attributive. For example, the verb phrase hit me, consisting of a verb and a pronoun, functions in English substantially like any verb expression, cf. (John) ran and (John) hit me. We describe the phrase hit me as endocentric, with hit as the head or principal word, and me as the attributive. The constituent me is thus subordinate to the verb hit.

Some combinations of words are neither subordinate nor coordinate. For example, in the prepositional phrase for me, we recognize that the preposition and pronoun are not coordinate, for they do not consist of the same types of constituents. Certainly one is not subordinate to the other, for the combination does not function as either a preposition or a pronoun. To be perfectly correct in our analyses, we must therefore recognize three types of structure: coordinate, subordinate, and noncoordinate and nonsubordinate.

6.3.4 Paratactic and Hypotactic Constructions

Some combinations of words are very loosely and others are very closely joined in their structure. For example, we may have such sentences as It's late; I must go. Formally, the component expressions could constitute two independent utterances if it were not for the fact that they are combined in one overall intonational phrase. Such loosely combined sentences are described as paratactic, while a corresponding sentence Because it is late, I must go is said to be hypotactic. The first clause of this latter sentence is formally combined with the second by means of the conjunction because.

Parenthetical expressions inserted in sentences are also described as paratactic, e.g.,
   1. Parenthetical sentences: The boss (I think he is a rascal) ordered him to leave.
   2. Parenthetical phrases: that is, namely, in other words.

Appositional expressions are also paratactic, e.g., Mr. Smith, the carpenter, helped us.

A type of duplicative parataxis[31] occurs between noun subjects and pronominal subjects. For example, in the French expression Jean, est-il venu? (cited in section 6.2.5) literally "John, is-he come?" the noun subject Jean is paratactically combined with the expression est-il venu, because a part of this latter expression, namely il "he," is a substitute for the noun subject. In Bantu languages the subject is always paratactically combined with the verb expression, for the verb always contains an included subject pronoun. In some Bantu languages the object is also combined paratactically, for the verb may contain an object pronoun referring to a noun object in the same sentence. See section 6.2.5.

In contrast with paratactic constructions, which are rather loosely combined and whose parts may duplicate one another, the hypotactic constructions are structurally more integrated. These are the combinations of words with which we are much more familiar, and hence they require no further illustration.

6.3.5 Immediate Constituents

There are two structural facts which impress us when we begin to observe the different types of expressions in any

---
[31] Parataxis is the noun equivalent of the adjective paratactic.

language: (1) expressions of quite different length appear to contain essentially the same kinds of units, and (2) the pertinent environment of items follows definite divisions of structure. Perhaps this seems unduly complicated, but it can be easily illustrated. For example, compare the following English sentences:
1. John ran.
2. The man died yesterday.
3. All the people departed in their cars.
4. Almost all the old horses were rounded up in the canyon.
5. All those people who were unable to manage successfully attempted to get some job with low pay but plenty of security.

Despite the fact that these sentences have all the way from two to twenty-one words, they are essentially alike in that they consist of subject expressions plus predicate expressions.

The problem of the pertinent environment of words may be illustrated by the second sentence The man died yesterday. If we were to explain the composition of this sentence, we would not describe the as going with the verb died, or say that yesterday is an attributive of man. Rather, we would say that the goes with (or modifies) man and that yesterday goes with died. Then we would describe the sentence as consisting of the subject the man and the predicate died yesterday. We could symbolize this relationship as follows:

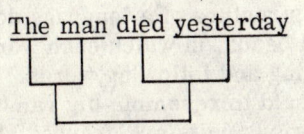

The man died yesterday

What we have done is simply to identify the constituents which immediately combine to form this sentence. These sets of constituent items we call the "immediate constituents."

The same procedure may be applied to the third sentence with the following result:

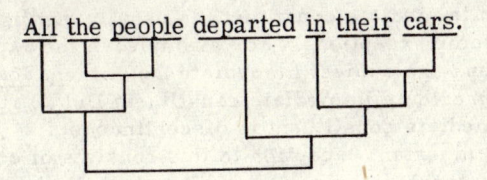

All the people departed in their cars.

These same principles of dividing according to immediate constituents may be applied to the structure of other languages. For example, we may describe the immediate constituents of the Spanish expression cited in section 6.3:

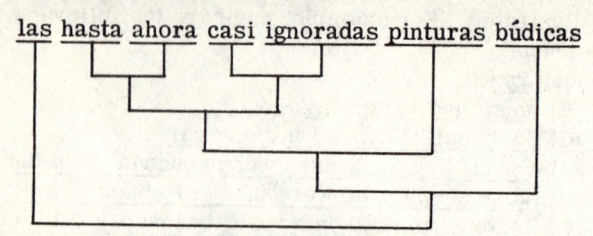

las hasta ahora casi ignoradas pinturas búdicas

This diagrammatic analysis helps us to describe the pertinent environment of constituent parts of any expression. For example, we would not describe the preposition hasta "until" as related to las "the," even though it immediately follows the article. Rather, we describe hasta as going immediately with ahora "now," and then we note that these two are in turn attributive to the verbal expression casi ignoradas "almost unknown." The pertinent distributional environment of hasta "until" is not its being postposed to las "the" but its being preposed to ahora "now." The analysis of the data into immediate constituents is essential if we are to describe the significant linguistic environment of forms. Otherwise we have a hodgepodge of information.

The syntactic structure of a language does not resemble strings of identical beads, in which each word is equally related to the preceding and following words. To the contrary, sentences may be said to resemble big rambling apartmenthouses in which various units are grouped closely together, and then these are combined into larger and larger units.[32] Furthermore, the combining process usually consists of uniting just two structures at a time. That is to say, there are usually only two immediate constituents in any one construction,[33] but, of course, there may be many layers of immediate

---

[32] Each immediate constituent is usually continuous, but there are some exceptions. For example, in the expression Did John run? the subject immediate constituent John occurs within the predicate immediate constituent Did ... run. This second immediate constituent is discontinuous.

[33] The important exception to this consists of coordinate endocentric constructions such as Jim, Bill, Dick, and Peter.

constituents, representing successive ranks of constructions. As practical linguists we are not so much concerned about the technical details of procedure and the many complications which arise in working out the intricate problems connected with the analysis of immediate constituents. Our task is to understand the general way in which languages build up expressions and then to make use of such patterns in the construction of our own sentences. The more we understand of the language structure, the more successfully we can use this structure in conveying our ideas.

6.4 Discovering the Syntactic Structure of a Language

Our first observations about the syntactic structure of a language begin when we start to expand the frames of phrases and clauses (see section 3.2.3.2.10). We must note the characteristic order of words, the ways in which the relationships between words are indicated (e.g., by concordant morphemes as in Bantu), and the types of words which may be combined. These preliminary observations must be confirmed or modified and expanded when we study the native texts. In texts we must distinguish between various types of syntactic usage, for we find that conversational forms are quite different from poetic forms, and personal narrative style usually differs from "proverbial style." But underlying all these differences are the fundamental patterns of the language structure with which we must become perfectly familiar.

We may not find it possible to give the necessary time to a detailed analysis of the syntax, but we must observe certain types of detail:

1. The average length of sentences.
2. The ways in which clauses are combined, e.g., paratactically or hypotactically.
3. The order of principal units in the sentence, e.g., the subject, the object, and the verb.
4. The degree of fixed vs. free order of elements. For example, the order of words in English is much freer than the order of words in most Bantu languages.
5. The kinds of constructions which may constitute sentences and those which normally do not constitute sentences.

These syntactic features are a bare minimum upon which to base our further study.

We must not overlook the necessity of making syntactic patterns just as automatic as morphological ones. Hesitating between words in a sentence is not as fatal to intelligibility as stopping in the middle of a word to figure out the proper ending. Nevertheless, all features of a language must become perfectly automatic. Some people attain an easy control of morphological features by means of pure memorizing of paradigms and lists of forms. However, it is not possible to acquire the same mastery of syntactic details without practice in listening to the language. We must become so accustomed to hearing expressions that in speaking we automatically express ourselves by means of these natural phrase patterns. Some people never learn a thing about formal syntax, but they learn to speak foreign languages with great facility because they have acquired through practice a thorough knowledge of the syntactic framework. They could never diagram the sets of immediate constituents of any sentence, and yet their speech is completely natural. This does not mean that formal analysis is without value, but it does mean that objective studying about a language is only one of the means by which we may acquire greater facility. It is no substitute for automatic mastery of the structural framework. A person may be ever so clever in the handling of tools, but the tools are not the equivalent of a house. They are only instruments for building a house more easily than we could with our bare hands.

6.5 Correcting Syntactic Errors

If in speaking we employ the wrong form of a word, almost any native speaker can correct us, for the mistaken form is so obviously out of place in the linguistic context. However, many of our syntactic errors of word order and choice of words cannot be so readily corrected; for though they seem wrong to the native speaker, he may not be quite sure what the mistake is. This problem is very acute in the process of translating. It is the rare missionary indeed who does not bring over into his translation many idioms and syntactic patterns from his own language or the language from which he is translating. The natives may be able to understand what is written, for the words are all there and obvious grammatical errors are not to be found. However, the word order may be quite artificial. It is not enough for the missionary to read over his translation and ask if the people understand it. If only the word order is incorrect, the chances are that the people will claim that the translation is fully intelligible, despite the fact that it may sound "like a crooked trail" as some have called such errors in word order. To straighten out forced speech, the missionary must usually suggest certain alternative orders and possibilities. By asking which of the alternatives sounds "better" or "sweeter," it is often possible to get very helpful corrections; but the initial suggestions for such alternatives must usually come from the missionary. After he has done this often enough and has trained some native helpers to assist in the task of reorganizing his awkward expressions, the native assistants may become very expert in suggesting improvements. It is too much, however, to expect untrained native speakers to be able to suggest changes from forms which are permissible, though awkward, to forms which are natural and fully acceptable. Constant attention to such details of speech, as unimportant as they may sometimes seem, will prove immeasurably valuable to anyone who is desirous of mastering a foreign language—the most effective means of making vital contacts with people.

Chapter 7

7. DISCOVERING THE MEANINGS

The practical linguist must direct his attention to four phases of language: (1) the sounds, (2) how morphemes are put together to make words, (3) how words are put together to make sentences, and (4) the meanings of morphemes, words, and combinations of words. Where there are adequate dictionaries one is fortunate indeed, for most of the aboriginal languages with which missionaries work have very incomplete dictionaries or none at all. In many instances the missionary must make up his own dictionary, and in others he must make additions to existing fragmentary lists of poorly defined words. Where there are good dictionaries, the missionary must understand how to use them properly. Regardless of our situation, we need to rid ourselves of some of the popular misconceptions about languages and their meaningful units and to understand the principles which underlie the meanings of words.

7.1 Popular Misconceptions

As we have noted in the previous sections 1.4 and 2.1, some individuals still think that primitive peoples have very simple languages. This may be the result of our rarely admitted, but socially dominant, concept of racial superiority. On the other hand, such an idea may just reflect our ignorance. Contrary to popular belief, the evolutionary hypothesis cannot be demonstrated by comparing the languages of peoples throughout the world. Our discussions in Chapter 4-6 should clear up any such ideas. All languages are extremely complex systems of symbols, so complex that a comprehensive and detailed description of any one of them would require a lifetime of study by a professional linguist.

Some missionaries who have become discouraged because of the abundance of vocabulary and intricacies of idiom in a native language, have thought that something should be done about constructing a basic vocabulary for the native language.

They have assumed that since Basic English has been devised with only 850 words and since its supporters claim that it is adequate to discuss all types of ideas and relationships, certainly it would be worth while to reduce some of the aboriginal languages to a limited vocabulary and thus make translation work and the process of language learning simpler. The mistake is in assuming that Basic English is actually English. Rather, it is a very artificially constructed dialect of English which requires great skill to write and amazing ability to speak. It is useful in some very limited practical situations, but its limitations are evident. For one thing, the 850 primary words have more than 12,000 principal meanings in the unabridged Oxford Dictionary. This means that though there are a limited number of symbols, these have many different meanings; and what one gains in not having to learn many different words is lost in the inexactness of expression and in the artificiality of idiom. We should not attempt to restrict languages artificially. It is our task to take languages as we find them and use their rich variegated patterns of expression to explain the matchless story of the Good News.

One of the difficulties which missionaries have is the apparent inconsistency of their native informants. An informant may say one thing on one day and quite the opposite the next day. Other speakers may contend for something still different. As a result, some missionaries have given up in despair, arguing that since the natives themselves do not know how to use their own language, how can a foreigner ever learn to speak it? For example, in Ngbaka, a Sudanic language of northern Congo, one may ask for the native equivalent of "he will see the lion," and informants may give two different forms: (1) ă· zŏ· nē gbɔ̄gbɔ̄ and (2) ă· zŏ· sɛ̄ gbɔ̄gbɔ̄. Both of these forms are perfectly correct in reply to the sentence requested, but the natives will argue at great length as to just which Ngbaka sentence should have been given in response to the missionary's request for information. This does not mean that either form is wrong or that the natives use them indiscriminately. Actually there is a difference in meaning, but a rather subtle one. The form with nē is a simple future statement, and the form with sɛ̄ is a statement made in reply to a question which has been asked about the possibility of someone doing something. The first translation would be given as a completely literal equivalent, but the second would be proposed by one who assumes that anyone wanting such a sentence would need it to use in response to a question. It would be useless to quiz natives about the differences in meaning between n$\bar{\text{e}}$ and s$\bar{\epsilon}$. They would be at a complete loss to explain the contrasts. However, they preserve the subtle distinctions with complete precision. If we are to discover the differences in meaning, we must either examine many pages of text material, particularly conversations, or we must be on the alert to catch such distinctions as they are made in ordinary speech. Sometimes we can ask our informant to demonstrate to us just when and how he would use such-and-such a form. If he is clever at reconstructing situations, we may discover immediately the slight difference which seemed utterly meaningless to us at first and concerning which even natives would argue, since they might not understand precisely what we wanted to know.

We must remember that there are many ambiguities and obscure distinctions in all languages and that English is no exception. Many of the formal contrasts in English appear to foreigners to be very inconsistent. It would not be easy for us to describe the different situations in which we would use I _have_ _finished_ _the_ _book_ and I _finished_ _the_ _book_. We might argue that the second is a more remote past than the first, but we could use either of these expressions the moment we finished reading. The differences between the so-called perfect and the simple past in English depend upon the actor's relationship to the accomplished fact, not just the time of its completion. Minute distinctions of meaning should neither discourage us nor cause us to believe that native speakers are inconsistent. They should rather stimulate us to master them as a means of speaking effectively with people.

One further misconception about language is the belief that aboriginals are wholly unable to talk about the mechanical developments of our modern world. Of course, if such things as airplanes, railroads, motorcycles, electric lights, and ice-cream cones are unknown to people, they will have no words for them; but when such features come into their experience, they can very readily develop adequate designations. For example, when the novelties of a mechanized civilization came upon the Kutenai Indians of the Northwest, they had no difficulty in employing or combining their own words to indicate new things.[1] For example, a tire is literally "the shoe of the car," a motor is "the head of the car," a train is "a fire wagon," coal is "a raven's stone," a watch is "a little sun," a sparkplug is "a little bone," a fan of a car motor is "that which blows the fire away," the low gear of a car is "that which pulls hard with," a key is "that which is forced into by a point with," and a pool room is "where pushing around with a point is done."

All languages have the potentialities of describing and identifying any type of phenomenon.

7.2 Basic Principles

The science of meaning, which is called semantics, rests upon some important and definite principles which we must understand if we are to discover the meanings of morphemes, words, and phrases. Many of the following principles are very closely related, and some are simple correlatives of others; but they are stated here in considerable detail since they are so fundamental to all our attitudes and procedures in the study of a foreign language.

7.2.1 There Are No Exact Synonyms within a Language

It may seem strange for us to deny the existence of "exact synonyms," for we so often hear people talking about them. What we mean, of course, is that there are no two words which are completely equivalent in meaning. All so-called synonyms are simply partially equivalent words. For example, the words truth and verity are listed as synonyms, but they are not equivalents. We can say he spoke the truth, but we would not say he spoke the verity. Neither in English nor in any other language can we expect to find completely identical words.

7.2.2 There Are No Exact Equivalents between Languages

We must learn that each word in every language has its own special meaning and that we cannot assume the two

---

[1] These data are from Paul L. Garvin, "Kutenai Lexical Innovations," Word, Vol. 4. No. 2. pp. 120-126.

languages ever fully agree in any detail. For example, we may be told that in Spanish <u>amar</u> means "to love" and <u>querer</u> means "to like." But these two words do not parallel their English translations. The word <u>amar</u> would be perfectly correct in talking about "loving the brethren of the church," but to use <u>amar</u> in courtship would sound terribly bookish and poetic. In saying "I love you" the romantic lover uses <u>te quiero</u>, not <u>te</u> <u>amo</u>, to declare his affection.

One of our difficulties comes from assuming that words which resemble English have the same meanings. For example, French <u>demander</u> appears to be similar to English <u>demand</u>, but the French word means simply "to ask" or "to request." There is not the slightest suggestion of "demanding" involved. Similarly in Spanish the verb <u>entender</u>, which is the common verb meaning "to understand," resembles the French verb <u>entendre</u>, meaning primarily "to listen to." The French equivalent of Spanish <u>entender</u> is <u>comprendre</u>, not the verb <u>entendre</u>.

In many instances words may look and sound alike but have entirely different meanings. For example, Spanish <u>destreza</u> might seem to resemble English <u>distress</u>, but it actually means "dexterity." Similarly Spanish <u>ropa</u> resembles English <u>rope</u>, but it means "clothing."

As students of a foreign language we cannot keep ourselves from thinking of new words in terms of similar words in English, but gradually we must break this habit of conscious or unconscious association of similar words. We need to think, speak, and react entirely in the native language. Otherwise, when we see such a Spanish expression as was cited in section 6.3.5, we might instinctively assume that <u>ignoradas</u> means "ignored," while in such a context it actually means "unknown."

7.2.3   <u>Ambiguities Occur in All Languages</u>

No language is perfect, and one must not assume, as some proponents of New Testament Greek studies have claimed, that Greek is any exception. Greek has its numerous ambiguities, and ancient playwrights made full use of them in providing clever puns for the enjoyment of their audiences. The habit of constructing jokes about resemblances between words appears to be almost universal.

DISCOVERING THE MEANINGS

We are sufficiently acquainted with ambiguities in English to realize that they are frequent enough. For example, in the phrase to slip on a sock we do not know whether the action is one of dressing or slipping. Similarly, the sentence he was run down may mean that a person was struck by an automobile, that he was being denounced, or that he was physically worn out.

In Spanish the words los puros may mean "the pure (ones)" or "the cigars." This type of ambiguity of meaning may give rise to all types of puns. In Mixteco, a language of southern Mexico, there are numerous puns developed on the basis of tonal differences between words.[2] For example, in one story a person who wishes to confuse his interrogator replies to the question "Where are the entrails?" (Mixteco hitə̀-tə̀ "its entrails") by purposely substituting the form hitə́-tə́, which describes a kind of walking with bent knees. The answer given is "Right here, its knees keep giving way while walking." It is not difficult to see how puns can be constructed when there are such sets of minimal pairs as the following: žàʔá "this," žáʔá "brown," žáʔa "here," žaʔa "pepper," žaʔà "soot"; kʷèdú "story," kʷèdù "liar!"; čáà "is coming," čaà "will come," čáa "is writing," čaa "will write," and čàa "man."[3]

7.2.4 All Languages Exhibit Changes in the Meanings of Words

Some people think that because a language has not been reduced to writing, the meanings of words are subject to all sorts of radical changes in meaning. That is to say, an unwritten language is regarded by many as being very unstable. This is, of course, not true, for unwritten languages are relatively more stable in forms and meanings than written languages; for the latter are subject to many more cultural influences tending to modify them. In most aboriginal languages[4] we have no way of tracing the history of words, but we can

---

[2] These data are from Kenneth L. Pike, "Tone Puns in Mixteco," *International Journal of American Linguistics*, Vol. 11, No. 3, pp. 129-39.

[3] Mid tones are unmarked.

[4] In some instances there are closely cognate languages with recorded histories.

make many inferences on the basis of cultural evidences and from what we know of the general tendencies in all languages.

For example, the Maya word tsimin means "horse" and "tapir." From what we know of the history of Latin America prior to the coming of the Spanish conquerors, we must assume that tsimin originally designated only a tapir, but it was later applied to the horses which were brought over by the Europeans. At present in some localities the word tsimin means only "horse," for tapirs are practically unknown in those areas.

Often the meanings of words change with the developments in techniques. For example, in the King James Version of the Bible we read in I Samuel 20:40 that Jonathan gave "his artillery to his lad," whom he dispatched to the city. The word artillery in this passage means a bow and arrow, and it was employed in the 16th and 17th centuries to identify almost any instrument for hurling missiles. As the instruments improved and changed, the name continued. Now the translation seems almost ludicrous, for uninformed people may picture the small boy struggling off with a cannon. Old words may also be used to describe quite new processes. For example, in Mende, a language of West Africa, one speaks of shooting a gun as "throwing a gun." This idiom is fashioned after the expression "throwing a spear"; and though only the bullet is propelled, nevertheless, the idiom does very well in Mende despite what seems to us contradictory.

7.2.5 Forms Have Areas of Meaning

We are entirely too accustomed to thinking of words as having precise points of meaning, while we should regard them as having areas of meaning. Some areas are very extensive and others very restricted, but all are areas, even though their limits may be difficult to define. For example, the word love in English covers a great area of meaning. Compare the following expressions: I love my wife, I love to do it, I love apples, I love God, I love that sunset, love 'em and leave 'em, love me love my dog. Where English could use one word to describe various phases of such emotional situations, Greek would use at least three: $era\jmath\cdot$ physical love, $p^{h}ile\jmath\cdot$ love resulting from association, and $agapa\jmath\cdot$ love resulting from appreciation of worth. Nevertheless, these three Greek words are not covered entirely by the English word love, and there are some uses of English love which cannot be translated by these three Greek words.

In Zulu[5] the word hamba has a very wide area of meaning "to travel, move along, walk, proceed, flow, live, behave." Zulu also has many ideophones which distinguish many different gaits and methods of walking or moving. The following are a few of more than 120 ideophones which characterize the general action of hamba: báda "of walking with an unsteady gait, as when exhausted or when traveling on a slippery surface," bódo "of walking clumsily (of a tall or awkward person)," búshu "of walking about naked or in tight-fitting garments," chéke "of the sound of leg-rattles or of walking with a superior, arrogant gait," cótho "of walking with shod feet," dáfa "of trudging along slowly," dúnsu "of a swaying gait," féshe "of loose-jointed movement," gídi "of the sound made by the walk of a quadruped," gúxa "of rickety motion," húqu "of dragging along," khéle "of hopping along on one leg," and xúbu "of walking in water." The verb hamba has a very wide area of meaning, and the ideophones have much more restricted areas; but all designate some areas of activity or form.

In certain instances it is very valuable to be able to describe such areas of meaning in terms of a central meaning and several peripheral meanings. For example, we may describe sucker as having a central meaning "one who or that which sucks," but there are also several peripheral meanings, e.g., a particular variety of fish, a type of hard candy, a shoot rising from the main body of a plant, and a person who is easily cheated. Whether we should relate all these meanings to a single word or consider that we have more than one word with the same form depends upon a number of technical factors which cannot be discussed in the limited study here.[6] However, for all practical purposes it does not matter

---

[5] C. M. Doke and B. W. Vilakazi, Zulu-English Dictionary (Johannesburg: Witwatersrand University Press, 1948).

[6] For a full discussion of such problems see Eugene A. Nida, Morphology, (Ann Arbor: University of Michigan Press, 1949), pp. 151-74.

much. We may either list one word or several, but we must be certain that we are properly identifying the areas of meaning of each.

7.2.6   <u>Languages Subdivide Phenomena in Different Ways</u>

In analyzing a language one cannot predict the manner in which the phenomena of the native culture will be subdivided by the words of the language. For example, the Tarahumara language, spoken in northern Mexico, has only five words for color, but these words cover the entire range of color distinctions, from violet on the one extreme to red on the other. Of course, each word covers more of an area of meaning than any corresponding word in English. For example, <u>siyóname</u> means both green and blue. On the other hand, Tarahumara often makes many distinctions which we do not make. For example, there are five distinct stems to describe different types of placement: <u>maná</u> "to place a bottle or container," <u>riká</u> "to place something in a lying down position," <u>wirá</u> "to place something in a standing position," <u>ačá</u> "to place something in a fixed location," and <u>učá</u> "to put a liquid on something." There are also three stems for "carry," each distinguishing a different manner of carrying—in the hands, on the back, or on the shoulders. In relating Bible stories it is imperative that a missionary distinguish carefully just what was done, or he may have the paralytic carried on four men's backs (a ridiculous thing for any Tarahumara) rather than on their shoulders.

In Bambara, a Sudanic language of West Africa, there are only three principal words for color: white, red, and black. These words, however, distinguish shades more than actual color. For example, a yellow object would be termed "white," but if a white piece of paper were contrasted with it, then the yellow object would be called "red." If one wishes to denote actual colors, then some comparison is used, e.g., a green object would be said to be "grass-like" in color.

In Totonac there are eight stems (including nineteen different words) to distinguish various types of smells. For example, there is one word which distinguishes "the smell of corn mush which has too much lye," and another word which denotes "the smell of mould or mushrooms."[7] On the other hand, Totonac does not have different stems to distinguish the four senses of hearing, seeing, tasting, and smelling. In place of separate stems there are compound forms of the following type: "to ear-taste" meaning "to hear," "to eye-taste" meaning "to see," "to mouth-taste" meaning "to taste," and "to nose-taste" meaning "to smell."

On the one hand, English seems to many peoples to be woefully deficient in adequate distinctions. For example, in Huichol, a language of central Mexico, there are fifteen different terms used to distinguish varieties of grasshoppers, of which only three are regarded as edible. Our total disregard for such distinctions would be considered inexcusable by Huichol speakers. Similarly, in Mazatec, a language of southern Mexico, there are two words corresponding to English "in." One designates such relationships as "in a shoe, a dish, or a house," while the other denotes a state of being mixed in something, e.g., yeast mixed in dough. In speaking about the Spirit of God indwelling the Christian believers, the missionary must make certain that he is saying that the Spirit is "mixed in" rather than just occupying some vacant receptacle hidden some place inside the body.

On the other hand, some peoples regard the distinctions made by English as being entirely unnecessary and even illogical. For example, a Kwango-speaking native from Congo would not be able to understand why we have four different words lamb, calf, son, and colt, when it would seem much easier to relate each offspring to its parent as is done in Kwango, e.g., "child of a sheep" meaning a "lamb," "child of a cow" meaning a "calf," "child of a person" meaning a "son" or "daughter," and "child of a horse" meaning a "colt." Similarly, a Kwango native would feel that we greatly underrate the semantic value of the verb "to bite," since we do not use it in the extended meanings which he does, e.g., "a wound bites the man" (i.e., he is suffering from a wound), "a man bites the king" (i.e., the man is speaking against the king), and "a sadness bites his heart" (i.e., he is suffering from grief). The Shilluk language has similarly extended the meaning of

---

[7] See Eugene A. Nida, Morphology, p. 158, for a full treatment of these details.

the verb "to kill," e.g., "to kill a hole" means "to fill the hole," "to kill a marriage" means "to get a divorce," and "to kill a law" means "to break it."

The phenomena of human emotions are described in many ways. In some languages the emotions are regarded as centered in the heart, in others in the stomach, the liver, the intestines, the kidneys, or the insides, but rarely in the head. In certain instances the various emotional and intellectual faculties are distributed among the physical organs. For example, in Acooli[8] the liver (cwińy) is regarded as the seat of the emotions, affections, inmost feelings, and will. In the liver reside the moral qualities and faculties for moral decisions. The insides (iĩ) are the seat of the nonmoral feelings and responses. The head (wiĭc) symbolizes the manner of activity. The eye or face (waàŋ) denotes the perceptive faculty, the power of conception, and is a means of expressing one's attitude of mind. The ear (iĭt) indicates the intellectual grasp, understanding, and manner of yielding, and the mouth (dóg) stands for the expressed will and one's language. All of these words may be modified by various adjectives to describe features of the emotional states, activities, and attitudes. Note the following expressions with the adjective teèk "quick":

Acooli Expression	Literal Meaning	English Equivalent
1. cwińyé teèk[9]	"quick liver"	"courageous, calloused"
2. iĩe teèk	"quick insides"	"reluctant in yielding"
3. wiĭe teèk	"quick head"	"nimble of motion"
4. waàŋè teèk	"quick eye"	"alert in grasping a situation"
5. iĭté teèk	"quick ear"	"good apprehension and memory"
6. dógé teèk	"quick mouth"	"stubborn in his opinion"

Many of these Acooli expressions are very specialized in meaning. That is to say, we cannot predict just what will be the meaning of the combination by knowing the principal mean-

---

[8] These data are from J. P. Crazzalara, A Study of the Acooli Language (London: Oxford University Press, 1938) pp. 79-85.

[9] Certain grammatical changes occur when the nouns are followed by an adjectival attributive.

ings of the constituent parts. This is always an important problem in all attempts to analyze the meanings of words, for words are not semantically fixed elements. Rather, they are exceedingly plastic and lend themselves to innumerable changes and modifications. For example, in the following expressions from Chol, a Mayan language of southern Mexico, one can readily note the various specializations of meaning which have become attached to the verbs and the noun "heart"

Literal Chol Expressions	English Equivalent
1. "to lose one's heart"	"to feel intense joy or fear"
2. "to be stuck in one's heart"	"to be sad"
3. "to enlarge one's heart"	"to feel pleasure"
4. "to fix one's heart on something"	"to have faith in"
5. "to have a heart"	"to be intelligent"
6. "to have a quiet heart"	"to be at peace"

In certain instances languages appear to be contradictory in their use of words. For example, in Shilluk one can say "good bad" and mean "very good." The word "bad" becomes a modifier of "good" in the sense of a great degree of something. This apparent contradiction in terms is, however, not very different from what we have in English, when a person says, "He wasn't only bad, he was good 'n bad!" In this English expression "good" occurs as an attributive to "bad" and indicates a considerable degree of badness. Compare also good 'n tired and good 'n lazy.

7.2.7 Words Reflect Cultural Differences

It is only natural that words should reflect cultural differences, for they symbolize the features of different cultures. In fact, we cannot understand the language of a people unless we also understand their culture. For example, if in East Africa one should hear a Kipsigis say that a family had "put leaves on a man," he might regard such an expression as having little or no significance other than the literal meaning of the phrase. However, to restrict this expression to its literal meaning and thus to miss the social significance of the term is to ignore one of the most crucial events in Kipsigis clan life. Before the coming of white men, any native caught stealing was first warned severely. On the second offence, he

was branded on the cheek, a sign for people to beware of him.
If he continued to steal and violate the traditions of the tribe,
he could be disowned by his own clan, and this act was symbolized by "putting leaves on the man." When that was done,
all the other members of the tribe were at liberty to stone and
beat the culprit to death; for by the act of laying on leaves the
clan renounced all claim to blood money or revenge for the
death. This practice has been discontinued for the most part,
but the phrase "to put leaves on a person" still remains and
signifies the complete repudiation of a fellow clansman.

The degree to which various languages subdivide phenomena generally reflects cultural differences. In English we
have no special reason for distinguishing different types and
forms of fallen snow, but in Barrow Eskimo there are many
reasons why specialized terms would be employed. Compare
the following: apu "snow" (a general term), kimuzuk "a snowbank," kaguḵłaič "snow drifted in rows," aḵiluḵaḵ "fallen
fluffy snow," and kanik "snowflakes."

In many instances the variations in languages reflect differences of belief, rather than contrastive cultural settings.
Fox example, in Miskito, a language of Honduras and Nicaragua, one describes the eclipse of the moon by saying "the
moon has caught hold of his mother-in-law" (cited in section
3.2.3.2.16). Such an idiom reflects legendary explanations of
natural phenomena. The eclipse of the sun in Bolivian Quechua
is described as "the sun dies," and in Zoque, a language of
southern Mexico, one says "the sun gets tired." Such terms
are slightly more prosaic than the Miskito, but they are certainly not scientific analyses.

Sometimes a cultural feature may have died out long before, but the terminology reveals its former significance.
For example, in Bolivian Quechua one may speak of a "year"
as "tying up the sun." This expression, of course, goes back
to the use of quipus, cords of various colors in which knots
were tied to record events and to keep accounts in the ancient
Inca empire. At the end of each year, a special quipu by
which the years were counted was tied to indicate that another
year had past. From this practice has come the expression
"tying up the sun."

In many instances the meanings of native idioms are quite
contrary to our interpretation of their literal translation into

English. In Shilluk, for example, one uses the phrase "small heart" to characterize a generous man and a "big heart" to denote a stingy or selfish man. This seems quite contradictory to our own metaphorical analysis of the situation. The Shilluks, however, are able to explain their idiom quite satisfactorily as follows: A man with a small heart is one who has been so generous in giving things away that as a result he has very little for himself. Therefore, his heart is small. The selfish and stingy man, on the contrary, has sought everything for himself and stored it away in his heart, and therefore he has a big heart. Certainly their reasoning is as good as ours.

Another contradictory type of expression occurs in Bolivian Quechua, in which one must speak of the future as being "behind oneself" and the past as being "ahead of oneself." That is to say, the future is always behind and the past always ahead. Some people have mistakenly philosophized about the "false orientation" of the Quechuas, but there are no philosophical implications whatsoever. The idiom results from a very simple interpretation of psychological phenomena. The Quechuas reason that since one can "see" the past through the eye of the mind, therefore, one must be facing the past. On the other hand, since the future cannot be "seen," it must be behind one.

Many idioms reflect quite closely the cultural patterns. For example, the English word hypocrite is a borrowing of a Greek word meaning "actor." This word developed from the stage of ancient times, and it undoubtedly appeared very natural for one to use such a phrase to designate any person who was acting a part in the everyday affairs of life. In Malagasy, the language of Madagascar, the equivalent of "hypocrite" is "one who spreads a clean raffia carpet." This expression comes from the practice of housewives who spread a clean raffia carpet over a dirty floor when they discover unexpected visitors coming up the path. The Greek and the Malagasy terms have quite different cultural histories, but functionally they are very similar.

Once a missionary realizes that each word of a language has its own special history and area of meaning, he will avoid many of the serious errors which come from ignorance or negligence. One must not translate words literally from one language to another, and this is particularly true of religious vocabulary. For example, one missionary called a refined Latin American gentleman un hombre perdido, literally "a lost man," but the word perdido in this context means a profligate, dissolute person and is a direct insult rather than a statement about a man's spiritual condition. The missionary soon realized his mistake, but no amount of explanation ever seemed to remove the violent reaction to that uncalled-for slander. It is not enough to memorize forms from a grammar; we must learn the cultural settings of words as well.

We often make mistakes in learning a foreign language because we assume that borrowed words keep their original meanings. This is by no means the case. Though English borrowed chant from French chanter "to sing," it would be quite wrong for us to assume that the English and French terms are now equivalent. In the Tetelcingo dialect of Aztec the Spanish word gloria "glory" has been borrowed in the form gluria, but it means something quite different. As the result of constant association with religious festivals where great quantities of liquor are consumed, it may now designate a religious drinking bout. Similarly, the Spanish word ayuno "a fast" has been borrowed into Bolivian Quechua, but because such "fasts" generally last only until noon, after which the day is given over to riotous eating and drinking, the word no longer has the Spanish meaning, but rather denotes a kind of fiesta. English borrowed a Spanish word vamos "let us go" and changed it to vamoose meaning "to scram, get out quickly." This inflected form of the Spanish verb is borrowed as though it were a root, and we have made it a perfectly regular verb, e.g., vamoosing, vamooses, and vamoosed.

Many borrowings from foreign languages are almost unrecognizable in their form, even though they do preserve some of the original meaning. Compare, for example, the following Mixteco proper names with their Spanish equivalents: tólo from Sp. Bartolomé (Eng. Bartholomew), čéè from Sp. José Eng. Joseph), pélú from Sp. Pedro (Eng. Peter), and múù from Sp. Simón (Eng. Simon). In some instances the words are almost entirely changed because of morphological reinterpretations. For example, in Chiluba, spoken in the Belgian Congo, the English word matches and the French words biscuit and diplôme have been borrowed as mačisi "matches," bisikiti "biscuits," and diploma "diploma." The corresponding singulars and plurals have been developed as though the first syllables of the English and French words were gender classifiers (see section 6.2). The results have been dičisi "match," čisikiti "biscuit," and maploma "diplomas." Once a word has been completely borrowed into a foreign language, it undergoes all sorts of formal and semantic changes, and ultimately it becomes so much a part of the language that it is indistinguishable from any other word. This, for example, has happened to the word thug. One might expect to find such a word coined by American gangsters, but it actually comes from Hindustani, having been used as the name of a professional group of robbers and murderers in India who made it a practice to strangle their victims.

It is a great temptation for some people to see in onomatopoetic forms a basic resemblance between languages. It would seem that in such types of words one would find certain universal characteristics if they were ever to be found, and yet we do not find them. Onomatopoetic forms are as diverse as any other part of the language. For example, in English the onomatopoetic form for the barking of a dog is bowwow, but in French it is ngaf-ngaf or toutou. In Spanish the corresponding form is guau. In Loma, a language of Liberia, the form is aó·ʔaó· (the final tones are extra high); and in Kipsigis, a Nilo-Hamitic language of Kenya, it is ʋ̀·ʔʋ̀ʔ. Even with such a relatively simple nonhuman sound, languages exhibit very little similarity in the manner in which they phonetically symbolize it. The following list of onomatopoetic forms in Chontal of Oaxaca, Luvale of Northern Rhodesia, and Malagasy of Madagascar, will demonstrate even more obviously the basic nonconformity between systems of phonetic symbolization:

Chontal

fuyfuy	"to drizzle"	nafnaf	"to rinse"
hoR̄hoR̄	"to snore"	tʸoftʸof	"to bust"
kuškuš	"to be curly"	hashas	"to split wood"
caʔcaʔ	"to sift"	cɛʔcɛʔ	"to break pottery"
tiltil	"to shine"	fʔansfʔans	"to bounce"
gofgof	"to hit clothes on rocks during the process of washing"		

226 LEARNING A FOREIGN LANGUAGE

Luvale[10]

mbé	"of firmness"	kú·kà·	"of trampling"
zwá	"of splitting"	mbólóngó	"of hanging downwards"
lwí·	"of suddenly appearing"	húlúlú	"of openness"
fwápù	"of floating"	ndú·lù·lù·	"of drooling saliva"
ndúpù	"of plopping into water"	kèlekéte	"of gnawing"
ngélé	"of the sound of a ringing bell"	wélèwéwé	"of a cock's crowing"
pèlyá	"of staggering"	tàmbakané:	"of protracted calling"

Malagasy[11]

mipàtrapàtraka "to patter (as rain on leaves)"
mibòbobóbo "to make a bubbling noise"
mikinàonàona "to howl (as wolves)"
mibàrarèoka "to bleat"
migònongònona "to mutter"
mikorìntsandrìntsana "to jingle"
mingòdongòdona "to make a trampling noise"
misáosáo "to make a rustling noise (as of silk)"
mitsàmontsámona "to make a chewing noise"
mikìtrakìtrana "to creak"
migòroròana "to gurgle"
midòbodóboka "to make a gobbling noise (as a turkey)"

7.3   The Process of Finding the Meanings of Forms

In most instances it is not too difficult to determine the meaning of a form in the one context in which we most usually find it, but we often encounter trouble because the same forms seem to occur in entirely different contexts. In order to handle such problems we should construct a dictionary file if there is not already an adequate dictionary in the language.

---

[10] A. E. Horton, A Grammar of Luvale (Johannesburg: Witwatersrand University Press, 1949), pp. 152-53.

[11] The Antananarivo Annual and Madagascar Magazine, Vol. 4, No. 8 (1889), p. 10.

DISCOVERING THE MEANINGS

This dictionary file may consist of paper slips, 3 inches by 5 inches, filed alphabetically.[1][2] Every new use or meaning of a word should be filed under that word, and on the basis of a number of occurrences in different contexts one can discover the various areas of meaning. It is important that every slip of paper contain enough of the context of any form that the minute distinctions based on context may be readily noted.

In certain instances one may be puzzled about the meaning of a form for a long time since the evidence may seem contradictory or obscure. For example, in Cherokee, an Indian language of the southeast United States, there is a pluralizing affix which is restricted to certain animals, e.g., pigs, rabbits, dogs, cats, and rats. It does not occur in the Cherokee words for calves, colts, sheep, goats, or humans. At first one might think that the distinction is primarily one of size, but actually the difference depends upon whether or not the young of the animal in question are born in litters. Only by collecting many instances of the occurrence of such a morpheme could one possibly discover such a subtle distinction.

One procedure which should be rigorously avoided is our habit of asking "What does it mean?" Of course, to an extent such a question is valid, but often the informant's answers are misleading. What we should inquire is, "How is this form used?" One should always attempt to get the informant to think of a word or phrase in terms of some context. As a result, his explanations will be more concrete and helpful to us, and he is much less likely to indulge in some fanciful explanation which may have little or no bearing on the real problem. Furthermore, words only have meanings in terms of the environments in which they occur, and for us as foreigners the

---

[12] The native language may not have the same symbols as in English, but they can be arranged in approximately the traditional order, despite some slight differences. For example, if one has regular stops, glottalized stops, and aspirated stops, it is possible to alphabetize by listing first those words which begin with a simple stop, e.g., p, then those with a glottalized stop, e.g., p', and finally those with an aspirated stop, e.g., ph. This same type of order should then be followed for all the different stops. If there are two kinds of e sounds, the regular e may be listed first and the open ɛ second. Similarly, the regular o would then precede the open ɔ.

possible environments of a form are the important features. The person who memorizes words but does not know when and how to use them is in a hopeless predicament, for he cannot depend on translating similar English expressions. If he does so in Malagasy, he can be quite wrong. For example, to say that someone is "orange" is to denounce him as cruel and ill-natured. "To whiten something" means actually "to disregard" or "to make light of it," but a person who has a "white soul" is a lewd vulgar individual. In Malagasy one does not speak of "dark colors" or "light colors" but rather of "old colors" and "young colors." Even in such details involving only the semantic area of color, the person who does not fully appreciate the context and environment of words will blunder tragically.

The words and idioms of a people often reveal much of their history and life. For example, the Bambaras of French West Africa speak of "redemption" as "having one's head taken out." To us such an expression may seem strange, but not to them, for in the memories of the old people are vivid scenes of long processions of slaves driven by the cutting lash of the Arab slave traders, who sold their victims to the Portuguese at the coast. These slaves were usually chained together and had iron collars around their necks. However, it sometimes happened that a local king might take pity upon some slave as he passed through a native village; and if the king could pay the Arabs enough in gold, silver, iron, or ivory, the slave would be set free. To describe this process of redeeming a man, the Bambara people used the vivid phrase "to take his head out," that is, to release him from the galling iron collar. The missionary may use these very words to tell the story of the Good News, for it is Christ, who by His atoning death has "taken our heads out" of the iron collar of slavery to sin and self. There is no language in which the message of the Bible cannot be told, and there should be no language in which it is not told. Furthermore, this message should be proclaimed so intelligibly and so clearly that men will know for a certainty that God was in Christ reconciling the world unto Himself.

INDEX

Aboriginal, definition of: 16
Aboriginal languages, typical difficulties in learning: 51-5
Acooli: 220
Adair, James: 19
Additive morphemes: 169
Africa: 7, 20, 23, 60, 76, 78, 85, 114
Afrikaans: 87
Age, as a liability in language learning: 2-3
Agreement, grammatical: 194
Agricultural missionaries: 4
Allomorph, definition of: 164
Alphabet, phonetic: 33
Alphabet problems, practical solutions to: 144
Alphabets,
  inconsistencies in: 141
  necessary distinctions: 144
  phonemic: 39
  phonetic: 22, 141-44
  usable for students: 139
Alveolar: 90
Amazon Indians: 60
Ambiguities: 214-15
Analysis, purpose of: 153
Anglo-Egyptian Sudan: 2, 60, 110, 129
Annamese: 19, 39, 112
Apache: 114
Aphorisms: 200
Arabic: 1, 82, 87, 133, 140
Arabic, Egyptian: 170
Areas of meaning: 216
Asia: 112
Aspect, grammatical: 179
Aspects: 66
Aspirated consonants: 127, 135
Aspiration: 86, 125, 145
Attributive expressions: 69-70
Auditory learning, importance of: 22-3
Auditory perception: 175
Automatic facility: 24-6
Aztec: 16

Back consonants: 145
Bambara: 190, 218, 228
Bantu languages: 17, 20, 66, 67, 94, 97, 100, 109, 115, 127, 140, 143, 154, 157, 174, 177, 187, 190, 198, 204, 207
Basic English: 211
Beach, D. M.: 93, 133
Belgian Congo: 8, 9, 12, 59, 86, 93, 111, 114, 116, 128, 148, 155, 224
Berlitz method: 33
Beym, Richard: 137
Bible: 23
  antequated language: 31
  English: 16
  King James Version: 48
  number of languages in which published: 51
  reading it in a foreign language: 47
  Societies: 30
  Spanish: 48
  translation of: 228
  translators: 30
Bible translating: 11, 52, 55, 141
Bible translations, characteristics of: 31
Black Thai: 113, 155
Blade of the tongue: 90
Bloomfield, L.: i, 164, 170, 195
Bound forms: 175
Breathy vowels: 110-11
  indication of: 146
Breton: 18
Burmese: 35, 70, 112, 113, 155
Bushman: 114, 133

California, University of: 35
Case: 194
Categories, grammatical: 177-80
Celebes: 193
Centralized vowels: 126
Centrals: 99-100
Change, in languages: 18

229

Changes in meaning: 215-16
Chatino: 114
Cherokee: 227
Chichewa: 131, 187-88, 194
Children's learning of languages: 1-2
Chiluba: 115, 224
Chinantec: 114, 116
Chinese: 22, 35, 39, 49, 112, 113, 140, 155
Chipewyan: 114
Chol: 221
Chontal: 225
Chontal of Tabasco: 68
Classification of languages, incorrect: 20-1
Classifiers,
    in Navaho: 156
    numerical: 70-1
Clicks: 91, 94, 132-33, 154, 155, 175
Colloquial Arabic: 60
Comanche: 110, 196
Composition, value in language learning: 48-9
Compounds: 169
Concord,
    grammatical: 194
    in Bantu: 17
Conditioned alternation, of morphemes: 164
Conditioned variation: 142-43
Congo Swahili: 16, 65, 67, 157, 158-59, 160, 161, 169, 174
Conjunctions: 199
Connectives in sentences: 74
Consonants: 91-126
    chart of: 101-2
    frictionless: 99
    voiced and voiceless: 125-26
Constituents, immediate: 204-7
Constructions,
    coordinate: 203-4
    endocentric: 201-3
    exocentric: 201-3
    hypotactic: 187, 204
    immediate constituents: 205
    non-sentence-forming: 200-1
    paratactic: 187, 204
    sentence-forming: 200-1
    subordinate: 203-4
Contour tone languages: 112
Conversation, importance of: 28
Conversational fluency, importance of: 11
Coordinate constructions: 203-4
Cornell: 35, 51
Cornyn, William: 113
Correction in speech, obtaining such: 82-3
Correctness, criteria of: 55
Correctness of form, conventional ideas: 52
Crazzalara, J. P.: 220
Cross reference: 197-8
Cuicatec: 114, 116
Cultural factors,
    in meaning: 221-26
    in vocabulary: 60
Cummings, T. F.: i

Denoeu, Francois: 34, 138
Diacritical marks: 93
Diacritics,
    for tone languages: 116-17
    systems: 147
    their use: 144
Dialectal differences: 54
Dictation, writing from: 75-6
Dictionaries: 16
    elementary: 53
    making of: 81-2, 227
Dinka: 2, 110, 140, 144
Dinka, Abwong dialect: 70
Doke, C. M.: 16, 82, 94, 112, 217
Drilling: 25, 39-40
Drilling, phonetic: 134-6

Egyptian: 20
Egyptian Arabic: 170
Elementary grammar, formation of: 68
Ellinghausen, M. E.: 177
Endocentric constructions: 201-3
English: 14, 15, 26, 67, 86, 96, 98, 99, 103, 106, 111, 124, 127, 133, 137, 143, 151, 153, 159, 163, 164, 167, 169, 170, 172, 174,

INDEX

English: (contd.), 175, 178, 191, 193, 198, 199, 200, 202, 203, 204, 205, 216, 224
   dialectal differences: 54
   idioms: 82
   pluralization: 167-68
   restricting one's use of: 50
   verbs: 15-6
English intonation: 119
English stress: 121
Errors, in syntax: 208
Eskimo: 2, 123, 144, 155, 157, 161, 169, 221
European languages, retaining fluency on the field: 49-50
Exocentric constructions: 201-3

Failure to learn a language,
   excuses for: 1-4
   reasons for: 8-12
   results of: 1
Fang, Cheoying: 113
Filing of data: 68
Flaps: 100-1
Flemish: 28
Frames,
   construction of: 72-5
   expandible: 73
   for tonal analysis: 149
   grammatical use of: 68-9, 72-5
   in narrative series: 74
   simple: 72
   syntactic: 208
Free variation: 142-43
French: 19, 22, 28, 35, 37, 39, 49, 87, 124, 125, 126, 127, 135, 138, 151, 173, 197, 204, 214, 224, 225
French Guinea: 108, 131, 148
Fricatives: 97
Frictionless consonants: 99
Fries, Charles C.: 13
Front consonants: 145
Futa-Fula: 131, 132

Gabon: 95, 127
Garvin, Paul L.: 213
Gender: 189, 194
   grammatical: 179

German: 5, 22, 39, 87, 95, 98, 106, 133, 154, 182, 195
Gestures, importance of: 151-52
Glottal stop: 93
Glottal trill: 133
Glottalized clicks: 133
Glottalized consonants: 132
Glottalized vowels: 108
Gold Coast: 7
Government, grammatical: 194-97
Grammar,
   function of: 153
   historical: 15
   irregularities in: 14-5
   Latin: 9
   relationship to speaking: 22
   traditional: 3, 13
Grammar books,
   preliminary survey of: 55
   proper use of: 30-1
Grammar-dictionary: 68
Grammars, tradition: 36
Grammatical frames,
   construction of: 72-5
   use of: 68-9
Graphic symbolism: 175
Greek: 17, 25, 30, 48, 160, 171, 186, 194, 197, 201, 214, 216-17, 223
Grooved tongue: 91
Guatemala: 97, 122, 132, 177
Gutterals: 133
Gweabo: 116

Habbe: 130
Hall, Robert A., Jr.: 34, 138, 177, 178
Hausa: 18, 170-71
Hebrew: 20, 21, 30, 186
Hindustani: 225
Hockett, C. F.: 113
Hodge, Carleton T.: 170
Homeric poems: 19
Honduras: 82, 122, 222
Honorifics: 168, 179
Horton, A. E.: 198, 226
Hottentot: 94, 114, 133
Huichol: 219
Hupa: 9, 178
Hypotactic constructions: 204
Hypotaxis: 187

Ibo: 112, 189, 196
Ideophones: 217
Idioms, listing of: 82
Ilamba: 17, 143, 188-89, 194
Immediate constituents: 204-7
Implosives: 97
India, characteristic language features: 93, 95
Indian languages, United States, 6, 18
Indiana, University of: 51
Indo-China: 19, 113
Indo-European languages: 15, 176, 189
Indo-Hittite: 15
Industrial missionaries: 4
Infixes: 169-70
Informants,
 learning from: 55-84
 use of: 32-4
Inhibitions: 24
Interjections: 199
International phonetic system: 58, 144
Interpreters: 6
Interrogative expressions: 67-8
Intonation: 24, 58, 118-21
Intonation,
 difficulties with: 119
 English: 119-20
 importance of: 120-21
Irish: 18
Irregularities,
 in grammar: 14
 in language structure: 53
Isolating languages: 154
Italian: 100, 152

Jabo: 116
Japanese: 5, 155
Jespersen, Otto: i, 88
Jita: 141, 142
Juncture, types of: 192-94

Kahane, H. R.: 137
Kekchi: 122, 132, 177
Kennedy School of Missions: 51
Kenya: 116, 125, 190, 225
King James Version: 216

Kinship terms: 61
Kiowa: 60
Kipsigis: 116, 125, 126, 171, 190, 196, 221-22, 225
Kissi: 108, 148
Korean: 155, 179
Kpelle: 163
Kroeber, A. L.: 16
Kutenai: 212
Kwango: 219

Language,
 literary dialects: 31
 misconceptions about: 30-1
 "missionary dialects": 52
 practical use of: 43-4
 textbooks: 38
 trade: 1
 use of: 26-7
Language ability,
 evaluation of: 4-5
 value of: 5-8
Language data, filing of: 68
Language facility, as a skill: 27
Language instructors, their function: 34
Language learning,
 aboriginal language: 51-84
 by listening: 78-9
 degrees of: 10
 drilling: 40
 nonaboriginal language: 35-50
 order in procedure: 21-2
 principles of: 13-29
 reviewing: 40
 textbooks: 34
 value of mimicry: 23-4
Language learning programs, reforming of: 55
Language proficiency,
 evidences of: 84
 importance of: 81
Language programs, availability: 35
Language structure, irregularities: 53
Language study, before going to foreign country: 38
Language teachers, types of: 31

INDEX

Language training, Armed Service approach: 32-4
Languages,
  attempts to relate: 19-21
  fundamental characteristics: 19-20
  number not written: 139
  phonetic differences: 86
  trade: 19
Larynx: 96
Laterals: 99-100
Latin: 17, 30, 48, 160, 191, 195-96, 197
Latin America: 7, 12, 78
Law Courts: 78
Lax vowels: 110
Layers, of grammatical structure: 205-7
Learning,
  by drilling: 25
  methods of: 22-3
Learning a language, from older missionaries: 9
Learning processes, relationship between: 23
Lectures, value of in language learning: 46
Length, confusion with stress: 109-10
Liberia: 116, 163, 225
Lingala: 18
Linguaphone, value of: 79
Linguistics, location of courses in: 51
Lip rounding: 90
Listening to reading, value of: 40-1
Lisu: 155
Literature, in aboriginal languages: 19
Living with foreign peoples, problems of: 79
Logic, in languages: 14
Loma: 116, 192, 225
Long vowels: 108-10
  indication of: 147
Luba-Lulua: 115
Luvale: 198, 226

Madagascar: 225

Maladjustments of missionaries: 7
Malagasy: 223, 225, 226, 228
Malay: 18, 35
Maninka-Bambara: 116
Marshallese: 177, 201
Masai: 116
Maya: 9, 16, 18, 71, 108, 175, 176, 177, 216
Mayan languages: 62, 97, 122, 132, 169, 171, 177, 187, 221
Mazatec: 95, 107, 114, 116, 127, 219
Mbanza: 114
Meaning,
  and cultural differences: 221-26
  changes in: 215-16
  discovery of: 226-28
  misconceptions about: 210-13
  study of: 210-28
  subdivisions of: 218
Medical missionaries: 3-4
Memorizing: 25, 39-40
  of native stories: 77
Mende: 216
Methods of language learning,
  Berlitz method: 33
  diversity of: 31-84
Mexico: 9, 14, 62, 66, 68, 71, 95, 97, 122, 152, 164, 169, 171, 187, 218, 219, 221
Michigan, University of: 35
Mimicry: 23-4
Miskito: 82, 122, 222
Mission stations: 10
Missionaries,
  causes of maladjustments: 7
  dialects of: 5
  language teachers: 9
  task of: 11-2
  technical: 3-4
Mixteco: 114, 116, 215, 224
Mode, grammatical: 180
Modes: 66
Modifiers,
  of nouns: 69
  of verbs: 69
Modifying expressions: 69-70
Mongbandi: 9, 12, 59, 62, 128, 162, 172, 178
Mongondow: 193

Monolingual approach to language learning: 32
Moras: 108-9
  of length: 109
Morpheme,
  practical definition of: 153
  technical definition of: 164
Morphemes,
  additive: 169
  different forms: 163
  discovering meaning of: 226-28
  discovery of: 158-61
  reduplicative: 170-71
  replacive: 169, 172-73
  structural types: 169-73
  subtractive: 169, 173
  tonal: 161-62
  types of phonemes which constitute: 161-63
Morphemic differences,
  morphologically defined: 167
  phonologically defined: 167
Morphology, definition of: 154
Musical ability: 3
Muskogee: 9, 70

Nandi: 126
Nasalization: 96
  indication of: 146
Nasalized vowels: 107, 126
Nasals: 99-100
Native culture, importance of knowing: 8
Native stories,
  memorizing of: 77
  uses for: 75-76
Navaho: 2, 70, 107, 114, 115, 154, 155, 156, 157, 179
Negative expressions, eliciting of: 67
Negro Africa: 10
Negroes: 87
Newspapers, value in language learning: 41
Ngbaka: 88, 93, 96, 111, 112, 114, 120, 148, 149, 150, 155, 157, 161, 165, 167, 170, 183, 186, 201, 211
Nicaragua: 82, 122, 222

Nida, Eugene A.: i, 32, 66, 141, 154, 173, 179, 192, 219
Nilo-Hamitic languages: 116, 125, 171, 190
Nilotic languages: 116, 129, 172, 186
Noel-Armfield, G.: 88
Nonprincipal sentences: 200
Nonroots: 169
Nosu: 155
Number: 194
  grammatical: 179
Numbers: 69, 70-1

Object words, lists of: 60
Old English: 15, 194
Onomatopeia: 90
Order, of words: 191-92
Orders, alternative: 192
Organs, vocal: 89
Orient: 23
Orthography, problems of: 21

Palatal: 90
Palatalization: 96
Palau: 19
Palmer, H. E.: i
Pame-Chichimec: 66, 122
Paratactic constructions: 204
Parataxis: 187, 204
Parts of speech: 176-77
Passive voice: 66
Passy, Paul: 88
Person, grammatical: 179
Personality, as a factor in language learning: 28
Persons,
  grammatical, types of: 156
  inclusive and exclusive: 178
Pharyngealization: 96
Pharyngealized vowels: 110
Pharynx: 88
Phonemes, suprasegmental: 163
Phonemic alphabets: 135, 139, 142-44
Phonetic ability, misconceptions about: 87-8
Phonetic alphabet: 33
Phonetic problems, types of: 123
Phonetic proficiency, attainment of: 133-35

INDEX

Phonetics,
    ability in: 87-8
    average tutors' knowledge: 37
    comparable value: 87
    importance of: 85-7
    need for study: 37-8
    textbooks on: 88
Phrases,
    learning vocabulary by: 43
    use of in language learning: 40
Pike, Eunice V.: 95, 107, 117
Pike, Kenneth L.: i, 88, 91, 95, 102, 107, 111, 117, 119, 135, 139, 148, 215
Pitch distinctions: 58-9
Plural formations: 63-4
Pluralization: 14
Polite forms of speech: 56
Portuguese: 35, 49, 87, 107
Possession,
    grammatical: 179
    obligatory: 62
Possessive expressions: 61-2
    confusion in eliciting: 63
Practical alphabets: 175
Practical expressions: 56
Prefixes: 169
Prepositions: 199
Principal sentences: 200
Processes of learning,
    auditory: 22-3
    motor: 23
    visual: 22-3
Pronunciation,
    criticism of: 41-2
    mistakes in: 85-6
    vs. grammatical correctness: 42
Proto-Germanic: 15
Proverbs,
    cultural significance of: 76
    linguistic forms of: 76

Quechua: 129-30, 143, 155, 157, 161, 169, 176, 184-85, 186, 222, 223
Questions: 67-8

Radio, listening to: 45
Reading, relationship to speaking: 9-10
Reading aloud, value of: 40
Reciprocal voice: 66
Recordings, mechanical, proper use of: 79-80
Reduplicative morphemes: 170-71
Reflexive voice: 66
Register tone languages: 114
Religious vocabulary: 47
Replacive morphemes: 169, 172-73
Restrictions,
    primary: 195
    secondary: 195
Retroflexion: 91
Reviewing: 39-40
    methods for: 57
    value of: 57
Rhodesia, Northern: 225
Rippmann, W.: 88
Roman alphabet, limitations of: 140-41
Romansch: 18
Roots 169
Rules,
    grammatical: 13
    learning of: 36

San Blas: 19, 170, 181
Sandhi, definition of: 193
Sapir, E.: 116
Scotch Gaelic: 18
Semantic equivalents: 213-14
Semantics,
    basic principles: 213-26
    misconceptions about: 210-13
Sentence connectives: 74
Sentence-forming constructions: 200-1
Sentences,
    non-principal: 200
    principal: 200
Shakespeare: 16
Shedd, L. M.: 130
Shilluk: 129, 144, 172, 219-20, 221, 223
Siamese: 112
Slocum, Marianna C.: 170
Sound mechanisms: 88-91
Sounds,
    domal: 93
    mistakes in pronunciation of: 85-7

production of: 88-91
similar to English: 123
types of: 91-111
Spanish: 18, 22, 25, 28, 35, 39, 48, 71, 83, 84, 86, 87, 99, 122, 123, 125, 126, 128, 135, 140, 143, 152, 154, 182, 189, 192, 194, 196, 198, 200, 206, 214, 215, 224, 225
intonation: 58
Mexican: 137
negative expressions: 67
Speed of utterance, attaining of: 59-60, 136-37
Stop, glottal: 93
Stops: 91-7
affricated: 95-6
aspirated: 94-5
double: 93
glottalized: 96-7
Stories,
memorizing of: 77
uses for: 75-6
Stress: 121-23
in English: 121
Stresses, types of: 163
Structure, of language: 17
Subordinate constructions: 203-4
Subtractive morphemes: 169, 173
Sudan Colloquial Arabic: 140
Sudanic languages: 9, 14, 59, 93, 108, 114, 116, 120, 130, 140, 148, 154, 162, 190, 211, 218
Suffixes: 169
Sukuma: 67
Summer Institute of Linguistics: 51
Suprafixes: 170
Swahili: 18, 117
Sweet, Henry: i, 88
Syllabaries: 139-40
Syllabic nasals: 131
Symbolizing, graphic: 175
Symbols, supplementary: 140-41
Synonyms: 213
Syntactic errors, correction of: 208-9
Syntactic structure, discovery of: 207-8
Syntactic units, types of: 199

Syntax,
definition of: 154, 181
in Bible translating: 181

Tanganyika: 17, 67, 109, 118, 141, 187, 188
Tarahumara: 14, 218
Tarascan: 179
Technical missionaries: 3-4
Tense: 179
Tense vowels: 110
Tenses: 66
of verbs: 66
Tepehua: 164
Textbooks in phonetics, limitations of: 87
Textbooks on languages: 34
Texts,
listening to: 77
reading of: 77
types of: 75
uses for: 75
Thai, Black: 113
Thai languages: 19
Thinking in the foreign language: 26
Time, as a factor in language learning: 3, 8-9
Tojolabal: 171
Tonal changes: 190
in morphology: 166
Tonal distinctions: 58-9
Tonal languages: 3
Tone,
importance of marking: 148
lost in some languages: 117-18
relative pitch: 111-12
vs. intonation: 130-31
vs. stress: 128-29
Tone deafness: 3
Tone languages: 111-18
basis of distinction: 111-12
errors in: 117
types of: 112
Tones, indication of: 146
Totonac: 108, 218-19
Trade languages: 1, 18-9
limitations of: 11
Translationisms: 181
Trevino, S. N.: 59

INDEX

Trill, glottal: 133
Trimingham, J. Spencer: 133, 140
Trudinger, Dr.: 2
Tsotsil: 187, 197
Turu: 190, 193
Turkish: 177
Tutorial programs, supplements to: 38-50
Tutors,
   difficulties with: 36-8
   function and use of: 35-8
Tzeltal: 62, 169-70

Unaspirated consonants: 135
United States: 9
Use of a language: 80-1

Velic: 90
Velum: 90
Verb expressions, forms to elicit: 64
Vibrants: 100-1
Vilakazi, B. W.: 82, 217
Vocabulary,
   cultural factors in: 60
   extent of distinctions: 60
   extent of in aboriginal languages: 16
   introduction of: 34
   methods of acquiring: 44
   object words: 61
   organization of: 42-3
   religious: 47
   simple verbs: 64
   supplementary: 42
Vocal cords: 88
Vocal organs: 89
Voegelin, C. F.: 177
Voice, grammatical: 66, 179
Voiceless vowels: 110
Vowel length, indication of: 147
Vowel modifications, in morphology: 166
Vowel phonemes: 145

Vowels: 102-11
   basic diagram of: 105
   breathy: 110-11
   chart of: 104
   factors in analysis: 103
   glottalized: 108
   long: 108-10
   nasalized: 107
   voiceless: 110

Ward, Ida C.: i, 88, 189
Ward, William: 13
Watkins, Mark Hanna: 131, 187
Welsh: 18, 100
Westermann, Diedrich: 88
Words,
   agreement between: 189
   arrangements of: 187-92
   determining extent of: 173-76
   order of: 191-92
   types of: 176-77
Word classes: 199
Word order: 183
Writing a language, relationship to hearing and speaking: 48-9
Writing down the language: 150-51

Yale: 35, 51
Yaqui: 152
Yellow-Knife: 114
Yipounou: 94, 127, 183
Yucatan: 18

Zanaki: 118
Zande: 116
Zapotec: 114, 122, 181
Zero, structural: 156
Zero allomorph: 167
Zinza: 109, 187
Zoque: 66, 222
Zulu: 16, 19, 81, 94, 95, 97, 99, 108-9, 112, 115, 116, 127, 131, 132, 154, 181, 217